THE OPERATIC STATE

Since its beginnings in the palaces of sixteenth-century Italy, opera has developed not only as an élite art form, but has also served as an arena of civic performance.

The Operatic State examines the cultural, financial and political investments that have gone into the maintenance of opera and opera houses in America, Great Britain, Italy, France, Russia and Australia. Ruth Bereson explores why opera has remained almost unchanged throughout wars, revolutions, and vast social upheavals, and questions why governments of all kinds give priority to the funding of opera and the maintenance of state opera houses. *The Operatic State* argues that by legitimising the power of the state through recognised ceremonial ritual, opera enjoys a privileged status throughout the world, often to the detriment of popular and indigenous art forms.

Ruth Bereson began her career as an arts manager and has since incorporated that practice in research and studies on arts and cultural policy in Australia, Singapore, Britain, France and the USA. She is the editor of *Artistic Integrity and Social Responsibility: You Can't Please Everyone!* (Ethos Books, 2001). She is currently Associate Director of the Program in Arts Administration and Assistant Professor of Practice at Teachers College, Columbia University.

ROUTLEDGE HARWOOD STUDIES IN CULTURAL POLICY
Edited by Jim McGuigan, Loughborough University,
and Oliver Bennett, University of Warwick

FRENCH CULTURAL POLICY DEBATES
Edited by Jeremy Ahearne

THE OPERATIC STATE
Ruth Bereson

THE OPERATIC STATE

Cultural Policy and the Opera House

Ruth Bereson

London and New York

First published 2002
by Routledge
11 New Fetter Lane, London EC4P 4EE

Simultaneously published in the USA and Canada
by Routledge
29 West 35th Street, New York, NY 10001

Routledge is an imprint of the Taylor & Francis Group
© 2002 Ruth Bereson
Typeset in Baskerville by Taylor & Francis Books Ltd

Printed and bound in Great Britain by Antony Rowe Ltd, Chippenham, Wiltshire

British Library Cataloguing in Publication Data
A catalogue record for this book is available from the British Library

Library of Congress Cataloging in Publication Data
A catalog record has been requested for this title

ISBN 0–415–27851–1

IN MEMORY – JEAN-MARIE HÉNOT

CONTENTS

ACKNOWLEDGEMENTS

The Operatic State began with the phrase 'opera over the barricades', which was uttered one afternoon at the Barbican in London during a lunch with Emeritus Professor John Pick, Dr Michael Hammet and myself. We were discussing the extraordinary fact that, however much civilisations change, and however much fashions in literature, art and drama may vary, opera consistently reinvents itself in precisely the same way and in the same form. So why was 'opera' so different from the other arts? This conversation triggered what would prove to be many years of research which have culminated in the present book.

I would like to thank many people who have provided much help and constant support during the very long period of gestation which produced this work. In particular this work would not have been possible without the unwavering interest and enthusiasm of Emeritus Professor John Pick, who provided me with support, assistance and inspiration. The pages which follow are the product of many hours of enjoyable conversation with him concerning opera, theatre and the inevitably challenging questions which concern the study of arts policy and management.

I am indebted to the contributions from many colleagues and fellow researchers who have assisted me during the various stages of the work. I would like to thank: Dr Desmond Allison, Dr Malcolm Anderton, Jo Caust, Professor Ian Eagles, Dr Doranne Fenoltea, Alison Fraser, Dr Fujin Gao, Professor Caroline Gardiner, Sarah Gardner, Dr France Guillemonat, Dr Michael Hammet, Joan Jeffri, Dr Leong Wai-Teng, Robert Lewis, Louise Longdin, Dr Paul Marriott, Dr Edward McDonald, Dr Robert Protherough, Dr Srilata Ravi, Dr Chitra Sankaran, Mark Stapleton, Paolo Tangucci, Professor Linda Thompson, Professor Samuel Weber, Wee Liang Tong and Dr Paolo Zedda.

Many friends have supported me in this project, in particular Ginou Lacroix and Ann Pick, who willingly and often offered me friendship, support and hospitality. Others who have provided immeasurable assistance and whom I would like to thank are Helmut Bakaitis, Paolo Cimarosti, Didier Delettre, Linda Duboscq, Goh Su Lin, David Herbert, Alistair Kyle, Allanah Lucas, Scot Morris, David Murray-Smith, Tisa Ng, Bill Snow, Bob Taylor, Graham Walne, Lynette Yeremiyew, Alfredo Zanolla and Georgina Zervudachi.

ACKNOWLEDGEMENTS

My interest in the arts in general, and opera and theatre in particular, was fostered by my parents, who gave me season subscriptions to the opera when I was still at school and supported my interests in theatre from an early age. More recently my father's assistance in gathering supporting material was particularly appreciated.

For their help in the preparation of this book I would like to thank Fintan Power, for his meticulous editorial eye, which has considerably enhanced the original manuscript, Oliver Bennett and Jim McGuigan for their support, and Phillip Harvey, who assisted me in checking many details. It is certainly hoped that all sources are correctly referenced and properly attributed. However, should any errors remain, they are, of course, entirely my responsibility.

1

INTRODUCING THE
POWER BROKERS

If financial support by the state is the prime yardstick of importance, then opera must certainly be the most important of the arts. Where the arts enjoy considerable state subsidy, opera receives the most significant share. This is true not only in countries such as Italy, Germany, France and the United Kingdom, where there is a long history of opera, but also in newer countries, both in Europe and outside of it, where there is no indigenous operatic tradition. Finland, for example, opened its new opera house in Helsinki in 1993. It has already by far the largest state grant of any arts organisation in Finland.[1] In Australia opera receives 26.9% of total government arts funding, the second largest group to receive funding after music companies and orchestras. Opera accounted for A$23.23 million, with Opera Australia (the national company) receiving the greatest amount of funding from government at A$10 million.[2] In the United States private foundations supported by government in the form of generous tax subsidies support the Metropolitan Opera, and the National Endowment for the Arts contributed US$1.27 million for the financial year 2001, up from US$1.25 million in 2000.[3] In China opera is soon to become a major state-supported art form, as witnessed by the funding of new opera houses in Shanghai and Beijing. The new Beijing Opera is already projected to cost 4.7 billion yuan[4] or over half a billion dollars.

When this kind of weighting is discussed, it is usually explained by politicians and funding bodies as if opera is, self-evidently, the superior art, somehow rising above the narrower traditions of drama, music and dance, from which it borrows, to form a whole which is, seemingly, much greater than its parts.

Yet this account does not go far to explain the extraordinary fact that governments, intent upon curtailing public expenditure elsewhere or otherwise indifferent to the arts, will go on supporting opera, and that companies will sponsor opera, and seek benefits from that sponsorship, even when they neglect the other arts. Nor does it explain why in Britain, where the argument that opera is consistently underfunded compared to continental Europe is regularly used, the Royal Opera House should be amongst the first recipients of national lottery funds and to date have received the largest share of any arts organisation.[5] Furthermore, it does not explain why opera is supported by governments which,

1

it might be imagined, would consider the art and its associations antithetical to their political vocabulary. In 1793, for example, at the height of the terror of the French Revolution, the Paris Commune supported the view that the opera be maintained, as did Napoleon Bonaparte, who closed the doors of other theatres.[6] Neither does it explain why, immediately after the Russian Revolution in 1917, the new rulers of the USSR determined to keep the Bolshoi Opera House intact, while subjecting all the other arts – drama, painting, music and literature – to rigorous reappraisal.[7] Nor does it explain why the first socialist government in France since the 1930s should decide in 1982 that the design and construction of a new opera house was of supreme national importance, developing it under the aegis of a major presidential project.[8] Nor why a left-wing Australian State government should decide that an opera house was so essential to post-war Sydney that an international competition be set up to create it and a source of funding generated and designed specifically in order to finance it.[9] Finally, it does not explain why in the year 2000 the Chinese government should choose to raze a central part of Beijing in order to construct a French-designed opera house. In every instance, the powers in question attributed to opera a significance much greater than that traditionally invested in an entertainment, a cultural institution, or a venue. These operas and many others performed the function of national showcases representing a physical demonstration of each of these states' political, social and economic status or coming of age, through the maintenance or construction of a cultural monument.

Even more critically, however, the view that the opera is just another of the arts does not begin to account for the extraordinary way in which the history of opera, and the grand opera houses, is intermingled with the history of power brokers, most particularly with the rituals and public displays by which those who hold the reins of power demonstrate and reinforce their authority. In times of change, it is the opera, both the institution and the house, which remains constant, while constitution, governments, ministries, the stock exchange[10] and even the church are in flux. This is most pertinently in evidence in France, where over the past three centuries the state has veered dramatically from absolute monarchy to republic, empire, different forms of constitutional monarchy and democratic enfranchisement, yet where opera as designed by a monarch has been ever present, a constant in a fluctuating society. We see too in the perceived home of opera, Italy, which until the nineteenth century was an agglomeration of states, that one of the unifying symbols was that of the opera house, whether it be the opera house of Palermo, where Garibaldi made his first great declaration, or the boxes of La Scala in Austrian Milan or San Carlo in Spanish Naples, so frequented by Stendhal and finally by Vittorio Emanuele and Mussolini, or La Fenice in Venice, the domain of Lord Byron's trysts. Although its meaning was adapted in terms of superficial changes in society and taste, at no time was its role fundamentally challenged. In changing political contexts its meaning remained constant.

Again and again, successful revolutions, victories in battle, peace agreements and national commemorations are celebrated in the opera house. One spectac-

2

ular example of this was on 19 June 1815 on the occasion of the return of the King of Naples to the 'brilliantly lit' theatre of San Carlo, which had been constructed by his father.

> The king was moved to tears; and when his bust appeared on the stage amid the banners of all the Allied Powers, the theatre resounded with applause and continued cheering for half an hour.[11]

But this kind of event is not relegated to the annals of history; one need only look towards the opera house in twentieth century Europe to find many other examples, as opera houses were turned into venues of state celebration by those whose aim it was to symbolically reinforce their power. Indeed, the liberation of Milan was announced from the stage of La Fenice in Venice during a performance of *Madam Butterfly*, and the liberation of Hanoi by The People's Executive Committee was declared from the balcony of the opera. Göring and Hitler understood the importance of such practices well, as did Lord Harewood in planning the opening of a new English opera, *Gloriana*, to celebrate the coronation of Queen Elizabeth II, by looking at the reign of Queen Elizabeth I and bedecking the Royal Opera House, Covent Garden, with all the right paraphernalia for the occasion but not taking into account the 'old practices' of his audience. Certainly the use of opera houses by the power brokers makes over time for unusual historical alliances for the only element linking them is that they have a pre-eminent role in their society and that they act out their power on the operatic stage.

Plainly, opera is not merely the best supported of the arts, it is also a symbol of the continuity of governments and, most important of all, an integral part of state ceremonial. Like the grandest form of monarchy or religious rite, the operatic institution is an environment of complex ceremonial traditions, as expressed by the kind of audience which traditionally attends it and the monumental architecture which houses it. Opera is more than a composite art, or a social experience, it is a state ceremony and has important political consequences, giving it wider and richer significance than the other 'arts'. In this way, opera can be seen to represent the quintessence of the establishment arts and patrician culture.

The intention of this book is to demonstrate that opera has performed the function of legitimising the power of the state through the use of ceremonial ritual since its beginnings as entertainments performed in the ducal palaces of Italy in the sixteenth century. These events served to support the spatial hierarchy of the audiences' seating structure and contributed to demonstrating the power and glory of the court. In the present day these conventions have been adopted by and translated into the terminology of the modern democratic state. The Australian cultural historian Donald Horne highlights the ritualistic role which the British monarchy plays out with its coaches, uniforms, palaces, ceremonies and jewels.[12] Such performance is operatic in dimension, and these legitimations are in fact played out by all states with or without a constitutional monarch. It is this physical and functional iconography that the state makes use of which is worthy of consideration.

Opera houses constructed today sometimes disguise the codified structures of old. For example, in France the new 'people's opera', Opéra Bastille, was designed with the specific intent of increasing accessibility to the house and creating an equality of distribution within it,[13] and the house itself was situated in a popular quarter of the city, thus appearing to take into account the precepts of contemporary cultural vocabulary. Nonetheless, although the Bastille district is steeped in strong political, republican and popular historical associations, the new opera house reinforces, in the same way that all French opera houses have done, spatial configurations which denote ranks of hierarchy. One enters the house by ascending a massive staircase framed by a traditional arch. Certainly, there are no boxes in this new house and the aisles are kept to a minimum, thus divesting the traditional audience of certain privileges formalised in the structure of older houses. Yet its hierarchical configuration is well demonstrated on evenings when the opera house is used as a venue for a state event. The aristocracy and bourgeoisie of old may have been transformed into corporate clients by the 1980s, but the head of state has not been divested of his rank and the ceremonial duties which accompany it. Thus, one could witness, at the inauguration of the house on 13 July 1989, on the eve of the bicentennial of the French Revolution, the Presidents of France and the United States, representing democratic leadership of both the right and the left, seated in the central row of seats in the first level of tiers, the traditional position for the Royal Box. They are placed on the first balcony and receded, facing the stage directly, so that the audience is obliged to turn 180 degrees to pay its respects (often in the form of applause accompanied by fanfares, or the playing of the national anthem), as occurs on the occasion of state ceremonial presentations such as galas, before turning to the ceremony of the stage. But this kind of opening is not confined to the corridors of the European power brokers. The *New York Times* described the opening of the Lincoln Center in 1966 in the same register as that of European opera houses:

> It was also an affair of state. Three boxes had been converted into a state box, in which sat the wife of the President of the United States, the secretary of defense, the ambassador to the United Nations, and President Ferdinand E. Marcos of the Philippines and his wife, the tiara-topped Imelda.[14]

And in 1974, at the opening of the Sydney Opera House by Queen Elizabeth II, we find yet again the 'tiara-topped Imelda'. On such occasions, attendance and spatial segregation are no more democratic or popular in form or meaning today than they have ever been.

Opera in all senses of the word was not merely a backdrop for state ceremonial but sometimes took on an acute political dimension. It is no accident that establishment figures were often targets of assassination attempts at opera houses. In Sweden, for example, in 1792 the reigning monarch Gustavus was shot in the opera house; in 1820 the heir apparent to the French throne was fatally stabbed there; and Napoleon III survived an anarchist's bomb on his way to the opera. The young Queen Victoria chose to mark her successful escape from an assassination attempt by appearing the following evening in full regalia at the opera. The opera manager Benjamin Lumley describes the scene:

> Far more interesting in its way ... was the appearance of the Queen in the theatre (Her Majesty's) on the 31st May, being the evening after an insane attempt upon her life. The visit of Her Majesty had been expected. The opera house was filled in every part to overflowing; and on the entrance of the Queen the expression of enthusiasm was electrical. The whole audience rose to its feet, and one loud deep burst of congratulatory applause burst forth from the vast concourse of human beings. Hats and handkerchiefs were waved. Many ladies sobbed aloud. During this demonstration the Queen stood at the front of her box and curtsied repeatedly, while Prince Albert bowed in reply to the deafening congratulations. The audience would not allow the opera to proceed till the 'National Anthem' had been sung. ... At the words 'Scatter her enemies', in particular, the most deafening acclamations arose, and one cheer more was raised when Her Majesty resumed her seat in the corner of the box.[15]

The opera house was a fitting arena for the monarch to demonstrate permanence and power. The opera houses in turn were sometimes closed by governments as precautionary measures if political ferment seemed too great, and their symbolic importance seemed likely to attract trouble. Sometimes the entire theatre was razed, as was the case under the orders of Louis XVIII after the assassination of the Duc de Berry, the intended successor to the crown of the ailing monarch.

Such events raise an inevitable question: how can an institution such as the opera at one and the same time represent certain formalised traditions which are steeped in the prescribed behaviour of past social and political systems, as well as assimilate a new meaning – that is, the arena of the enfranchised, the public which believes it has access to culture as a right? Furthermore, is this paradox compatible within the current subvention structures and is opera really competing on the same terms as the other arts for the same pounds, francs, dollars, deutschmarks, yuan, dong, roubels or kroners? In other words, is 'opera' an art in the sense that contemporary dance, theatre and painting are 'arts'?

It is highly significant to this study that opera houses so closely resemble each other physically. Until the nineteenth century they contained iconographic references displaying classical conventions: porticos, grand staircases, allegorical sculptures, traditionally significant colour schemes of gold, crimson and blue, the private spaces of boxes and the more public foyers. The buildings themselves were of monumental design, resembling temples and palaces. Writers throughout the centuries have described the universality of the experience both as a building in the heart of a city and as an event, by making a connection between opera's past and present imagery. And the similarities do not stop there; going to the opera in any century, whether one is transported to the opera by coach, métro or motorcade, anticipation and expectation are common factors in the experience. Catherine Clément unites the deceptive elements of time and display succinctly:

> The House with its Greek pediment – the temple for music begins to quiver. Coaches, carriages, cars, taxis, subways discharge a delighted populace. Sometimes official retinues led by helmeted motorcycle escorts arrive in pomp. The brilliance of all the chandeliers is visible through the tall windows.[16]

The role of the opera house and the changing function of spatial configurations within the house, its benefactors and its site within the city are also of significance. Sir Christopher Wren, architect of St Pauls Cathedral in London, outlined in 1750 the political potential and purpose in the construction of such monumental works:

> Architecture has its political uses; public buildings being the ornament of a country; it establishes a nation; draws people and commerce; makes the people love their native country, which passion is the original of all great actions in a Commonwealth.[17]

This factor remains as true today as it was in the eighteenth century. The form of great monuments is commonly acknowledged to be a physical manifestation of a building's meaning, especially if the building is designed to house a state institution, so that it is possible for contemporary historians to espouse ideas such as 'Institutions like individuals, must parade and display their glamour if they are to keep their glory alive'[18] as acceptable truths. Opera houses were traditionally placed at significant axes in the cities, close to courts or amusement centres of the aristocracy, their location shifting as focal centres of power changed. Roland Barthes wrote of the connections between the Opéra Garnier and the demography of Paris, describing the Opéra and the district that surrounds it as the heart of 'materiality, business, commerce'.[19] These are distinctive signs of its topological meaning.

During the twentieth century opera houses have simply translated these motifs into the arena of the symbolic monument. The tablets of stained glass designed by Marc Chagall (once arts commissar in Vitebsk in the Soviet Union)[20] at the new Metropolitan in the Lincoln Center in New York, and the Sydney Opera House, its sails dominating the harbour of the city and defying the engineering principles of the day, well illustrate this point. Even the much criticised, recently constructed, Opéra Bastille, which failed to convey the all important quotient of 'architectural marvel', contains the elements of portico and staircase so necessary to communicating the acceptable meaning of an opera house. The colour scheme of the fabric for the chairs, for example, was chosen by the incumbent president of the Republic with the absolute intention of breaking from the traditional connotations which red, blue or green implied in the symbolic iconography of previous regimes. The polemic surrounding the choice of colour for the seating fabric in the Opéra Bastille well illustrates the importance of such objects to the creation of a language that reflects the meaning of the opera house which is valid for today but also reflects its history and tradition. Michèle Audon, one of the directors of the project, comments on her reasoning behind this choice, stressing the symbolic importance of the chosen colour:

> I could have agreed to grey or a blue, but I couldn't accept red. We even found a justification: red corresponded to the theatrical interiors of the nineteenth century, the blue to those of the eighteenth, another colour was needed for our century.[21]

It is also significant that state ceremonies take place in opera houses more often and with greater ceremony than in other kinds of theatres. The purpose of the state gala is to display the finery and importance of the personages in attendance and the hierarchy of the political structure.

The chronicler of the British monarchy's association with the stage, Ian Bevan, describes the first attendance by an English monarch at the theatre. He notes that as early as 1636 Charles I attended the earliest of operatic works, *The Siege of Rhodes*, making it 'a gala affair by going in state'.[22] This reference to the monarch's attendance at the opera adding to the experience and turning it into something more than simply the performance of a mixed media work on stage could equally well describe the experience of going to the opera in early eighteenth century England or of going to the opera in Moscow, Sydney or Paris in the twentieth century. Describing Covent Garden in post-war austerity Britain, he notes that the same principle applies as 'Covent Garden is chosen for state galas because it provides a rich background for ceremonial occasions.'[23]

The coronation celebrations of George V at Covent Garden also demonstrate the association between the monarchy and the opera house in the twentieth century. Bevan describes the scene emphasising the importance of the decorations, seating arrangements and rank of those in attendance:

> The artistic extravagance on the stage was matched by the opulent decorations in the house and 5,000 orchids were used to make a frieze of mauve and gold and white in front of 11 centre boxes where the royal party sat. The rest of the theatre was decorated by a hundred

thousand fresh roses and innumerable artificial ones. Watteau panels and Gobelin tapestries transformed the foyer into an art gallery. The air was cooled by blocks of ice hidden amid banks of hothouse flowers.

The King's guests and his suite filled a third of the available seats. On his left sat the Crown Prince of Turkey. There were more than 100 people present of royal rank – a pageant of Hohenzollern, Habsburg, Bourbon and Savoy, together with princes of the East, such as events of a few years later made impossible ever to be seen again. Even in the glittery history of royal occasions at Covent Garden, there have been few nights to compare with this.[24]

In virtually no other sphere of activity except, significantly, some areas of state military ceremonial and pageantry can this kind of display be witnessed.

The opera represents a continuity of pageantry and display of a state institution linking its present meaning powerfully with its original one. No modern state has neglected this use of the opera house and, even if the performance is not billed as a gala, if an important political person is in attendance, they, their dress and those who accompany them are commented upon in contemporary journals.

Opera is remarkably ageless. There is, for example, no eighteenth century poem, or novel, or painting, or building design, which could be taken for a contemporary design. The way people have customarily described the opera throughout several centuries and through many political changes shows an astonishing coherence of view about what opera actually is, which is central to this work. What does at first glance appear to be different today is the language employed by respective states to justify subvention. Language is designed with the intention of making the public believe that 'accessibility', 'accountability' and 'excellence' are the criteria for support of such institutions, but these terms also serve another purpose; they denote the changing language of the new powerful élites who derive their sense of power from a mix of 'democratic principles' and the waft of new money. By changing the language or terminology which is used, they do not change the meaning of opera any more than did the new élite of nineteenth-century New York manage to change the nature of the institution when they constructed a new opera house where Mrs Vanderbilt could reign supreme, as so eloquently described by the New Zealand opera singer Frances Alda.

It had been Mrs Astor's custom to arrive at the opera at exactly nine o'clock. And this no matter at what hour the curtain rose. As what she did was copied slavishly by the rest of society, it developed that the opera's first act was sung to a house more than empty.

As nine o'clock drew near, there would be the swish and rustle of silk trains, the tramp of feet coming down the orchestra aisles, the scrape of chairs being moved to better positions in the boxes.

Interest in happenings on the stage dwindled. Opera glasses were raised and focused on the curtains of Box Seven.

Nine o'clock.

A hand parted the curtains.

Mrs Astor came in and took her seat.

An audible sigh of satisfaction passed through the house. The prestige of Monday Night was secure. Only then was the attention of all but the ardent music-lovers in the audience turned to the singers and orchestra.[25]

The similarity of contemporary statements about opera to those of, for example, the first *privilège* accorded to opera by Louis XIV in 1669 (which stressed the importance and need for the creation and maintenance of a national institution) will be examined. It will be demonstrated that there has been no real evolution in the intention behind the language used and reasons given for the creation and support of state cultural institutions. Thus when the 1998 *Eyre Report on the Future of Lyric Opera in London* states that 'Britain deserves to have an opera house in the first rank of international excellence';[26] or the 1994 *Annual Report* of the Department of National Heritage sets out that its brief is to 'provide for institutions of national importance entrusted to the Government's care'[27] 'which contribute to a sense of national identity and national pride' and 'help to shape the future',[28] they will be read with the knowledge that the substance of such articles and government reports are little different from treatises devised three centuries previously and across the Channel, and can indeed be shown to be part of a linguistic tradition of governmental rhetoric.

The perspectives of politics and history are not the only form in which opera's remarkable continuity can be demonstrated. This book will investigate what the opera represented to those who attend it, as well as taking note of the opinions of those who do not. The inclusion of descriptive examples written by commentators on the appearance of opera houses, its audience, their social mores, codes and traditions will contribute to the argument from another perspective. It is not surprising that those who traditionally attend state opera houses are part of establishment culture and that attempts made to adjust the social structure of audiences in France, England, the United States and Australia, even if seriously intended, have largely failed.

Audiences often attend opera to make a statement about their social position to either act as or be seen to mingle with the power brokers, as much as to see the performance itself, and demonstrate that they are prepared to pay handsomely for this privilege. It will be shown how the transport they take, the clothes and ornamentation they wear, the food and beverages they consume, the programmes they buy, indeed even the tickets themselves, distinguish the act of going to the opera from that of an ordinary social activity.

Even the fictional realms of literature and cinema repeatedly reinforce such a view by representing scenes of opulence and traditional privilege at the opera.

The dramatic scenes during the Risorgimento at La Fenice in Venice in Luchino Visconti's film *Senso*, set against the backdrop of the opera *La Bohème*, the Austrian occupation of Venice and a dramatic love affair, are of a similar ilk to those of Count Vronsky seeking Anna Karenina in her box and thus scandalising St Petersburg society, or Emma at her first opera being seduced by the provincial bourgeois world in *Madame Bovary*, or Julien Sorel's desperate sighting of Mathilde at the Paris Opéra in *Le Rouge et le Noir*. Even Charles Dickens, not known for championing élitist institutions, supports this view as he made Mrs Sparsit the object of derision by Mr Bounderby in *Hard Times*:

> '… Why, what do *you* know about tumblers? At the time when, to have been a tumbler in the mud of the streets, would have been a godsend to me, a prize in the lottery to me, you were at the Italian Opera. You were coming out of the Italian Opera, ma'am, in white satin and jewels, a blaze of splendour, when I hadn't a penny to buy a link to light you.'
>
> 'I certainly, Sir,' returned Mrs. Sparsit, with a dignity serenely mournful, 'was familiar with the Italian Opera at a very early age.'
>
> 'Egad, ma'am, so was I,' said Bounderby, '– the wrong side of it. A hard bed the pavement of its Arcade used to make I assure you. People like you, ma'am, accustomed from infancy to lie on down feathers, have no idea *how* hard a paving-stone is, without trying it. No, no, it's of no use my talking to *you* about tumblers. I should speak of foreign dancers, and the West End of London, and May Fair, and lords and ladies and honourables.'[29]

Indeed, criticism of opera is often centred on those extraneous characteristics which appear to signify opera and what it denotes rather than on the performed work itself. In Britain there is a long history dating from the late seventeenth century in which opera is frequently and vehemently chastised as being an institution distinct from contemporary British culture. These arguments have frequently been couched in nationalistic terms, the complaint being that it is a foreign institution serving an élite, the tastes and linguistic preferences of which are apart from that of the general public.

It is true that traditionally the nobility did build and support opera houses. During the nineteenth century entrepreneurs took the risks but looked towards 'society' to support the institution. The importance the government placed on financial management and attendance are themes which have never ceased to preoccupy the political aspects of operatic management and, as will be demonstrated later, remain unchanged today. Thus Dr. Véron could describe the social and musical life of the Paris Opéra of which he was director in the 1830s as being 'the triumph of the bourgeoisie'.[30]

Later in the century the English theatre entrepreneur Sir Augustus Harris recognised that it was very much the whole operatic experience which attracted his audience, and therefore the kind of venue in which it was performed counted very much indeed. He stated to the operatic chronicler Hermann Klein 'I shall recoup myself … with the aid of society', and when Klein asked, not without cynicism, 'Do you expect the leaders of fashion and their following to come to Drury Lane?', Harris's reply was most firm: 'Certainly not, … I have every intention, all being well, of taking Covent Garden at the earliest practical date.'[31]

This principle held true under the entrepreneurial management of Sir Thomas Beecham at the beginning of this century, who recounted in his memoirs that he was strongly advised to perform his opera season at Covent Garden because this theatre 'had been associated in the public mind with opera for over 200 years' and thus would attract a traditional audience.[32]

Thus the opera and opera house have not only served as a metaphor for political pundits of all persuasions who, from the early eighteenth century, have felt that to deride it was somehow to criticise those in power, they have also been used successfully by entrepreneurs to harness the support of those in power. The current debates about opera, which continue to treat it as an art form like any other, are therefore essentially misleading, as they do not take into account its special historical relationship with the state and social critics. To argue about subvention policy and not to take into account these important historical factors based on tradition and convention is at best limited and naïve and at worst fraudulent. Such conditions define its meaning even in contemporary society and funding patterns demonstrate this. It is evident that opera has, throughout centuries of continued debate, been consistently maintained by the state. Thus the Arts Council of Great Britain, or its successor arts councils, may appear to quibble about the proportion of the cake which they allocate to opera, and the Ministère de la Culture in France may appear to be unconcerned by the recent squabbles over the management of the Opéra Bastille, yet both have ensured that establishment figures, drawn from the great corporate pillars of respectability or members of the aristocracy, head these institutions, and direct them along political lines consistent with their government's philosophy.

It could be thought to be an insidious claim by governments when they say they treat opera as 'just one of the arts'. They are certainly trying to meet immediate objectives in a contemporary political jargon. This may be convenient but sorts ill with their behaviour, for they *act* as if opera is overwhelmingly more important than other arts. Moreover, this deception greatly harms the other arts as arguments over funding become distorted, as false and inflated esteem are bestowed on certain categories of designers and artists, which thus serve to denigrate arts which may be more intelligent, critical, relevant and life enhancing to today's public than the ten thousandth performance of *La Bohème*.

Nothing in the book should, however, be taken to imply that opera is, or opera-lovers are engaged in, an art that is *inferior* to classical theatre, orchestral music, great literature or painting. Such comparisons between the arts are difficult to make, but it must nevertheless be emphasised that it is when governments claim that opera ostensibly gains their support simply because it is the supreme art that the public is being misled. Opera matters to governments for different and important reasons, and that must be made clear. It must also be understood that whatever the motives might be of the monarchs, prime ministers, presidents, generals, the political and economic power brokers who attend the great opera performances, elsewhere in the house there will certainly be many who are there simply and solely because they love the art. It will, however, be argued in these pages that although such opera-lovers exist in large numbers, they are not necessarily the most important factor in the essential opera experience which European states promote, and that many of the well known 'opera-lovers' have provided some of the most valuable comparative critiques of social mores and political intent. The heart of this argument is thus to investigate the source of opera's political context and not to debate musical aesthetics.

Opera is of course sung in many places other than the great state opera houses. Europe has many specialist opera houses which are of private foundation, such as Bayreuth and Glyndebourne. It has many touring companies such as Britain's Opera North, which turn theatres into opera houses by their visits, and it has many successful opera houses in its cities, supported by local populations, such as the recently renovated theatres of Lyons and Bordeaux. The arguments in this book may well help to explain some curious phenomena in such houses, such as the way in which the audience behaves and the price it is prepared to pay to attend such performances. They may also help to explain the many opera houses funded by German municipalities which provide a repertory of opera that, some argue, is another form of opera although it is clearly not state opera. This book, however, essentially seeks to make its case by concentrating upon those great national opera houses which are so curiously – and, to some in arts management, irritatingly – close to national governments.

The argument rests upon the European operatic tradition, but it will be found (and demonstrated in some detail in the case of the Metropolitan Opera and the Sydney Opera House) that the argument generally can be applied to *all* opera houses which are related, even loosely, to Western cultures. Thus the crisis which took place in the Bastille Opera House in Paris in the 1990s bears an uncanny similarity to the 1957 crisis in the Teatro Colón in Buenos Aires, when the Argentinian government confronted the artists and closed the theatre.[33] Although the United States is a federation and lacks a strong recent tradition of state subsidy for its arts, the organisation and presentation at the Metropolitan Opera House are still in many respects more like those of its European counterparts than the other performing arts in the United States.

Finally, it is worthwhile to pause and consider the question of why opera houses continue to be built today. At the time of writing the design and construction of the opera house in Beijing are very much being reported. It will be of great interest to observe its evolution. Singapore is currently building two theatres of over 1,800 seats each which will perform the function of monumental theatres hitherto lacking in that young and now wealthy city state, which has started to call itself 'vibrant' and boasts a state-initiated 'cultural renaissance'.[34]

The Sydney Opera House is an enlightening case study, as such a project highlights the real meaning of opera in the twentieth century. It reveals the apparent incongruity whereby a country which veers ever more sharply to republicanism, and which prides itself on its 'new world' image, has been sufficiently impressed by the European cultural tradition to provide what is, in effect, a national opera house built to represent its traditional meaning.

The Labor Premier of New South Wales, John Cahill, who was largely responsible for the promotion of the project, equated democratic principles and traditional symbolism in his justification of the construction of such a house:

> the building when erected will be available for the use of every citizen, ... the average working family will be able to afford to go there just as well as people in more favourable economic circumstances, ... there will be nothing savouring even remotely of a class conscious barrier and ... the Opera House will, in fact, be a monument to democratic nationhood in its fullest sense.[35]

The example of the Sydney Opera House thus well illustrates the confusion inherent in the construction and maintenance of opera houses in today's modern states. It can be seen today in the United Kingdom that the equally ambiguous domain of subvention and funding allocation to opera is being played out between two traditionally rival operatic establishments. These are now being pitted against arts organisations of all kinds for funds from the national lottery. The argument inherent in such a policy is that there is one cake to be divided up into socially equitable parts and that the previous 'have nots', the non-establishment arts, have seemingly equal rights to the resources of a finite cake. Traditionally, however, this cake has not been finite where opera is concerned; nor indeed is it today. Opera is expensive. The very nature of the resources required to produce it, as well as the funds needed to maintain its premises, render it so. Even the renowned La Scala opera house in Milan at the height of the Bel Canto period experienced severe financial difficulties. When opera has run into financial difficulty, ways have been found and assurances have been given by incumbent powers to support the maintenance of the institution. Indeed in 1923 Mussolini instructed Alberto de Stefani, his Minister of Finance, to find a way of supporting the opera house. When the reply was tardy and unfavourable, he was simply told unequivocally to do so.[36] Another example of such an occasion was the assurance given by the Chancellor of the Exchequer Sir Hugh Dalton to Sir John Anderson, Chairman of the Covent Garden board, in August 1946 that 'the State will be assuming a definite obligation to see to it that ... Opera is not let down'.[37] The pledge of such support for opera, in postwar austerity Britain, was by no means an inconsiderable nor lightly proposed commitment, particularly as commitments of this kind are traditionally binding upon successor chancellors.

Yet what does the term 'opera' tell one of an institution interwoven in the European tradition of ceremonial display, ritual and particularly culture, which has been maintained throughout its four hundred year history by powerful political forces and which is so often critically at the forefront of social experience and public conjecture? What does this broad term really signify?

It is impossible absolutely to define a word which means so many different things. Thus to avoid confusion and to distinguish between its separate and overlapping meanings the terms 'an opera', 'the opera' and simply 'opera' can be taken to describe each part of the event: the work; the experience; and its function.

This books rests its argument on the important distinction between these three elements, for so much of the confusion surrounding opera stems from an incomplete understanding of their separate and yet overlapping parts. These distinctions can be described in terms of:

i)   'an opera' – the performed composite musical work;

ii)   'the opera' – the social connotations of the venue, the people who frequent it, their modes of dress and behaviour; in short the many events external to the work itself and yet so intrinsic to the notion of going to 'the opera'; and

iii)   'opera' – the widest and hence most difficult meaning of the word. When 'opera' is referred to, it will mean an operatic institution which emulates state ceremonial, disseminating the images closely aligned with any legitimation of power. It is at 'opera' that the glory and ceremonial of state can be suffused from a seemingly non-political venue. Simply put, it is the extended meaning encompassing the first two elements of 'performance' and 'experience' as well as including its political meaning, where 'opera' becomes an arena of civic performance.

The first meaning, 'an opera', has frequently been investigated and is identified but not discussed in depth in this book. The realm of the performed work is nonetheless important but has too often taken precedence, casting a veil over wider and, I argue, more significant meanings of the word 'opera'. The second meaning has been addressed by social commentators and opera-goers throughout the centuries who describe the buildings and their audiences, their behaviour and traditions. Thus the intention of this book is to stress not only that opera, the third meaning of this word, occupies an unusual position in the continuum of state-funded arts organisations, but also that its position is unique in that there is a demonstrable continuity of political intent throughout European opera. It is this continuity which is central to opera's meaning over time and under very different regimes.

The term 'power brokers', which is used throughout this book, simply refers to those who at any particular time control the levers of power in any of the countries under consideration.

Just as this book addresses the important aspect of the third meaning of opera and therefore is not a discussion of operatic works, it is also advised that it should not be read as a 'history of opera'. There are many excellent accounts of its chronological history. The historical argument rests on those moments when the house and its uses display the political and ceremonial purpose of the power brokers and as such is selective in its use of historical examples. It is the essential contention of this research that opera houses are useful to the state, and supported by it, for purposes quite other than cultural. Moreover, it will be demonstrated through compounded historic example that governments treat state opera houses as monumental constructs which serve to legitimise, through the use of ceremony and ritual, the power of the state. Furthermore, such an assertion is prescriptive. This research does not end with that which has occurred until now for, if such a trend is accepted, opera's meaning will be projected further into the socio-political structures of societies to come. The question which prompted the initial research is a very simple one. Why does opera – unlike theatre, music and literary forms – change its nature so little but retain such powerful support from all kinds of states? The hypothesis attempts to reconcile its inherent complexities by suggesting that it is the nexus between opera and the state which determines the central nature of opera, attracts such unwavering state support, and draws such powerful reactions from its supporters and detractors.

2

PRINCELY PLEASURES

Princes and Power – The Birthplace of European Opera

'Opera' – 'Italy'; to an opera enthusiast these words might seem almost synonymous. When we think of Italian opera, we think of the great composers, and so too of the great opera houses and their grand traditions: La Scala – Milan, La Fenice – Venice, San Carlo – Naples, Teatro Regio – Parma, Teatro dell'Opera – Rome, Teatro della Pergola – Florence, Teatro Carlo Felice – Genoa, this proliferation of musical art and of a great tradition with its roots firmly planted in the Florentine renaissance and the princely courts of its patrons. Yet this unified image flies in the face of the history of this modern country. Italy as we know it comprises states which have been ruled over and influenced by many different powers, before being finally unified in 1870, with central power vested in Rome. The grand theatre of La Scala owes much to Austrian and French occupation; the great San Carlo is a scion of the Bourbon's great Spanish empire; even Carlo Felice of Genoa was under the rule of the kingdom of Sardinia. La Fenice, one of the few remaining public theatres created by the wealthy Venetian merchant classes, soon to be dominated by the Austrians, has its roots in a very different history. Yet when we speak of 'Italian opera', it would seem to mean that there is one homogeneous entity in the modern state of Italy and that these very real differences do not exist.

Of course opera is undeniably a recognisable art form, but even that art form has changed considerably through the years, from the intimate counterpoint of its inventors (or re-inventors if the notion of renaissance is to be believed) to the verissimo of Verdi or the atonal musings of the twentieth century. It is of course a profession comprised of singers, managers, impresarios, directing committees and its own public. Opera is also a mode of social behaviour. Etiquette in the box has been particularly commented on in Italy by local and foreign observers.[1] La Scala, however much it changes, remains 'La Scala', the foremost operatic institution in Italy in the minds of many and a point of reference not only within Italy but far outside it. No matter that Venice once boasted over 20 public opera houses and that its one remaining house has been recently razed, in keeping with its prophetic name, La Fenice will rise like a phoenix and become, once again, *the* opera house of Venice. We recognise these houses as symbols. We know that once within their walls stood such different figures in the history of opera as da

Ponte, Rossini, Verdi, Boito, Puccini, Toscanini and Callas, and that their beginnings were fathered by the likes of Monteverdi. They are in themselves a tradition.

Could then this opera, this Italian opera, be something quite different from opera in other countries? This book will set out to prove that it is remarkably similar to the opera of other European countries from the sixteenth to twentieth centuries. That its genesis was in the northern Italian states is without a doubt but its essential meaning cannot be locked into the time and place of its birth. Those circumstances no longer exist, but opera does.

Perhaps the apparent superiority of Italian opera has to do with language. After all, there has been much literature over the centuries about the essentially lyrical nature of the Italian language, which should guarantee its aesthetic superiority for operatic purposes. Jean-Jacques Rousseau and many French intellectuals certainly espoused this view, as too did many English supporters of Italian opera. But if this were a natural state, why then throughout the centuries have operas been written and sung in French, German, English and Russian? The Italian language was deemed for the most part (except in France) to be the most prestigious language for the singing of opera. Indeed in 1709 the English satirist Thomas Addison, in a very well-known essay, points out that although the language is massacred beyond recognition, it predominates on the English musical stage. In the nineteenth century Covent Garden was, of course, the Royal Italian opera and Paris had a Théâtre Italien. Covent Garden premièred Bizet's *Carmen* in the Italian language (although it was written in French and contained French recitative) and in 1888 Wagner's *Die Meistersinger* underwent the same fate. Certainly the great Monteverdi and many other composers were Italian, but they were often paid by such noble families as the Gonzaguans with firm allegiances to the Austro-Hungarian empire. The eighteenth century produced, alongside great Italian composers and librettists, Mozart (an Austrian), Handel (a German who worked mainly in England) and the great librettist da Ponte, a man of northern Italian birth whose career stretched from Venice to Austria, Germany, England and finally the United States. Or perhaps our memories are more selective and rooted somewhere in the nineteenth century, where the great Italian names we now identify with bel canto opera dominated the world stage: Verdi, Donizetti, Rossini, Boito, Puccini. True the great Paris Opéra of the 1830s hosted many Italians who had left their great (if it was) cultural tradition to flock to the Théâtre Italien. John Rosselli, the Italian opera historian, reports that 'it has been said, only two per cent of Italians could speak Italian when the country was nominally unified in 1870 and few had any real sense of belonging to a new nation'.[2] He believes that this view is an oversimplification and that 'much of the urban population – admittedly a minority in the peninsula – could handle Italian, as well as the local dialect, for some purposes',[3] but nonetheless it does demonstrate that the notion of national cohesion through a shared common language was hardly the case as recently as the nineteenth century.

If opera is so loved by the Italians over every other people, and subject to other rules, then why in the late nineteenth century did La Scala find itself in a situation which so resembles that of the Metropolitan in New York at the same time, in encountering significant financial difficulties whilst maintaining a reasonable artistic success, which forced some to argue for the need for state subvention, though this was not in fact bestowed on La Scala until the mid-1920s. The arguments used do not differ significantly from those of the Paris Opéra at the time, nor from the repeated pleas for subvention which have come from English opera managers over the years.

Some romantic commentators say that it is because opera is understood and 'cherished in the hearts of the Italian people' that it is so important. Perhaps that is a convenient myth? True, today in the arenas of Caracalla and Verona one can be part of an audience of 30,000 made up of a wide diversity of spectators. Some, of course, are opera enthusiasts, although many would argue that the event is what brings the audience as musical purity cannot be controlled or sustained in these arenas of epic proportions. Are these traditional opera-goers? Certainly the great theatres of the nineteenth century did not house such hordes. In fact many of the large musical theatres in the United Kingdom housed more people than the Italian opera houses of the nineteenth century. Why has opera shared finan-cial difficulties if it is so universally popular within the Italian borders?

It is the very nature of opera which determines such things and, although popular opinion would have it otherwise, that nature is not state specific. It does seem that some countries can produce a greater number of singers, librettists, composers than others, but managerially, economically, socially and monu-mentally the Italian opera behaves as all other opera houses have done. The mystique is perhaps Latin, or Italian, but the reality is essentially bound up with the real meaning of opera.

That Italy has often been recognised as a plunder house for Europe is well evidenced by Austro-Hungarian, Prussian, French, English and Spanish behaviour. It is not only the ruins of Rome which have attracted the attention of others. The French had set up their Academy in Rome in the late seventeenth century, making its most prestigious arts prize the *Prix de Rome*, a coveted two-year stay in that city. Marriages of French royalty to Italian princes were celebrated by operas in the late sixteenth century and the French very quickly, as they did with many of the trappings of Italian taste, chose to adopt these enter-tainments. François I of France brought the loggia and Leonardo da Vinci to Amboise in France, where he died, and the *Mona Lisa* remains in the former royal palace, the Louvre, to the present day. Furthermore, Louis XIV would bring opera to his court, making it distinctly French under the supervision of an Italian musician, Lully, and Napoleon I would enter Milan as a victor and remain there for almost two decades,[4] as later would Napoleon III. The Austrian and Spanish courts were full of prizes of what we now call Italy. And yet somehow this pillaged ground would retain a heritage distinctly its own. And it would become known as the birthplace, if not the home, of opera.

Thus one can understand how and why Garibaldi should have chosen (almost operatically) to cry out 'O Roma o morte' from a box of the Palermo opera house, and how over a century later the English critic Spike Hughes would claim that La Scala in Milan was 'not so much a theatre as an idea, an attitude of mind',[5] maintaining that the bombing of 1943 represented only a destruction of bricks and mortar but not of the spirit or essential meaning of the building. Thus, he argued, the damage to the institution was not of great significance, especially as the very process of reconstruction was to serve as a metaphor for the rebuilding of international alliances.[6]

That the institution of opera is important to the modern Italian state is undeniable and that this is not vested in only one house due to the nature of Italian history. But, with the emergence of the new state, other more basic needs were pressing on its governors. Thus in 1868 Parliament withdrew subsidy from opera houses and actually imposed a 10% tax on their takings. Only wealthy municipalities could support the art form, and Milan therefore could use its prosperity to ensure that its opera house retained its 'position of leadership'.[7] The traditional forms of support from society and gambling thus disappeared in the latter part of the nineteenth century and the debate, so familiar to the British and French, was heard in Italy about whether opera should be subsidised when the poor needed more basic amenities, and, if so, how this should be done. Almost a century later we find, however, that the state has not relinquished its support for opera and found a role for 13 public opera companies:

> in 1967 Law no. 800 (still in force), dealing with the organisation of the 13 public 'Enti Lirici' (opera authorities), acknowledged to the Teatro dell'Opera in Rome a special role *'for the representative function carried out by the theatre in the capital of the state'* but went on to declare La Scala, an autonomous 'Ente Lirico' since 1920, to be 'a body of particular national interest in the field of music'.[8] (my italics)

Thus the modern state recognises within its statutes the role of this institution and the significance of the theatres themselves. Its source can be located in the very origins of opera, embedded in the renaissance search for antique examples of greatness. Notably, these contained architectural references which from an early stage were interwoven into the meanings of the houses. Leacroft's study of European theatres, complete with designs of the Italian theatre of Sabbioneta and the Farnese theatre in Parma, well illustrates this.[9] Few were the operas of the eighteenth and nineteenth centuries which did not incorporate the traditional pillars, pediments, statues and monumental staircase so associated with the greatness of past eras. These symbols were perceived to be fundamental to the meaning of the house and, by some, to be more important than the operatic event itself.

Thus opera houses were built in a sense to upstage each other; each aimed to establish itself not only as the foremost theatre within a nation but as the most remarkable theatre in the Western world. This is reinforced by the position they hold within urban configurations or morphology. The eighteenth century San Carlo Theatre in Naples was placed next to Charles III's palace and connected to it by private corridors,[10] and the Regio opera in Turin was attached to the royal palace so that the king could be found 'munching breadsticks, thoroughly at home'.[11]

This notion of grandeur is further reinforced by Lalande, who gives us an interesting account of San Carlo in Naples, opened on 4 November 1737, the feast day of both the saint and King Carlos III, King of Naples and eventually of Spain:[12]

> 'The boxes,' he says, 'were large and comfortable for people who pass a quarter of their life in them are naturally careful to furnish them agreeably.' There was a restaurant and there one could have warmed up one's dishes (presumably brought from home when one wished to sup in one's box); in which one was waited on by the staff of servants. But boxes could not, like those of Venice, be closed off from the theatre by a shutter. The archduke's box had attached to it a private sitting room and even a bedroom. The performances were extremely splendid, the enormous stage sometimes being occupied by 400 persons and 40 horses.[13]

This is an insightful description, as Lalande places emphasis on the ceremony of restoration and segregation of Italy's aristocracy, with its taste for the spectacular and 'splendid' on its stage.

In 1767 Ferdinand IV, aged 16, ascended the throne. Ferdinand entirely renovated the theatre in 1768 on the occasion of his marriage to Marie-Caroline, daughter of Maria-Theresa of Austria, constructing new stage boxes and increasing its gilded and mirrored splendour.[14]

The following description, written on 4th September 1771 by Charles Burney, the British chronicler of musical traditions on the European continent in the eighteenth century, on the occasion of a gala performance at San Carlo, gives us a very good idea of the grandeur of such an event:

> It is not easy to imagine or describe the grandeur and magnificence of this spectacle. It being the great festival of St. Charles and the King of Spain's name-day, the court was in grand gala, and the house was not only doubly illuminated, but amazingly crowded with well-dressed company.(*)[15] ... The King and Queen were present. Their majesties have a large box in the front of the house ...[16]

But Burney the musician does find fault with this regal display, where voice and instruments are very evidently not the fundamental reason for attendance at the opera:

But to return to the theatre of S. Carlo, which, as a spectacle, surpasses all that poetry or romance have painted: yet with all this, it must be owned that the magnitude of the building and noise of the audience are such, that neither the voices or instruments can be heard distinctly. I was told, however, that on account of the King and Queen being present, the people were much less noisy than on common nights.[17]

The year 1797 brought further decorations to celebrate the marriage of Prince Francis to the Austrian Archduchess Marie-Clementine. The Italian opera historian William Weaver therefore could unhesitatingly assert that:

> Thus in the eighteenth century it can be seen from these selected examples that size, site, architecture, decoration, spatial requirements and social significance were undeniably perceived to be essential elements of an opera house. The commentators were drawn to comment as much on these factors as any discussion of performance.[18]

However, the century was not entirely over and social orders were bound to change; the close of the century in Naples, as in most of Europe, heralded a very new era. 1799 proved to be a revolutionary year, as French republican armies won a victory over the city and forced the king to flee to Sicily. A republican government, the *Repubblica partenopea*, did not manage to ban Ferdinand's birthday celebrations in the theatre on 12 January but closed the theatre shortly afterwards for a fortnight. The republicans promptly renamed the San Carlo as the *National Theatre* and took up residency in the Court Theatre of the royal palace, planning amongst other things to celebrate their new-found power with a grand ball to be held that June in the liberated National Theatre. However, the King returned to Naples in June 1799 and the San Carlo quickly reacquired its familiar name.

During the years 1806–1808 Joseph Bonaparte was to rule Naples and, although under this administration the interiors were not changed to reflect the new ascendant powers, a more fundamental change took place: 'the theatre was remodelled on that set up by Napoleon in Paris'.[19] No longer were the Bourbons and their administration to be responsible for the running of Neapolitan opera. Joseph Bonaparte was succeeded by Joachim Murat, who brought with him French officials whose intention it was to make their mark on the Teatro di San Carlo. The most significant of these men was M. Lecomte, who 'planned to construct a new facade and renovate the exterior of the San Carlo'. These plans were seen by one of the San Carlo's scenographers, Antonio Niccolini, who managed to convince Murat, whom 'the Emperor had installed as King of Naples', that 'an open competition for designs' should be held.[20] Thus the era of competitions, which we hold so dear in our age, in which the bywords of accountability and access seem so strong, has its origins in infinitely non-democratic environments. The king agreed to this scheme and it was won by the very same Niccolini, who created the façade which still stands today as well as a new foyer and interior decorations.

In 1815 Napoleon and, with him, the French Neapolitan King Murat fell from power. The Bourbon King Ferdinand IV returned to the city. On 19 June he appeared in his box at San Carlo and was 'enthusiastically welcomed'.[21] Weaver's unnamed observer commented that:

> all reports agree that the theatre had never been so brilliantly lighted, nor had there been, as one observer wrote, 'more perfect or more seemly joy'. The king was moved to tears; and when his bust appeared on the stage amid the banners of all the Allied Powers, the theatre resounded with applause and continued cheering for half an hour.[22]

Yet again the opera house becomes the scene for a legitimisation of power. This king, so aligned with San Carlo from the first, as his father, the Spanish King, had been its constructor, was shown fealty within the very walls of this house that was so intimately connected to his palace.

On 12 February 1816 the Teatro di San Carlo was burnt down but, as has become customary after such events, witnessed in recent history by the reconstruction of the Teatro Real in Barcelona, or La Fenice in Venice, or La Scala and the Staatsoper after the war, it was rebuilt with remarkable speed as well as retaining significant features. In the case of the San Carlo, the 'specially constructed corridor connecting it with the palace' was retained.[23]

In less than a year, and on the occasion of King Ferdinand's birthday on 12 January 1817, the theatre was reopened with a gala occasion. Stendhal describes the event, noting that: 'This mighty edifice, rebuilt in the space of 300 days, is nothing less than a *coup d'état*: it binds the people in fealty and homage to their sovereign far more effectively than any constitution ....'[24] Such a statement demonstrates his absolute recognition of the meaning of opera. Known for his artistic critiques of opera in his diaries on Rome, Florence and Naples, it is significant that he acknowledges in language with which we are already familiar, 'awe and expectation', the function of the operatic venue and thus its real supra-artistic meaning, which like the coup d'état is a political event. Stendhal comments that: 'The magnificence of San Carlo marks adoration of King Ferdinand; we see him in his box sharing the delights of the public: this word "sharing" lets us forget many other events.'[25] He explains this enigmatic commentary from the point of view of a not-so-enraptured Neapolitan, who was less than pleased with his royalist sentiments: 'You see a theatre, he says, and you don't see the little cities', which was understood by Stendhal to mean that this man was a Rousseauean 'noble savage'.

Stendhal concludes that, although he was initially deceived by the splendour of this theatre, as a musical machine it is infinitely inferior to that of Milan but that it is important that it be maintained for national pride.[26] He describes the ceremonies which accompany the purchase of a seat, comparing it to the moeurs of La Scala:

> In Naples, San Carlo theatre is only open three times a week. You proceed through corridors with increasingly pretentious titles written on the doors of the boxes which tell you in large lettering that you are only an atom which an Excellency can wipe out. You enter with your hat; a hero of Tolentino follows you. Mme Conti enchants you and you want to applaud her but because the king is present applause is a sacrilege. You want to leave your seat but a grand noble emblazoned with medals ... murmurs that you lack respect. Bored by these pretensions, you leave and ask for your transport; but you have to wait and catch cold as the six horses of some princess obstruct the door for over an hour. (my translation)[27]

The first quarter of the nineteenth century was extremely volatile, and in 1820 the July Rebellion in Naples pushed the king into promising to grant a constitution. This promise took another two decades to honour and, according to Hughes, the performance of *Atilla* in that revolutionary year

> now gave the Neapolitans an opportunity to show their feelings and cheer at the stirring sounds of 'Avrai tu l'universo, resti l'Italia a me!' (You may have the universe, but let me keep Italy!) At the performance of the opera on the 29th January the theatre (according to a contemporary journal called L'Omnibus) was a mass of waving tricolour handkerchiefs from all parts of the house. It was the day on which, after years of promises broken by the Bourbons, the granting of a constitution was finally announced.[28]

This well-timed opera, which so captured the spirit of the *Rissorgimento*, was performed in a gala on 1 February to celebrate the granting of the constitution, and King Ferdinand II and all the royal family were in attendance to mark the occasion.

The rigours of censorship prevailing in all the Italian states during the nineteenth century are well documented and too numerous to comment upon here. Verdi, who composed for all the great theatres of Italy, had his work consistently subject to scrutiny for possible political associations. It is unusual, however, for an international event to affect the production of opera. But in 1856 an attempt was made on the life of Napoleon III of France and it was an Italian, Felice Orsini, who was responsible. The script of Verdi's new work was banned on the basis 'that neither title, subject, scene, characters nor verses were admissible'[29] by the prevailing Neapolitan authorities in order to prevent any more outbreaks of unrest in the opera house. Verdi, who was now aligned politically with the rissorgimento movement, withdrew the opera and demonstrations followed by the people of Naples, who cried out 'Viva Verdi', which was meant to be an acronym for *Viva **V**ittorio **E**manuele **R**e **D**'Italia* – Viva, Vittorio Emanuele King of Italy.[30]

Within a decade, however, responsibility for the management of La Scala was taken over by the Municipality of Milan and, within another decade, the theatre was closed and remained closed for two years until 1876 whilst a battle for subsidy was fought out. Such a downturn in the opera's history can be attributed to a number of factors: Naples' decreasing importance in the newly shaping European map, the fact that opera houses world-wide were facing economies of scale which rendered performances uneconomical, as one sees with the situation of the Metropolitan in New York, where the famous Neapolitan tenor Enrico Caruso spent most of his career, or the Carlo Felice in Genoa and even in La Scala in Milan, and the shifting power bases which made subvention rather more unstable. It was no longer 'de rigueur' to attend the opera to see and be seen, as other, newer entertainments were emerging which momentarily cast a shadow over the operatic experience. Certainly since the late nineteenth century there had been moments of great activity in San Carlo, and most notably between the two world wars, but during the Second World War Naples was subjected to blackouts and bombing, although the 1940–41 season went ahead. Here we see the new power brokers, the Minculpop (Ministry of Popular Culture), making their mark on this theatre by insisting that a comic opera be included in the repertoire of 1941. This is in many ways the first evidence that governments can shift absolutely the meaning of a house. Hitherto the reasons for opera houses were fairly respected. A comic opera, or volksoper, played popular works to entertain the public. Opera houses presented a very different kind of work, designed to uplift and to an extent dignify those present on the occasion of the performance. Since the Second World War the mixing of genres has been one of the arguments which governments use when trying to argue for the necessity of state subvention. The 'democratisation' and 'accessibility' of the operatic form have become a major tenet of modern government. That this seems no less problematic to a fascist, socialist or democratic government is a thought worthy of consideration.

Performances continued during the Second World War, but during the daytime, until the theatre finally closed its doors to the public in 1943. On 4 August 1943 the theatre received a direct hit, although only the foyer was destroyed. When the allied troops entered Naples, the British requisitioned the theatre 'with the sole intention of using it for concerts and operas' and, according to Harold Rosenthal, 'over 1 3/4 million members of the Allied Forces attended performances' between 1943 and 1946,[31] which Hughes claims 'provided thousands of British troops with their first experience of "Grand Opera"'.[32] Such a statement reveals much, as E.J. Dent was pursuing a similar policy under ENSA in the United Kingdom, educating those newly enfranchised to the refinements of music, theatre and opera.

The restoration of the foyer took place with great speed and by 1946 little evidence of the destruction could be found. The plaque thanked the occupying forces, the mayor and the management for 'keeping alive the flame of its traditions', which as we know is the essential meaning of opera. In 1946 the San Carlo Opera Company visited England, at once reinforcing the importance of Italian opera in Britain and also functioning as a cultural envoy of peace, as memories of that bitter war were erased through the vehicle of musical diplomacy.

Hughes describes the atmosphere he sensed back-stage at San Carlo ('It is an atmosphere which I can only describe as being aristocratic, gracious and elegant') and then being taken through the private passage from the palace into the theatre 'to reveal the full breathtaking beauty and splendour of the theatre'.[33] This account, written 150 years after Stendhal's exclamations of awe and expectation, differs little, and it is perhaps these sentiments which define the meaning of the house. Perhaps all this can be encapsulated in the central focus of that theatre – the royal box, which during the Second World War witnessed a gala performance in the presence of Vittorio Emanuele, Mussolini and Hitler, the power brokers of their age, who, flanked by their historical predecessors, demonstrated the legitimation of their power from this very site. No operatic work resonates with such meaning as this public display of power.

We move now to another great centre of opera in Italy, Venice. In so many ways this city distinguishes itself from other Italian cities. Its history and geography conspire to make all institutions of the city singular. The operatic history of Venice cannot be traced back to ducal courts but rather to that city state's merchant background. In 1637 the Teatro San Cassiano, the first public opera, opened its doors rather than remain a restricted court affair. In its heyday Venice boasted no fewer than twenty public theatres and today, sadly, as a result of a fire set deliberately in order to claim on insurance, there is momentarily none. Il Teatro del Fenice (Gran Teatro al Fenice), like the phoenix of its name, will, however, soon rise from its ashes and witness once more an operatic life.

In the revolutionary year of 1789 a competition was announced for the design and construction of a new theatre in Venice. The instructions 'defined the cultural environment and the logistical objectives' of the Società, which was comprised of a 'society of noblement together with a Council of Ten'.[34] Competitors could be national or international and were given considerable information about the restrictions which the site placed on them. (This is not very different from the announcement in 1952 in Australia of an international competition for an opera surrounded by water.) A young architect, Giannantonio Selva, was the winner of a competition in which 29 entries were submitted to construct a new opera house in Venice. The new house was opened on 17 May 1792. It was loudly and universally acclaimed as a masterpiece.

This newly constructed theatre was to be a focal point during the revolutionary months of May to November 1797. It was draped in banners, celebrating 'republican virtues' and friendship towards the French, and its doors opened free of charge for the first time in its history to gondoliers. It even hosted balls for workers of the nearby 'arsenale'. It has even been claimed that at this moment it 'represented democracy and a new national conscience'.[35] This early baptism was to establish the house as a place where the history of the Italian city state would be played out on its stage, in its auditorium, in its boxes and in its elegant halls. Venice was never to be the capital of the new unified state.

Indeed, within the opera house itself a symbol of the political changes was the royal box. From 1807 it has constantly been tinkered with to reflect the 'fortunes and lack of fortune of dynasties and diverse institutional forms, empires, kingdoms and republics, all anxious to signify in striking manner their often precarious triumphs. Alongside the structural change went changes in nomenclature, as boxes, for example, became known as Imperial Box, Imperial and Royal Box, etc.'[36]

The Bonaparte regime associated itself fully with the symbolic power of the opera house. On the occasion of Josephine de Beauharnais' visit, amongst the activities held were a parade by the National Guard, where a patriotic hymn was sung with full throat, balls and illuminations. Stendhal, whose interests were apparently more chaste, associates all this with the trappings of political power and fortune, concluding that the Fenice's significance rests upon its tradition and monumental stature, which themselves are a source of political legitimation.[37]

> This theatre, which gives onto the Grand Canal, has an original façade. We enter and leave by gondola, which are all of the same; what a fatal spot for envious beings. This theatre was magnificent during the time of the government of San Marco, as the Venetians say. Napoleon also gave to it some wonderful days, but now it is decaying like the rest of Venice. This city, the most original and vibrant of Europe, will be only an unhealthy village in 30 years from now unless Italy wakes up and gives itself one king, in which case I would give my vote to Venice, impenetrable city, for being Italy's capital.[38]

By 1828 the theatre was to be restored again by Borsato, who had been in charge of the first redesign of the imperial box. But that glorious theatre, so full of historic events and grand social displays, was not to last. On the night of 12–13 December 1836 the theatre was almost entirely destroyed by fire. The new Fenice, again true to its name, was reconstructed at extraordinary speed and opened on 26 December 1837. The new architects, two brothers named Meduna, were charged with making a faithful reconstruction of Selva's original work and yet modernised much of the internal workings and made the interiors much more ornamental. In 1843 gaslight replaced oil lighting. In 1848 the imperial boxes were transformed into six smaller boxes and were closed until Venice was integrated into Italy in 1866. Reduced from twenty to just one theatre, but undeniably one of the most beautiful theatres in Italy, La Fenice retained its significance within Italy's operatic infrastructure.

Between the wars, the Società was no longer able to finance the theatre, which was not in receipt of a subsidy, and so in November 1936 the Fenice became the responsibility of the Commune of Venice. In April 1938 the Fenice was opened again as an Ente Autonomo, the form of autonomous corporation which characterises the nine principal state-subsidised opera houses of Italy.

The fiercely independent Venetians were to maintain public performances of opera throughout the Second World War. In contrast to its ally, many of these works were in fact by artists and from countries with whom Italy was at war.

It was at La Fenice on 26 April 1945, during a performance of Puccini's *Madam Butterfly*, that the announcement of the liberation of Milan was made from the stage. The season was immediately suspended but on 6 May the theatre opened its doors for a performance, in honour of the partisans and allied troops, of *Madam Butterfly*.[39] In a matter of days the season recommenced and La Fenice could proclaim loudly that it was the first theatre in northern Italy to open after the liberation.[40]

But let us turn back to the history of the best-known and most acclaimed theatre in Italy and possibly the world, Il Teatro alla Scala, and briefly observe the way in which it maintained its role, remembering that great artists such as Verdi boycotted the venue for many years, specifically writing into their contractual agreements that performances were not to take place there, and that Mozart's *Cosi Fan Tutte*, although successful in its first season, had to wait almost half a century for integration into its repertoire.

In Milan opera can be traced back to the year 1598 in a theatre named Regio Ducale, in the ducal palace, in honour of princess Margherita of Austria, who was on her way to Spain to marry Philip III. Milan, a duchy ruled by such distinguished families as the Visconti, was part of the Austro-Hungarian empire. So when in the mid-seventeenth century there was a need to construct a new opera house after the former one had been razed in a fire, it was the Empress of Austria, Maria-Theresa, and Duchess of Milan to whom approval of the plan put forward by box holders for La Scala fell in July 1776. This theatre, officially named 'il nuovo Regio Ducal Teatro di Milano', was opened on 3 August 1778 and is the theatre which we call 'La Scala' today; it took its title after a member of one of the great Milanese families, Regina della Scala, wife of Duke Bernardo Visconti.

It was thus a monumental and purpose built house with special provisions, containing within its walls the only gaming houses allowed in Milan. It was designed to inspire awe in its public. The box holders 'were allowed to display their coats of arms on the front' and have passed these down until this day.[41]

The political events that swept across Europe soon after its construction also affected the house. Early in its history it was to host festivities by the power brokers. In 1793 the coronation of Emperor Joseph II was celebrated with free admittance to everyone, and in 1797 Milan was freed from eight decades of Austrian domination by Napoleon, who 'made (Milan) the capital of his kingdom of Italy'.[42] According to Anthony Gishford,[43] Napoleon's actions marked the end of the Austrian domination and the dawn of 'the age of reason' under the French. The large royal box was divided into six boxes which were to be 'reserved for the "liberated people" '. In addition, performances were given to mark Napoleon's coronation as emperor, as it was clearly important that the best-known Italian opera house, La Scala, lent support to and reinforced the credibility of this regime. The young Stendhal rapturously wrote: 'That it is impossible to imagine anything grander, more magnificent, more imposing and newer in any form of architecture.'[44] Its magnificence was without doubt a deliberate and successful strategy for marking its importance, and consequently the importance of the merchant city of Milan.

It is here that this opera house distinguished itself in its new role as a literal beacon for the changing political climate within the city. According to Hughes, the Milanese illuminated La Scala during the following decade to celebrate the following state events:

- The anniversary of the execution of Louis XVI in 1792
- The arrival of Napoleon in 1797
- The return of the Austrians (with the Russians tagging along as co-liberators)
- The victory of Marengo
- Peace with England
- The coronation of Francis I of Austria
- The visit of Caroline, Princess of Wales
- The victory of the Allies at Waterloo[45]

Furthermore, the following coats of arms were displayed in quick succession,[46] demonstrating which power brokers were in control:

- The French Republic
- The Cisalpine Republic
- The Italian Republic (under Napoleon)
- The Kingdom of Italy (King: Napoleon I) and
- The Austro-Hungarian Empire incorporating the Kingdom of Bohemia
- When the French arrived they stripped the arms and crests from the boxes of La Scala and demolished the centre royal box
- but when the Austrians returned they put it back together again.

In December 1815 Francis I, Emperor of Austria, made a solemn entrance into the city of Milan and on 6 January 1816 La Scala payed tribute to its new monarch, thus returning Milan to its original rulers and giving the opportunity for La Scala to play an important role in the emergence of the new Italian state. According to Sergio Segalini, 'Milanese society returned to the traditions of the Austrian Court and went to la Scala as if to obey a rite'[47] and that rite was a social obligation. Lady Morgan wrote in 1820: 'After the Duomo, there is no shrine in Milan so attended, no edifice so prized, as the Theatre of the Scala.'[48] That La Scala retained throughout this period its social importance was attested to admirably by Stendhal, who highlights the uses of boxes in other parts of the theatre by distinguishing the social reasons for attendance from the musical:

> La Scala can very comfortably house 3,500 spectators. It has, if I remember correctly, 220 boxes, where three people can be seated in front, ... and the rest of the box or small salon can accommodate nine to ten people who change frequently throughout the evening. One is silent during the first performances, and following that only for the more beautiful pieces. The people who want to hear the whole opera go and find places in the stalls...[49]

It is clear that the theatre was attended very much for the social opportunities it afforded rather than the musical, however many claims to 'musicality' might be forthcoming. The theatre during the Napoleonic era of which Stendhal was writing was to present countless galas and balls and was the place to which 'society' repaired.

But Segalini goes on to argue that Napoleon and his republican discourse were not forgotten in the minds and hearts of the Milanese intelligentsia.[50] Thus the Austrian police 'doubled its surveillance' in order to stop any discernible unrest.

The significance of La Scala was thus established in its early days as both a theatre in which to see and be seen as well as a barometer and indicator of the current political climate. That it was an extravagant and grand house was an element which was keenly maintained, and in 1830 the entire theatre was redecorated, replacing 'red curtains and drapes in the boxes by a uniform blue silk'.[51] In 1838 the furnishings and hangings were renovated in honour of the coronation of Ferdinand I.

The revolutionary year 1848 was keenly felt in Milan, one of the strongholds of the Italian nationalist movement, and the fading Austrian empire kept its thumbs very closely on the city. It closed a number of theatres but allowed La Scala to remain open, as it was understood to be 'a symbol of the city'.[52] Inside the house, however, it doubled the proportion of Austrians and uniforms were to become more numerous than ball gowns. For their part the Milanese stayed away, leaving boxes unlit and corridors and meeting places empty.

In 1853 the Milanese rose up against the Austrians and La Scala was forced to close its doors. And by 1859 the Austrian stranglehold was broken. War broke out on 27 May, and on 4 June the Austrians were defeated at Marengo. Six days after this, Vittorio Emanuele and Napoleon III entered Milan and were welcomed by a gala programme on 14 June. Significantly, in June La Scala 'became a Royal theatre and bore the arms of an Italian King.'[53] The kingdom of Italy therefore became a fact and La Scala was to be recognised as part of it, even though Rome was not yet an integrated part of the kingdom. On 26 February 1860 Vittorio Emanuele revisited the city and was honoured at La Scala by the composition and performance of a special hymn in his honour.[54]

But even though this theatre was the home, or claimed to be the home, of some of the greatest opera in the newly unified states of Italy, it could not sustain the economics of such a venture and eventually lost the patience of its creditors. In 1897 the City Council of Milan withdrew its subsidy 'and for the first time in its history of 121 years La Scala did not open'.[55]

That this state of affairs could not last was evident, especially when the local aristocracy was responsible for the institution. According to the New Zealand soprano Frances Alda, later wife of the opera impresario Gatti-Casazza, director of La Scala:

> The house was closed for nearly a year and a half when Duke Visconti, who was President of the Board, and the other directors, heard about Gatti. … The directors of La Scala offered him the position of Director of La Scala. The shareholders and the city of Milan advanced the money for the first season. And Gatti has made money for them. He has brought *il bel canto* back to Italy – he and Maestro Toscanini, his conductor.[56]

But Gatti-Casazza was to leave for the United States and the Metropolitan Opera in New York and take with him the great conductor Toscanini. The opera remained open during the First World War and on 20 November 1917, on the occasion of a 'Patriotic Evening Dedicated to the Allies', Mussolini addressed the audience within the house.

After the First World War the theatre closed its doors and, with the exception of the presentation of a short season in 1918, remained closed until 1921. It was in this year that the theatre became an autonomous corporation.[57] It was financed by a specially designed tax imposed on cinemas, theatres, football grounds and other forms of entertainment. In 1922 Mussolini became Prime Minister and by 1925 he had had all powers vested in him.

Toscanini returned to Italy and La Scala after falling out with Gatti-Casazza in New York and brought with him the reputation that the house had been so longing to re-acquire. But again the history of the house became significantly influenced by events which were far from musical. Mussolini, whose power was increasing, was insisting that his portrait and that of the king be placed in the foyer of the theatre. He also demanded that the fascist hymn 'Giovanezza' be played before every performance. This is not as surprising as one may imagine. During the French revolution 'La Marseillaise' and other revolutionary songs were demanded before theatrical and operatic performances, and within the culture of the British Empire 'God Save the Queen' was played before any presentation, be it cinema, theatre or opera. Toscanini, however, would not agree to this. The situation was exacerbated as Il Duce had expressed a desire to attend the opening of Puccini's posthumous opera *Turandot* on 25 April 1926. This, the directors argued, would be a great honour for La Scala. Toscanini refused and Il Duce did not attend. What is interesting about this event is that

Mussolini, the new power broker, had wanted to do what power brokers have done throughout history, to make his mark publicly in the opera house by the representation of his likeness, his anthem and himself.

In 1929 the company toured what were soon to be Italy's allies, Austria and Germany, but with the great anti-fascist conductor at the helm, Arturo Toscanini.

In 1943 La Scala was reduced to rubble by an RAF bomb and, like its counterpart in Vienna, was rebuilt with remarkable speed and in its predecessor's likeness. There was one significant change to the auditorium, however, as the new theatre no longer contained a royal box. Even La Scala has been influenced by this wind of change. Spatial configurations were subtly tampered with to reflect the new political order. We learn that:

> On 11th May, 1946 the mended Scala was opened again with the auditorium a faithful reproduction of what had been before – with one important difference: the centre box was filled with old men and women from Verdi's rest home for aged Musicians.[58]

This 'democratisation', almost adulation, of the new social order is most significant. It tells of the new priorities of post-war Europe, where terms such as 'democratisation', 'accessibility', etc. were to become bywords. Telling too is that the new power brokers appeared harder to find on that night, although they reasserted themselves shortly after in the magnificent seasons of the 1950s and 1960s. Another interesting characteristic of that opening night was that, although the celebrated Toscanini conducted, no opera was performed, merely an operatic concert. This is no accident. The house was being celebrated more than the opera. Nor was this something unique to Italy: the Palais Garnier was opened in 1872 by a concert, Covent Garden enjoyed a ballet, the Sydney Opera House a concert, and the Vienna Opera a concert (after its reconstruction in 1955). Perhaps this is more indicative of the real meaning of opera than all the 'musical successes' within the walls of the great opera houses.

In 1947 Wagner's *Tristan und Isolde* was due to be performed in this recently liberated Italian house. The lead singer was to be Kirsten Flagstad, wife of a former Nazi dignitary. La Scala became a place again of violent protest, with banners and a large demonstration on the opening night. But this was to be among the last of such manifestations. The Cold War made for subtle shifts of protest and La Scala was to become the bastion for society, as it had been for much of its history. The dress standards, and the ceremony and costuming of attendants, remain to this day amongst the most impressive of European opera houses:

> At about 8.30, the white marble foyer of the world's most elegant opera house began to fill. Not a pair of female shoulders was un-minked; not a female throat unbejewelled; not a head of female hair untinted. The

world's most elegant opera house is patronised by the world's most elegantly dressed women.

At the auditorium entrance, attendants, costumed to look half vesper, half lord mayor in black uniforms and silver chains of office, waited sombrely for admission tickets – and for the hundred lire tip they would receive as they ushered each utterly aristocratic Milanese couple into their seats.[59]

The political climate of 1968 briefly visited itself on the opera, which maintained its traditions of evening dress in the face of

student demonstrators pelting the elegantly dressed leaders of Milan society with eggs, fruit and paint – mink-coated ladies being the special targets.[60]

Later in the century mink coats were yet again to be a target for demonstrators, who this time saw them as symbols of animal exploitation. In 1992

A group of attractive animal-rights activists mingles with the crowd in the foyer of the opera house in La Scala. Suddenly the protesters unbutton their second-hand, imitation-mink coats, reveal their bare breasts and cry: 'Better naked than in fur'.[61]

But this is not just a protest about choices of clothing materials. La Scala remains a venue to which Heads of State pay homage and the notion of the gala political event is still very much alive today. For example, even when the venue for opera is not necessarily 'grand', the event may still have high symbolic importance, as the author of the following article acknowledges:

Now, until September they [Caracalla Baths] are the scene of Gian Paolo Cresci's ostentatious efforts to put Roman opera back alongside La Scala or La Fenice in Venice. 'I want to put this theatre in the spotlight,' he says. 'When heads of state, ministers and ambassadors come to Rome, where should they go if not to the opera?'[62]

Rupert Christianson's account in the *Daily Telegraph* of 11 December 2000 of the opening night of the season at La Scala tells us that the opera house still has the highest symbolic importance:

Quite aside from the performance, the spectacle of a prima is dazzling. Outside the building, a parade of Milanese wealth and station sashays past ruthless paparazzi, heckling protestors and wide-eyed fans. A ceremonial guard of honour mans the foyer. Inside the creamily sumptuous auditorium the six tiers of boxes are garlanded with flowers.

It is all wildly extravagant and dazzlingly wonderful. If only our own beloved Covent Garden could sometimes dress itself up like this. The inverted snobbery of Chris Smith and his apparatchiks drearily supposes that the whiff of grandeur around opera houses deters poten-tial audiences – but isn't the prospect of something gorgeous and extraordinary precisely what draws them in?[63]

Finally, if one were in any doubt about the significance of opera in Italy, one need only refer back to what the historian of the fascist era and musical institu-tions in Italy Harvey Sachs calls 'an isolated episode in the history of' Mussolini's Italy. It was the attempt to create a national opera house in Rome. According to Sachs, 'La Scala, glorious but intractable – at least throughout the 1920s – was located too far from the capital to be of use as a showcase for impressing visiting dignitaries; and Mussolini was determined to establish a company in Rome that would equal and, if possible, overtake the Milanese sanctum sanctorum'. Thus in September 1924, on the second anniversary of the march on Rome, the cornerstone for this new opera house was to be laid next to the Queen's palace.[64]

This chapter has suggested that the opera houses of Italy, whether they be in Venice, Milan, Naples, Rome or other smaller cities, served at least two masters. Undeniably they were to be 'temples of music', but their very existence and significance were ultimately dependent on the importance given to them by the state. That the states changed and political affiliations were shuffled like decks of cards from the late eighteenth century onwards did not affect, in the least, the significance of these houses. They are places in which society witnesses the performances of both the power brokers and the artists. In Italy, so adept at the art of spectacle, that they have reached in many ways their quintessential impor-tance is clearly seen. Carlos III, Ferdinand IV, Napoleon, Francis of Austria, Garibaldi, Mussolini and countless others have understood their dual role and played out their performances not just to the operatic world, but also to the world of political power.

3

OF KINGS AND BARRICADES

From the Heart of Versailles to the
Place de la Bastille

Opera has been one of the most traceable and continuous symbols of the French state. Louis XIV, Napoleon, Louis XVIII, Napoleon III, Thiers, Charles de Gaulle and François Mitterrand are all linked by their absolute commitment to the maintenance of an opera at the centre of their orbits of power. Louis XIV's opera was found within Versailles and its gardens. Napoleon Bonaparte's was in his capital. Louis XVIII's was an extension of the palace. Charles X sanctified his at the cathedral of Rheims. Napoleon III and Thiers sited theirs within the commercial heart of the city. And finally François Mitterrand took the symbolic step of placing the opera at La Bastille, in the very heart of the square which symbolises revolutionary Paris.

When one thinks of modern France, romantic notions of great monarchies, revolutions and empires spring to mind, and a smattering of heros and anti-heros. In such a complex nation, where politics veered from absolutism to revolution, one would surely imagine that opera would be at best a distraction from the affairs of the state or a mere entertainment. And yet we find it clearly placed in every important era somewhere near the centre of power.

Opera was first brought to France from Italy by Cardinal Mazarin in 1645 for a performance before the Queen to a select audience. That Cardinal Mazarin's motives for this action were 'very largely political'[1] is generally acknowledged by historians. He achieved a significant beginning for what was to become, before the end of the century, the art that most reflected the state 'politique', in terms of the works themselves, its venue and its public.

By the time Louis XIV had reached his majority and revolutionised the meaning of monarchy, the creation of a national image was compounded by the weight of its artistic individuality and splendour. Opera was to become a perfect vehicle through which the politics of absolutism were to make inroads into the cultural visage of the state.[2]

In seventeenth century France the rationale at the core of the absolutist 'politique' of Louis XIV was to produce social devices which enabled him to mould all elements of his kingdom after his fashion. Opera was to serve as a vehicle reflecting a codified image of the state. Distinctions between frontiers and language were not linked to definitive notions of sovereignty and identity in

34

France as they are today, and so it was vital for French opera to be associated with the French language from the first. The undeniable basis of Louis XIV's reign was the quest for unification and homogeneity and these became the hallmarks of his state. Cultural policy was thus an element of political rationale, as vanquished states were made to yield to the greater power and to adopt the forms of the dominant culture. Given this political strategy, it would seem that opera lent itself naturally to serving such a rationale and became a state art and a state institution and thus a state symbol incorporating in its meaning the image of itself that the state wished to impart to other nations.

Historians tell us that the intention of Louis XIV was evidently to create a grand, magnificent opera.[3] What therefore could be more useful to such a regime than a theatrical genre which could present a representation of society and its hierarchy and reinforce it with all that was the most refined in ballet, music and voice, as well as the display of extraordinary machines to astonish a public which had become accustomed to grandiose display? This meaning of opera, which incorporated not only the genre but also its relationship to society and its usefulness to the state, was clearly adopted from its inception in France. As will be demonstrated throughout this chapter, the French Opéra has undergone many changes in title, in mode, in the manner of its subvention and its position within the French cultural order, and yet it has remained virtually unchanged from its beginnings until the present day.

Opera was legitimised by royal *privilège*, published on 28 June 1669. This document is important. It identified unequivocally the reasons for the introduction of opera into France. It was primarily a matter of national pride:

> over the past few years the Italians have created some Academies in which there are performances which are called Opera. These academies are composed of excellent musicians of the pope and other princes, and even members of honest families, nobility and gentlemen of birth, who are knowledgeable and experiment with the musical art with singing, and are currently the most beautiful productions and the most pleasant entertainments, not only in the cities of Rome, Venice and other Italian courts, but also in those cities and courts of Germany and of England where there have been Academies created on the Italian Model.[4]

Thus not only did the text of the edict make reference to the fact that opera had its source in Italian principalities representing both temporal and spiritual power, and was frequented and appreciated by a cultivated and noble public, but it also drew attention to the fact that it was imitated by France's great rivals, Germany and England. The intention was therefore not only to integrate opera into France, but also to divest opera of any Italian authority. Opera was to be formally cultivated in France not as an Italian import but as a French Academy (*Académie d'Opéra*), central to the French State, and additionally a source of

French national pride. In this *privilège*, or royal edict, the importance the state placed on the role of the French language in national culture is specifically identified, and the requirement that French opera should emulate the attributes of Italian opera is stressed so that the state's role as a pre-eminent cultural and political power be recognised.[5]

This first *privilège* was refined, and the importance of opera to the state further clarified, when it was given to Jean-Baptiste Lully, the great musician of Louis XIV's court, in the *lettres patentes* on 29 March 1672. (Lully, one could say, died for his court and for his art as, whilst beating time during one of his performances, his great baton pierced his foot, which quickly turned gangrenous and then fatal.) The new *privilège* commences with an acknowledgement of opera's importance in terms of its position in relation to the state, claiming that 'science and art are the most important ornaments of States'.[6] At that time the 'Académie' was renamed the 'Royal Academy' (*Académie Royale*), thus further linking it with the state as something more than an 'ornament' but rather as a valuable state asset upon the scene of which state interests could be promoted with all the pomp and ceremony the court desired.[7]

Lully's *privilège* is distinct from the first *privilège* of 1669 in that it allows for opera to be performed in languages other than French.[8] Thus Louis XIV in 1669 first created a French opera and by 1672, after an interval of only three years, confident of having established the French tone and the ascendance of its national opera, had incorporated opera sung in foreign languages into the repertory in the form of a new *privilège*.

But as Louis XIV grew old and the firm arm of absolutism became visibly enfeebled, criticism about the role and nature and, to an extent, the allegiance of opera became prevalent. Lully organised and ran the *Académie Royale de Musique* in an autocratic manner much resembling that in which Louis XIV ruled his kingdom. Dissent was for the most part quashed, as contenders could not enter the realm. Argument about opera therefore focused on themes other than musical and had at its heart a desire to combat the exclusivity and autocratic autonomy not only of the Academy, but also metaphorically of the state.

Lully and later Rameau were to be labelled as turncoats and political pawns by the protagonists of Italian opera. It was as if what they composed was seen to take on a much greater significance than that of musical expression. It could be suggested that it was as much these composers' connection with the crown, and the institutions of the crown, as their compositions of French opera, which instigated the depth of venom that was directed both at them and at their work.

In 1702 the Abbé François de Raguenet published the *Parallèle des italiens et des français en ce qui regarde la musique et les opéras*,[9] the first of many treatises concerning the relationship between French and Italian opera, and the nature of musical expression and dramatic action, in which he supported Italian opera. He thus opened up the century in France with the issues which would preoccupy it in literary terms. Opera was to become the focal point of three pamphlet wars during the century,[10] which used the relationship between Italy and France as a pretext for literary, philosophical and political debate by the greatest writers and intellectuals of the period.

Raguenet highlighted the central paradox in the French/Italian debate, which renders the actual argument irrelevant, by focusing upon the origins of Lully's birth and the obvious irony that he, by birth an Italian, is deemed the originator of all that is great in French *tragédie lyrique*:

> We are daily admiring Lully's fertile genius in the composition of so many beautiful different airs. France never produced a master that had a talent like him; this I'm sure no one will contradict, and this is all I desire to make it appear how much the Italians are superior to the French, both for the invention and composition, for, in short, this great man, whose works we set in competition ... with those of the greatest masters in Italy, was himself an Italian. He has excelled all our musicians in the opinion of the French themselves. To establish, therefore, an equality between the two nations, we ought to produce some Frenchman who has in the same manner excelled the greatest masters in Italy, and that by the confession of the Italians themselves; but this is an instance we have not yet been able to produce.[11]

Raguenet also perceived the importance of grandness as part of the meaning of opera itself. He supported the view that the term 'opera' meant more than just a performed work, 'an opera', but was also inextricably linked to the grand architectural statements and magnificent decorations to be found within its walls:

> To conclude all, the Italian decorations and machines are much better than ours; their boxes are more magnificent; the opening of the stage higher and more capacious; our painting, compared to theirs, is no better than daubing; you'll find among their decorations, statues of marble and alabaster that may vie with the most celebrated antiques in Rome; palaces, colonnades, galleries, and sketches of architecture superior in grandeur and magnificence to all the buildings in the world ...[12]

Raguenet's assertions were not uncontested. In 1704 Jean Laurent le Cerf de la Vieville, Seigneur de Freneuse, published the first part of *Comparaison de la musique italienne et de la musique française*, followed in 1705 by a further addition amalgamating the *Traité du bon goût en musique* in which he defended French opera.[13] These arguments seemingly about the ascendance of French and Italian opera over each other may appear at their face value absurd, and yet their role in the development of opera in France is crucial to its development in all the senses of the word.[14]

Thus it is suggested that the schism of thought surrounding opera at the turn of the eighteenth century coincided with and reflected the devolution of power from the absolutist state. This enabled social critics to use opera as a metaphor to explore the changing political structures within French society. Moreover, in 1749 the *privilège* of the Opéra was given by Louis XV (1715–1774) to the city of Paris, thus divesting the monarchy of its financial responsibility for the institution at a time when the monarchy was clearly losing its previously tight hold on the reins of power.

By mid-century the debate took on the form of a theoretical battle in the guise of a pamphlet war entitled *La Querelle des Bouffons*. It took its name from an Italian company called the Bouffons, who performed *La Serva Padrona*, a work by Pergolese, on 1 August 1752. It was the performance of this piece and the presence of the 'Bouffons' in Paris, where they remained for two years, which served as the focus of the argument between the two sides. The vehemence of this debate is attested to by Jean-Jacques Rousseau, one of the chief advocates of Italian opera. Commenting on the level of sentiment surrounding the debate, he wrote:

> all Paris was divided into two camps and debate was so heated that it looked like an affair of State or religion. The strongest camp was composed of the great, the rich and women defending French music whilst the other, the more alive, prouder, more enthusiastic was composed of the real connoisseurs, people of talent and men of genius.[15]

Rousseau's position is indicative of the essentially political character of the *Querelle*, as he clearly delineates the two camps in socio-political terms, not musical.[16]

Grimm, who sided with Rousseau and the Encyclopedists, wrote a parody on opera in Paris in 1753, entitled *The Little Prophet of Boehmischbroda*, which derided the French opera establishment. In it he acknowledged one of the most significant precepts of opera, when as consolation to the losers (i.e. French opera) the prize of national glory is offered: 'And your glory will be resplendent on every side, and I myself will spread it among the nations; you will be called the people above all others, and you will have no equal, and I shall not tire of looking upon you because it will be pleasing to me to see you.'[17] Thus one of the fundamental meanings of opera, a meaning which allows it to be used by whichever party is ascendant, is glory. It is inextricably linked with opera and states notoriously seek and feed off glory. They strive to unite symbolic metaphors of glory with the rationale of their government.

In 1753 Rousseau virtually opened his work *Lettre sur la musique française* with an acknowledgement of national notions of opera and made reference to the operatic scene in Europe while advancing the same cultural chauvinism or desire for greatness which inspired Louis XIV to proclaim his very first *privilège*. Rousseau argues that the French language when sung gives rise to derision and thus a less than noble perception of the French state; the Lullists/Ramistes the opposite. What is important is that national pride is seen to be displayed by the opera, and thus it is empowered to make or break the image of a nation:

The Germans, the Spanish and the English have claimed for a long time to possess music which is proper to their language, in effect they had national operas ... which they admired and believed that it was better to ban all works which hurt their ears except their own. Pleasure was their vanity, or they had preferred to sacrifice their taste to the reason of their prejudices which often rendered nations ridiculous by the very honour which they uphold.

Concerning our music, we in France share roughly the same sentiments as those other countries but who can assure us that, even though we are more opinionated, our stubbornness is better founded?[18]

Grimm too reinforces this point when he attacks opera for being an institutional extravagance, rather than a place of performance:

And in the hardness of your hearts you have created an opera which has wearied me for twenty-four years and which is the laughing stock of Europe to this day.

And in your opinioned extravagance you have erected an Academy of Music, although it is none, which I have never recognised.[19]

The battle was not confined to literary or theatrical spheres. The supporters of the Italian opera were seen to be aligned with the interests of the Queen, and the supporters of the French opera were aligned with the King. The *Querelle* in fact provided a forum for these philosophers to expound their social and political theories, intermingled with comments on notions of harmony and melody. It served as a convenient mask for the beginnings of a new age of thought. As the *Querelle des Bouffons* was regarded as a vehicle for one of the great debates of the Enlightenment, it can be interpreted as being such.

In 1755 Francesco Algarotti wrote *Saggio sopra l'opera in musica* (Essay on the Opera), which provides a different assessment of the operatic situation in France at the time. He describes the nature of opera in France since its beginnings, using the denominating terms of 'magnificence', 'pomp', 'splendour', 'extravagance' and 'decoration', as if he is in no doubt as to the meaning of the term. He too sees the rivalry over Italian and French opera as having a symbolic political connection: 'No means could be hit on by our artists to make their execution agreeable to Gallic ears, and the Italian melody was abhorred by them as much as had been, in former times, an Italian regency.'[20] Writing in 1770, the English music historian Charles Burney takes a practical rather than philosophical view of the nature of the musical rift between France and Italy: 'The truth is, the French do not like Italian music; they pretend to adopt and admire it; but it is all mere affectation.'[21]

The Italian position taken up by Rousseau and the Encyclopedists, it has been shown, had at its heart political motivations, and *The Serva Padrona* served as a vehicle by which they could debate their philosophical viewpoints. The fact that the *Querelle des Bouffons* was barely dormant when a new operatic debate erupted in Paris lends support to the view that these debates were merely a pretext for other causes. The Gluckist/Piccinist squabble would at first glance appear to be a deliberately staged quarrel.

Gluck, having composed *Iphigénie en Aulide* for the Paris Opéra in 1774, was presented with a libretto by Calzabigi of *Iphigénie en Tauride*. Piccini was a Neapolitan composer who was brought to Paris under the protection of Marie-Antoinette. He was given the same libretto as Gluck and asked to compose the opera. The two works divided the Parisian operatic world into two more camps, dealing with issues of modernity (Gluck) and antiquity (Piccini) very similar to the philosophical and political demarcation lines upon which the very first great operatic debate was held. Burney describes the debate in the following passage:

> Party runs as high among poets, musicians and their adherents, at Vienna as elsewhere. Metastasio and Hasse, may be said, to be at the head of the principal sects; and Calsabigi and Gluck of another. The first, regarding all innovations as quackery, adhere to the ancient form of the musical drama, in which the poet and the musician claim equal attention from the audience; the bard in the recitatives and the narrative parts; and the composer in the airs, duos, and chorusses. The second party depend more on theatrical effects, propriety of character, simplicity of diction, and of musical execution, than on, what *they* style, flowery descriptions, superfluous similes, sententious and cold morality on one side, with tiresome symphonies, and long divisions, on the other.[22]

The quarrel was very much between Gluck representing Italian opera and the French school of so-called Italianate opera, which had been influenced by the Encyclopedists to look for a new simplicity in opera, as opposed to the older style Italian opera with few French references to taste represented by Piccini. Gluck transcends the petty nature of the debate, aligning himself with Rousseau in search of the creation of music over nationalism:

> With the aid of the famous M. Rousseau of Geneva, whom I was planning to consult, we might perhaps together have been able, by searching for a melody noble, affecting and natural, with an exact declamation according to the prosody of each language and the character of each people, to determine the means which I have in view of producing a music suitable for all the nations and of causing the ridiculous distinctions of national music to disappear.[23]

Thus it can be seen that the debate surrounding French opera not only has its roots in the art itself but stems from the very depths of its reason for existence, namely that it is a theoretical position put into practice. The operatic debates until the French Revolution had been essentially spurred on by intellectuals who used the opera as a forum to vent philosophical views on harmony and melody, language, nationalistic concepts and political precepts.

The nature of the debate would change during the Revolution and opera would be expected to demonstrate its utility to the state politic. The institution created under royal *privilège* 120 years previously was interpreted by the Communards as being a place of great industry and manual labour and thus a worthy symbol of state.[24] J.J. Le Roux, a municipal officer and administrator of public establishments, charged by the Commune to investigate whether the Opéra was a necessary state institution, raised some significant questions. In his report on 'whether theatre is absolutely necessary to the commerce of the capital' (*faire connaître si ce théâtre était absolument nécessaire au commerce de la capitale*) he firstly asked 'What is the Opéra?' His answer is indicative of the way in which the opera as an institution lends itself easily to any state purpose:

> it is the meeting point of a number of arts and embraces all dramatic forms. It has an established and solid reputation and has inspired sustained enthusiasm for more than a century. It carries the imprint of an unknown magic, it generates a kind of drunkenness by its behaviour on the senses. But it satiates and one cannot suffer from it. It requires singing, dance, orchestra, scenery, nothing remains to be desired. The operatic stage only displays chefs d'oeuvres. What work to put on one production, how many difficult rehearsals and what work on the part of the artists and workers![25]

Thus in this instance opera is seen to mean a laborious enterprise on the part of artists and workers. However it is in his answer to the question 'Is it in the interest of the capital and of the political mores to save the Opéra?' that Le Roux uses a reasoning which resembles very closely the *privilèges* of Louis XIV. It starts off by stating that the criteria of the ancien régime cannot be the criteria of the Revolution: 'We will no longer say as under the reign of abuse – the ancien régime – that Opera is the most beautiful spectacle of Europe, that it attracts masses of foreigners, that it contributes to the glory of the French and that, whatever expense it occasions, it is beholden on the grandeur of France that it is sustained.'[26] However, the criteria appear to be very similar, citing an argument made familiar by usage that it brings capital from abroad (notably England) and that money is useful to the state. Its reasoning is essentially 'modern' and based on capitalist principles. The opera generates work and is an industry which provides cultural prestige and monetary exchange:

> it assures the existence of more than 500 employees, without speaking of the incalculable number which benefit in commerce and industry ... (its) annual expenditure is some 1,100,000 pounds. Of this sum the major part is given voluntarily by the wealthy and is distributed in

fractions amongst thousands of hands, artists, writers, composers, workers. ... It attracts the curious from all parts of the country and abroad, especially England, and those who come for this purpose to Paris engage in many other expenses which fecund the capital. We said in previous times that Opera circulates 20 million pounds in Paris, we can evaluate that sum today to 8 million, of which a third comes from foreigners and a third from the provinces. ... The opera is a hive of artists of all kinds whose talent resonates throughout the provinces and in Europe. Its works are printed and sold everywhere.[27]

So it could be argued that in essence the opera has not changed through this period of social turmoil. What is different here are the criteria used to assess it. The language which justifies it has changed its terms from philosophic or literary to economic. As opera can be seen to fulfil its function economically, it is charged to remain as a part of the new order, enabling Le Roux to conclude that 'it is not only useful but indispensable for the Commune and should be aided'. He finishes with the cry: 'To abandon the Opera at this moment would be to play into the hands of the enemies of the Revolution. Do we not think that the public fortune is in danger? When foreigners will fix their choice under other skies.'[28] Thus it can be concluded that Le Roux, diligent servant of the Revolution, found within opera a symbol of continuity which should be preserved and supported by the state.

The reader should be reminded that the eighteenth century in France was unquestionably a period of tremendous political and social upheaval. At the beginning of the century the country was governed by an absolutist monarchy; it then underwent the throes of Revolution and closed the century as an empire and with a new political and social order. Opera acted, reacted and was integrated into these phenomenal political and social developments and at each stage it was used by the dominant power as a symbolic representation of the state. This at first glance appears remarkable given the disparate foundations and aims of these powers, but the opera proved to be most adept in the role of chameleon of public institutions and as such an asset to the promotion of the legitimacy of ascendant regimes.

It is also essential to recognise that opera was used by intellectuals who were vying for a political place in a hitherto closed society as a metaphoric battleground upon which the great thematic debates of the era could be fought. In this sense opera took on the greatest meaning of the word: a performance, a building, a political construct; all of these were challenged and yet the institution remained consistent to itself and permanent throughout.

On 10 October 1800 a plot to assassinate Napoleon Bonaparte was uncovered and the two would-be assailants were arrested at the theatre. On Christmas Eve of the same year Napoleon was the subject of an actual assassination attempt whilst on his way to the opera, narrowly escaping harm from the bomb, which hit his carriage and resulted in a large loss of life and property. The First

Consul not only arrived unscathed and apparently unconcerned at the opera house, where rumours of his assassination were already rife, but in the fashion of a true statesman displayed himself to the audience from his box, receiving resounding applause from the audience.[29] The performance that evening was at once suspended in deference to the political event and the house bore witness to Napoleon's triumphant escape. This event was itself operatic in character, combining spectacle and intrigue against a brilliant backdrop, a most vividly illustrative example of the connection between the opera and the state in France at the outset of the nineteenth century.

Napoleon's motivations for support of opera were far from 'artistically' inspired. His much-vaunted phrase 'Paris vaut bien un opéra' reveals the cardinal rule operating at least since the seventeenth century that a capital city requires a great opera.[30] The consummate collector of the spoils of military conquest was to make the opera in his capital a bejewelled casket of display for the arts and arts institutions, or yet another way in which Napoleon demonstrated the might of his regime. It was to the opera that Napoleon invited his generals and officers of high rank, and he determined a high level of pomp and state ceremony within the house.[31] Between the years 1806 and 1811 Napoleon decreed the closure of virtually all public theatres and implemented a formalised administrative system for the remaining national theatres.[32] Those which were permitted to keep their doors open were ordered to give 20% of their profit directly to the *Académie Impériale de l'Opéra*. Thus Crosten, one of the foremost historians of opera during this era, could comfortably assert that: 'The official lyric theater was now reinstalled more securely than ever in its former seat of privilege…'.[33] This security, he claims, was determined by the ever increasing levels of subvention accorded to the opera at the beginning of the century, a trend, he argues, that lasted for three decades. The opera was to be an important and highly visible state institution throughout this period.

In 1803 Bonet de Treiches, director of the *Académie Impériale*, wrote an article entitled *De l'opéra en l'An XII*, in which he stated that the Paris Opéra was not only superior to *all* the other opera houses, but that it represented the 'glory of the empire' as a 'permanent party which the Emperor gave to Europe'.[34] Furthermore, he stated unequivocally that the opera is important and should be supported by the state because 'it is a place of contact between the Head of the Nation and the Nation itself'.[35] This, in the days before the infrastructures of transport and mass communication were firmly in place, was a considerable claim.

De Treiches' reasoning for the continuation of state support of opera differed little from that of the intendant Le Roux during the Paris Commune only a decade earlier, or indeed that of Louis XIV's *privilèges* a century prior to that. Opera was, in terms which have now become familiar, a national institution of great importance to the French state, whatever the political persuasion of those in power. Opera, it was claimed, brought wealth to the capital, as foreigners and provincials were attracted to the city partly because of it and, once there, stayed and contributed to its economic and cultural wealth: 'What incalculable number

of spectators from the provinces and abroad do not go to the Opera, and consequently to Paris, where they remain for lengthy stays!'[36] Thus opera was seen to
be a significant economic escalator. This fully justified continued state subvention
of opera, he argued, as the returns from it far exceeded expenditure. This is a
particularly interesting justification for a notoriously loss-making enterprise. He
endorses subvention on the grounds that, even if opera were to continue losing
money, the commercial benefits from the circulation of income derived as spin-
offs from opera warrant a policy of continued subvention:

> From an economic perspective, one can consider that the Opera brings
> financial aid to the capital to the tune of FF6,000,000 and helps circu-
> late some 20 million annually. How many artisans, how many businesses
> aren't in some way owing their existence to lyrical productions![37]

Furthermore, de Treiches concludes that these factors signify that opera should
remain within the direct ambit of government, as entrepreneurs could jeopardise
its immeasurable value by looking after their personal interests rather than
'national glory'.[38] He asserted with equal vigour that 'the loss of opera would
wield a mortal blow to art',[39] although his justifications for supporting art and
staving off a 'mortal blow' appear transparently mercantile and political.

A quarter of a century later Dr Véron, the first entrepreneur to make a profit
from the opera (although it still received considerable state subsidy, even though
the terms of his contract stated that he was to run the opera at his own 'risk,
peril and fortune'),[40] supported de Treiches' analysis of the situation. Moreover,
he concluded with the extraordinarily frank and apparently unshocking statement that, although opera did not interest Napoleon I, he endorsed it thoroughly
as the premier state art.

> The Emperor Napoleon I rarely went to performances at the opera. He
> had little taste for French music, but he attached a serious importance
> to the question of theatres for the city of Paris, he believed that it was
> necessary to have progress in the arts and the existence of national
> glory and the splendour of the imperial Academy of Music. The
> emperor didn't like the Opera, but he funded it generously.[41]

> Not only did the Emperor support the institution, he also determined
> that he 'would not permit for there to be competition to operatic
> performances'.[42]

The fall of Napoleon Bonaparte did not lead to the demise of opera in
France. Véron concluded, as Crosten later would, that opera was maintained in
a very similar manner by the very different political regimes which held power in
France at the beginning of the century. He wrote that 'the decree of 13th August
1811 was maintained throughout the Restoration. The expenses of the Opera

under Louis XVIII and under Charles X were thus paid.'[43]

Whatever the inherent differences between the empire and the monarchy, opera continued to be supported by them. The one element which changed was its title. The tradition of naming the Opéra after the ascendant regime was maintained. As power moved from Napoleon Bonaparte to Louis XVIII and back, the Opéra's official title was duly changed from *Académie Impériale de Musique* to *Académie de Musique*, reverting once again to *Académie Impériale de Musique* with the brief return of Napoleon and then once more taking on the title which it held for most of the ancien régime, that of *Académie Royale de Musique*, which once more was controlled under the aegis of the king's household.[44] The stability of the *ancien régime* was well and truly undermined during the Revolution. It was hardly surprising, then, that the nineteenth century witnessed many tussles for political ascendance, which contributed to the volatile changes in the management and name of the Opéra.

Attendance at the Opéra became once again a formal part of French social structure. The opening up of the city to the newly wealthy classes and the creation of such public areas as the Palais Royal placed opera at the centre of the new dilettantism or dandyism of the era. Opera became once more the place to see and be seen, a haven for the patrician class. Its popularity was abruptly ended on 13 February 1820, when the Duc de Berry was assassinated at the Opéra. He was next in line to the crown of the ailing Louis XVIII (1815–24) and at the time thought to be the end of the Bourbon line.[45] France was in mourning and the opera house was razed by official decree of 9 August 1820.

It was in the new 'temporary' opera houses of 'la salle Favart' (1820–21), 'le théâtre Louvois' (1821) and finally 'la salle Le Peletier' (1821–73)[46] that the golden age of French opera was to begin. Ironically, or perhaps consistent with its history, it was foreign and essentially Italian composers who formed the backbone of the golden age of French opera. Meyerbeer, Auber and Donlevy were followed by Rossini and then Donizetti, Bellini and later Verdi, all of whom were acclaimed in the French capital. Once again Paris, this time because of its position as a prosperous city and cultural Mecca, managed to hold in its capital, and within the walls of its opera, the greatest composers of the era. This golden age coincided with the rise of the bourgeoisie and the changing nature of the opera house reflected its values.

Charles X (1824–30) also understood that opera was a convenient and suitable vehicle for state and self promotion. Rossini was commissioned to write *Le Voyage à Rheims*, a work which detailed the coronation of the monarch in 1824 and was steeped in symbolism designed to lend support to the new monarch's legitimacy. In this sense the opera was no more than a state-commanded work of propaganda.

The revolution of 1830 and the abdication of Charles X did not deter the endorsement of the opera by the bourgeois king Louis-Philippe (1830–48) as early as 1831, when he and his family behaved as previous monarchs had traditionally done and displayed themselves at the opera house, thus demonstrating their legitimacy to the public.

The change in government brought about by the revolution was also reflected in the organisation of the opera. It was hoped that direct subsidy could be diminished, perhaps even abolished, and that the new director of the Opéra would serve the state's requirements while also taking on some of the risks. In order to do this the opera house, like so many other state institutions, needed to change its image and become home to the bourgeoisie of the era.

The state no longer wished to be seen to shoulder entire financial responsibility for the opera and thus sought the services and income of an independent manager and financier. Dr Véron, the successful contender for the position of director of the institution, explains the way in which he argued his case and won the coveted position of 'directeur-entrepreneur'.

> I was allowed to explain in few words the political importance that, at the commencement of a reign, how desirable it would be to have a brilliant direction of the Opera. ... Foreigners must be attracted to Paris by the good execution of musical chef-d'oeuvres, and they would find the boxes filled with elegant society. The success of the opera and its finances are an insurance against riots.[47]

Véron not only calls upon the same sentiments as those spelled out in Louis XIV's initial *privilège*, while pleading his case to be taken on as director of the Opéra, but also makes no secret of the fact that opera is a reflection of the legitimacy of government. Thus the state, in bestowing on him the honour of the new position, made the nature of Véron's obligation to it very clear. Furthermore, the terms of his contract were most specific with respect to his obligations to the state: 'Article 4. The entrepreneur will maintain the Opera in all the pomp and luxury expected of a national theatre.'[48]

The state's interests and those of Dr Véron were, fortunately for opera, mutually beneficial. He exploited the new found wealth of the industrialists and invested the opera with references which displayed the mercantile success of this era. Véron even changed the spatial configurations of the house to reflect the new power structure by reducing the number of boxes to increase seating and thus reduce prices, as he reasoned that this would 'better accommodate the income and economical proclivities of the new grandees of the third estate, the new court of the bourgeoisie which had replaced that of Charles X'.[49]

Opera represented all that was most grand, magnificent and ceremonial. Thus Véron cleverly transformed it into one of the foremost representative symbols of the July Monarchy. He expressly set out to demonstrate that the meaning of opera in the 1830s was synonymous with that which Louis XIV had invested it with at Versailles.

> At first I refused to undertake, on the heels of a revolution, such a heavy 'fardeau' as that of the Opera. ... I hesitated almost a fortnight, but after reflection I said to myself: 'The July Revolution is the triumph

of the bourgeoisie: this victorious bourgeoisie wants amusement; the Opera will become its Versailles and it will come on mass and take the place of the grand lords of the exiled court.[50]

Again, he uses arguments similar to those of Le Roux and de Treiches by supporting the fallacy of its supposed economic viability as well as acknowledging its position within the fabric of the state and society:

> All the grand European capitals have opera houses which hardly hear the applause showered upon the chefs-d'oeuvres in Paris. The Imperial Academy of Music has at its heart a greater encouragement for more than industry, as it is seen as one of the glories of France abroad.[51]

Véron's interests were undoubtedly motivated by personal incentive, since the further the state diminished its subsidy, the less profit he acquired. Yet he declares, somewhat audaciously, what few have openly affirmed about opera's relationship to the state, which is that its funding is not simply a matter of the state arts funding levels which restrict the other arts. Opera's meaning and importance to the state are greater than the work performed or even the venue or event itself. Therefore, he concludes, it will always be supported financially by the state whatever restrictions are announced in official arts funding, and it is in the state's interest to do this. Opera which does not display 'splendour' cannot compete with that of the great capitals and therefore loses its most essential meaning. It is thus an expenditure which the state cannot rationalise.

> To reduce the subsidy of the opera is not a wise economy. It is firstly to compromise the splendour of the institution, it is to restrict necessary resources in the fight against competition from Germany, England and Russia. … And finally, when the deficits are passed on like inheritances from direction to direction, the supreme insolvency will cost the government greatly and the State Budget will always end up by paying up.[52]

Véron's direction of the opera lasted a brief six years, which was the only period that the opera did not run at a loss and thus as a financial burden to those responsible, which ultimately always meant the state, since the direction of Lully at the end of the seventeenth century. Véron did not extend his stay at the Opéra because he realised that this period of prosperity could only be short-lived, dependent as it was upon state subvention, and, having gained handsomely from the enterprise, he had the foresight to see that he could not achieve this for long.

Indeed, this grand era of French opera did not survive the revolutionary movements of the latter part of the 1840s.[53] In 1848 the Opéra was closed down but allowed to reopen with a production called *Les Barricades de 1848*.[54] This is a good example of the way in which, once a group gained power, the Opéra quickly became a venue in which its propaganda was displayed.

The nineteenth century witnessed many violent scenes in and around the opera house, which became increasingly associated with privilege and ceremony. On 14 January 1858, whilst travelling to the opera, Napoleon III's carriage was bombed by Orsini, a disgruntled Italian, killing and injuring 150 people. Orsini acted in the belief that by assassinating Napoleon III the way would be freed for the emancipation of Italy. By 1861 the unpopularity of Napoleon III was clearly manifested inside the Opéra itself at the opening of *Tannhäuser* in Paris. The Emperor had supported Wagner and financed this opera. Thus it was seen by those opposed to the Second Empire as being a politically suspect work. Furthermore, the establishment also had its own quarrel with the way in which opera (a euphemism for the regime) was being conducted, and the performance of the production was marred as members of the *Jockey Club* created a disturbance ostensibly because there was no traditional ballet in the third act. This disturbance had, in fact, other more basic nationalist origins and the elimination of the ballet was perceived as an invasion of German influence upon French grand opera, as well as an endorsement of the values of a corrupt and rigid and suspiciously internationalist regime.

It was, however, Napoleon III who most obviously changed the face of opera in France. The competitive era of great exhibitions had begun. The impact which the great exhibition of 1851 had on London, and thus England, will be treated extensively in Chapter 4. The universal exhibitions of the late nineteenth century were to mark the beginning of magnificent temporary structures in Paris proclaiming the might of the ascendant regime. The Second Empire, however, required symbolic venues of a more permanent nature, where the élite could gather and which would inspire others.

In 1860 Napoleon III called for an international competition to find the architect for this emblem of his regime. The specifications were clear. An opera house worthy of the city of Paris was to be designed, and spatial configurations were to take into account the ranks and numbers of the élite. The house was not to be too large for fear that it might become a less select, and therefore more public, meeting place. It was, however, certainly to be sumptuous to demonstrate the wealth and greatness of the nation. Although Charles Garnier's project was chosen in 1861, this mighty symbol of Napoleon III's reign ironically was not inaugurated until 1875, when France once again had become a republic.[55] The symbol of the empire became the symbol of the new republic, which emulated the pomp of the regime it had replaced. Indeed, this opera house was to demonstrate the might of the state, the ultimate institution. It was to be distinguished from all other theatres primarily by its title, as the use of the word 'palais' was infinitely more prestigious, linking it to those in power, than simply the word 'house'. Gourret suggests that Garnier's intention was that this new opera would resemble an Italian palace, perhaps a metaphoric architectural link with opera's origins in the ducal palaces of Italy.[56]

Frédérique Patureau, whose work *Le Palais Garnier* describes this new Opéra, suggests that it was a physical extension of the philosophy of that era in that it would act as a symbol of France well beyond its borders, assert the importance of opera over all other musical forms and offer to the wealthy and fashionable an exceptional meeting house.[57] She goes on to suggest that as the centre of power was being transferred from inside the court to the new industrialised society, so too was the position of the Opéra within the structure of the newly recreated city a fundamental design of the empire, with its site linking the court and the new bourgeois public areas.[58]

A century later the socialist government of François Mitterrand chose the site of its new opera house as the Place de la Bastille, linking it with the revolutionary past of Paris. The press release of 17 January 1983 by Mitterrand's Minister of Culture, Jack Lang, could easily have been written by a minister of Napoleon III, so closely do the rationales of these two governments concur:

> If the ordering of a new opera is an event, its locality within the most symbolic historical sites of France gives to this project an importance which must mobilise the greatest architectural talents. That is why the government is launching an appeal to men of art throughout the world.
>
> They must know that the aim is to make this opera, at the Place de la Bastille, a major event of contemporary architecture and urbanism fitting for the end of the XXth century.[59]

The Palais Garnier has remained to this day, however, a very identifiable symbol of the greatness and prestige of a state institution, whether opera is performed there or not. Indeed, it was duplicated on a smaller scale in Hanoi by the French colonial forces at the turn of the twentieth century. Certainly, according to Patureau, even in recent times the symbolic meaning of this opera house has been maintained:

> Prestigious state institution, musical museum charged with the job of transmitting to future generations the national musical heritage, the Palais Garnier is consistently at the heart of political life and the great debates which influenced it in an era of change which definitively consecrated the foundation of the Republic.[60]

Napoleon III (1852–70) was in exile when the symbol of his empire was finally opened to the Lord Mayor of London, a number of crowned heads of Europe and other political, artistic and financial personalities in a ceremonially stacked occasion which bore many similarities to that of the opening of the opera of the Bastille over a century later. The regimes which followed did, however, tacitly understand his purpose and by 1975 no fewer than twenty-four galas for royalty and seven galas for heads of state had been held within its walls, as well as galas in honour of companies from different countries. However, it is important to note here that the opening of the house did not involve the presentation of a new opera. A rather banal amalgam of the great successes of the 1830s and 1840s was presented to the distinguished guests. This eloquently highlights the significance which those responsible for the opening attributed to the experience as opposed to the art.[61]

The institution of the opera continued to represent the interests of the state. Towards the end of the century republicans would argue that its very existence was a blight on the nature of the republic as it represented all the vestiges of the monarchies and empires of old. Octave Mirabeau was one such critic. Writing in 1885, he suggested that state subvention of the opera was in opposition to the precepts of the republican cause:

> ...because its utility is obvious in the hands of a monarchy, because the sovereign gives fetes and galas and he presents to the public foreign personages who visit our shores. It's a de luxe institution, it's the only luxury which he can sustain, as it fades amongst the royal courts and faints in the rubble of the low republican courts. 'To shut the opera' ... and close the doors of its interiors would make a substantial statement. Shut because of the republic'[62]

This view, however, never took hold in political circles, as opera is supported precisely because of its role as a grand venue and ability to cause others to marvel. This is the very reason for a state, republican or not, to support it. Ernest Boysse, writing in 1881, details the significance of the Palais Garnier as a meeting place and in so doing demonstrates how at the end of the nineteenth century the opera embraced all ranks of society under its roof:

> We would see there successively, Princes of Blood, Dukes and nobles, marshals, grand dignitaries of the Crown, Parliamentary Ministers, Presidents and advisors and from other courts counsellors of State, masters of enquiries, farmers general, bankers, administrators of domains, the postoffice, the lottery, saving societies, lawyers, bourgeoisie and merchants and finally fashionable girls, the arrival of courtesans.[63]

No other state institution could so successfully bring together such disparate interests, all of which were necessary to the successful functioning of the French state.

Throughout the most varied forms of political regime in France during the nineteenth century opera remained an ever present venue for the social interaction of ascendant classes. The modes of interaction were elaborate, emulating the increasingly formalised ostentation in vogue during the century. During this time many opera houses and venues changed to reflect the age. The Palais Garnier was the culmination of the various elements which made opera so important to the French state. Not only was it to physically reflect the need to display the grandeur so intrinsic to Napoleon III's regime, but it was also to emphasise by its very configuration the size of the élite of that society by providing 2,000 seats and giving them a variety of public spaces in which to mingle. Never before had an opera house emphasised social interaction to such a degree. The performance space was arguably the least important element of the house. Even the auditorium was designed to provide maximum visibility from box to box and tier to tier. The traditional spaces of antechambers off boxes were retained and the capacity to deny entry to any unwelcome party more tightly guarded. But it was the grand staircase and the various marbled and stuccoed foyer spaces which allowed easy circulation and provided an incomparable environment in which to see and be seen. Then there were the spaces reserved for the inner sanctum of French society, where select male patrons could meet in the *foyer de danse*. Access was dependent on rank and young ballerinas acted as discreet hostesses.

Thus the nineteenth century opened to the fading embers of revolution and quickly transformed into an autocratic empire. It closed with the steady, respectable formulations of the Third Republic. But during this entire period opera was supported by the state in France in every sense of the word.

Much has been written by historians and commentators of all kinds about the dying years of the nineteenth century and the opening of the twentieth century, punctuated by rapid technological change and, later, two world wars which changed the face of the modern world. In France this transition is evident through an exploration of the cultural language employed since the First World War, when the state openly assumed full responsibility as 'patron of the arts'. Since this time one can witness the constant definition and redefinition of such responsibilities. The pre-eminent role of opera as a bastion of cultural excellence remained unchallenged over this period, supported by the socialist regimes of the Popular Front (1936–39) and François Mitterrand's government (1981–95) as well as that of the conservative government of Charles de Gaulle (1956–72) and his Minister of Cultural Affairs, André Malraux.

In his challenging study on the nature of the 'cultural state', Marc Fumaroli suggests that the role of the state became that of a cultural minder, determining in a paternalistic sense that which is good for the people and thus practising a demagogic cultural 'politique'. He ascribes to this the same significance as that of religious ceremonial, supporting the notion that the state was deeply influenced by the church's ritualistic methodology, which it went on to incorporate into its own ceremonial display. He challenges the notion of the supposed liberality of the democratic state, essentially arguing that this is a veiled linguistic subterfuge.[64] Furthermore, he advances the theory that what he calls an 'alibi' was designed to reserve for the traditional élite its conventional spheres of interest, and that it was in the field of culture that the state determined its ethic:

> Under the cover of 'democratisation' of the arts and letters, those in power reserved for themselves the export and consumption of the élite,

a privileged sector, which, because of its high protection and subsidy, would remain immune to the media's vulgarity 'for everyone'. It's a secret reserved for the oligarchy, but it displays fundamentally the hypocritical depths of cultural democratisation.[65]

The very basis of Fumaroli's hypothesis is that duplicitous rhetorical language is used by the state to disguise and determine its real intentions. Theodor Adorno demonstrates this situation well in relation to opera in his description of the twentieth-century conflict between the individual and the mass. Writing on the *Sociology of Opera*, he declares:

> As everyone knows, however, society after World War II is ideologically far too levelled to dare have its cultural privilege so crassly demonstrated to the masses. Today there is hardly any real old-line society like that economic backer of operas in which it found itself intellectually reflected, and the new luxury class eschews ostentation. Despite the economic flowering of the period, the individual's sense of impotence, if not indeed his fear of a potential conflict with the masses, is far too deeply ingrained.[66]

André Boll, in his work *L'Opéra de l'avenir* (*The Opera of the Future*), concurs with this view, suggesting that popular culture is no more than a bourgeois construct designed to protect that class's interests.[67]

Significantly, André Malraux's speech on becoming Minister of Cultural Affairs on 3 February 1959, in the early days of the Fifth Republic, is a flagrant example of the distortion of language to give an impression of cultural enfranchisement for the masses:

> The minister of the State ... has as his mission to render accessible the capital works of humanity, and firstly those of France, to the greatest number of French, and to ensure a vast audience to our cultural heritage and to encourage the creation of works of art and the spirit which enriched them.[68]

The notion of accessibility is extremely important and cannot be overlooked when considering twentieth century trends in the arts. It is a term which was to dominate cultural language. 'Access' and 'democracy' were employed by politicians and intellectuals alike as if they were 'natural' partners, in the same way as divine right was the natural order of Louis XIV's reign. The emphasis is of course on French culture, French works of art for French people. This is particularly interesting as Malraux, like his predecessors Napoleon and Louis XIV, had no qualms about lifting artistic works from other great cultures in order to appropriate them for his own. He was in fact a convicted thief of cultural artefacts from Cambodia, where he went in his youth with the express intention of enriching himself by bringing home parts of Cambodia's rich architectural ruins.[69]

The most unifying concept to come out of the polemic in terms of the state and culture was that the 'State as Patron' became the ethos of twentieth-century governments. By the mid-1930s both France and England had made important gestures in this domain and, although there is much divergence of opinion as to the manner in which to apply state intervention, the critical concept was accepted and applied: that is, that some form of state support through subvention was to become the core of support for the arts.

The decisive moment in which the French state took direct responsibility for the arts occurred on 14 January 1939, when the Opéra became part of the *Réunion des Théâtres Lyriques Nationaux* and, as Soubie remarks, 'thus placed itself firmly in the public sector'.[70] He furthermore identifies this decision by the state as an assumption of its 'royal heritage'.[71]

Boll questions the motivations of the Fifth Republic and concludes that the Opéra was preserved essentially for its emblematic value:

> Is the Opera an instrument of culture, a commercial theatre, a site for tourists, or a parade ground for foreign sovereigns? ... In truth the 5th Republic conserved of the Opera only the title and magnificent emblem of its prestige.[72]

Giscard d'Estaing, waiting in the wings to succeed Charles de Gaulle, stated this position clearly in *Le Monde* on 17 October 1967: 'subsidy of opera is an evident necessity'.[73] Thus the opera and its traditional audience knew that their order would not be challenged by this conservative successor. Certainly the man who would become President of France in 1974 did not question the utility of state subvention of the Opéra.

In this sense French and British support for the concept of state subvention appear to differ. It is hard to imagine a British head of state making such a candid claim as Giscard d'Estaing without an elaborate justification of its meaning. We have seen, however, that this notion of it being a necessity was clearly understood in Britain in 1946 by the Chancellor, who was prepared to promise support to Covent Garden, although in less public a manner.

The young conductor and composer Pierre Boulez, in an interview in *Der Spiegel* in the volatile year 1968, even suggested that opera houses should be blown up as they were emblematic representations of the conservative forces which the student riots were so vigorously rejecting. 'The most expensive solution would be to blow the opera houses up. But don't you think that would also be the most elegant?'[74] But closing down the opera was never a viable option, let alone 'blowing it up'. As has been demonstrated, the existence of an opera in Paris was integral to the French state, no matter who held the reins of power. We see that in 1976 such contestation about the role of the opera was no longer relevant. The new director of the Paris Opéra perceived opera's role as that of being a prestigious state emblem:

> Prestige, prestige before everything.
> For Mr. Liebermann, the Opera is 'a national institution in a city which could be the capital of Europe'. It is not correctly speaking the opera of Paris, but an Opera of France, a prestigious theatre, essentially for the foreigner.[75]

His understanding of the role of the opera was thus consistent with state thinking on opera since its beginnings. Opera in France yet again would be a venue which would attract foreigners to France, by demonstrating its cultural ascendance.

The Opéra Bastille is an excellent example of the gulf between the political language of democratisation and access and the reality of the meaning of opera. Patureau describes it as 'the achievement of secular will to democratise the opera'.[76] The socialist government of François Mitterrand clearly demonstrates the mixed objectives of politics and cultural policy. The conception of the Opéra Bastille was marked with all the problems endemic in its double objectives.

All these notions of accessibility and 'Frenchness' were well expressed in the brief given in 1983 by the French Ministry of Culture to architects competing to design the new opera house. Section II of the brief is entitled *The Objectives: Make Opera Accessible to All* and goes on to explain that the constraints of an opera house built for an oligarchic society no longer reflect the requirements of democratic society in this century. Therefore, a new house was needed in order to reflect this new ethos:

> I. The need for a new Opera House in Paris
>
> The building of a new Opera House is justified both by the expectations of a wide audience currently excluded from opera …
>
> The Paris Opera, the Palais Garnier, designed at the end of the Second Empire, was opened in 1875 in the sumptuous beginnings of the Third Republic by an oligarchic society, quite different from our own …[77]

As we have seen, opera's political significance has long held a prominent place in the French state's cultural policy. This is demonstrated in recent times by the opening remarks of Raymond Soubie's report to government on the running of the Palais Garnier in the 1980s,[78] where he distinctly makes the point that the Paris Opéra is closely linked to the fortunes of political power.

The Paris Opera has always been tightly linked with political power. As in Italy, lyrical art took its ascendance in France from the court, but its evolution is more notably marked by the upheavals which shook the country during the centuries from Louis XIV to the 5th Republic. Place for privileged ostentation of monarchs and heads of State, the Opera remains above all the shining symbol of Parisian life.[79]

He also lends support to this analysis of the evolution of opera's relationship with the state when he stresses the continuity of the institution and contrasts this with the changing fortunes of political power:

The fall of royalty did not bring about the fall of Opera. The Royal Academy became the National Opera during the Revolution. In the nineteenth century it changed its name a number of times and occupied many houses, but without contestation, since its birth the Opera has been placed under the sign of permanence, despite the changes in power which decided its future. ... It became, under the Second Empire, one of the foremost lyrical theatres in the world and it was once more those in power who decided upon its future. Napoleon III wanted to give to the opera a house worthy of it, in the centre of a quarter of business and salons. ... That is how, out of the imperial dreams of Louis III, the Palais Garnier was inaugurated by the 3rd Republic, which assumed without hesitation its heritage.[80]

Such an overt explanation to the socialist leaders of the Fifth Republic could not be ignored. Soubie understood that continuity of the opera was important and that in a sense those in power depended upon it in order to sustain a platform for legitimacy of their state. The socialists consequently added to the operatic infrastructure of the capital by designing an opera complete with the semiotic references and iconography of their age.

Firstly, it was a project to build an opera house and, secondly, it was a project to reform and create a system of operatic performance. Urfalino commented that in Jack Lang's cabinet the only thing of interest to the bureaucrats about the opera was its architectural aspect and certainly not its musical one.[81]

A lot of the troubles so frequently commented upon in the polemic surrounding this opera in fact revolve around these incompatible objectives. Government was interested in the first objective and the bureaucrats involved in its original conception had a vested interest in the second. Michèle Audon describes these links between establishment, public administration and the meaning of opera as a matter of fact.

We felt that the tenants of Garnier, the lobby of the 'two hundred families' attached to the old opera, were politically in a position of strength.

Some high public servants ... had belonged to this milieu for a number of generations and their families held subscriptions to the Opera.[82]

There was also discord in the political language surrounding the Paris Opéra. Mitterrand's new socialist government had begun a number of major public works to symbolise this new regime. Saint Pulgent demonstrates the continuity of meaning of the Paris Opéra:

> The Paris opera, born out of the desire of an absolute monarch, is today still a monarchical and Colbertist institution, admired and hated for its cultural domination of our capital and field of political manoeuvre and tyrannic bureaucracy.[83]

She identifies the fact that the characteristics of state opera during the Fifth Republic all too distinctly resemble those of Louis XIV's opera. This is amply demonstrated by an examination of the decrees of the President and his Minister of Culture announcing the decision to build an opera house and the published brief to architects. In the press statement of 17 January 1983 Jack Lang wrote that:

> The present opera house ... was built for the society of the Second Empire. In choosing to build a new edifice, the government desires not only to facilitate access to the opera for the greatest amount of specta-tors possible but also to adapt it to the aspirations of contemporary society.[84]

The earliest definitions of what this opera house was required to do were to increase audience numbers and provide more reasonable prices in order for more people to participate in the lauding of cultural heritage. Jean-Pierre Agrémy, writing under the nom-de-plume of Pierre-Jean Rémy, Cultural Attaché to Britain in the 1970s and Director of Theatre for the Ministry of Culture early in the 1980s, describes the initial enthusiasm and desire to fulfil these aims juxta-posed against the realities imposed by the art itself:

> We began by asking for the moon, advancing figures looking for a financial and sound breakeven with a theatre of 4,000 to 5,000 places. But, seriously, all those interviewed agreed on this formal point – the capacity of an auditorium shouldn't exceed 3,000 people, preferably it should have fewer than 2,500.[85]

And the experienced civil servant François Bloch-Lainé, who had recently retired from the Ministry of Finance, headed the team and saw the dichotomy posed by the terminology:

What was fundamental was to find a way for all citizens to have access to any élite by taste and habit rather than money and protection. Because this wasn't possible at the Palais Garnier, one had to either construct a new opera which could, for a roughly similar price, accommodate a greater number of spectators, or shut the old one from opera so that it doesn't generate a social and financial scandal, and with the good will of those responsible.[86]

Soubie emphasises the importance of political symbolism in the terms in which the creation of a new house was defined:

The Bastille should at least be a temple dedicated to a genre which belongs primarily to past centuries rather than a living place of culture, of music and of encounters as, in another domain, the Georges Pompidou Centre has successfully become.[87]

The following critics, all of whom were involved in the creation of the Opéra Bastille, describe their understanding of the term 'opera'. Gérard Charlet was an urban planner brought in during the early days of its development: 'Deep down no one knew what a new opera should be like. It was our unique chance.'[88] He naïvely viewed it as a unique possibility to determine a new meaning.

Bloch-Lainé's rationalisation was that this was a political term reflecting the aspirations of the early 1980s and focused on the experiment of opening opera up to a larger public. He openly wondered whether this implied utopian or demagogic principles:

In the beginning the term 'popular' wasn't too irritating, as it reflected the spirit of 1981. But its emphatic character engendered criticism. It indicated the intention which ... was taken for that of an ideology. The real question was to know whether the opening of lyrical art to a larger public made sense, or if it was lip service, or an Utopian vision, or a demagogy.[89]

The English press was quick to comment on all this and the relationship between France's regal past and 'democratic' present.

Of all the Presidents since Charles de Gaulle, the one with the most passion for building and rebuilding, whose architectural schemes most suggest a nostalgia for the imperturbable power expressed by Louis XIV's architects during *le grand siècle*, turns out to be a Socialist: François Mitterrand. ...

The most troubled Big Project is the Opéra de la Bastille, which everyone hates for different reasons. Its problems go far beyond the disputes over policy and repertoire that led in January to the firing of its artistic director. ...

Right from the beginning, the Bastille was declared a 'modern and popular' opera house, unlike the 'élitist' opera housed in the Palais Garnier's gilded whale of a building. But there has never been a coherent sentence from the Culture Minister Jack Lang and his cohorts as to what popular opera is supposed to be.

It may be Mitterrand's desire to make Paris the opera capital of the world – a recurrent theme of French cultural politics – has landed the city with more opera seats than it can possibly fill. According to a recent survey, opera is the least popular of all cultural activities with the French public. ... Yet in 1989 the state is subsidising opera to the tune of more than $70 million, of which 85% has been allocated for Paris alone.

But proportion is not the point. Mitterrand's cultural policies are enmeshed in symbolic spending. ...

When 21st century students of French politics want to know what his critics meant by the phrase 'presidential monarchy', they will consult, among other evidence, the Big Projects.[90]

In 1994, four years after the previous article, *Time Magazine* had not altered its opinion:

Like Renaissance Princes, French Presidents since Charles de Gaulle have indulged a taste for monumental architecture to mark their time in power. None rivals François Mitterrand in the pursuit of such *gloire*: in a country where culture and politics are inextricably intertwined, the socialist President has spent more lavishly than any of his predecessors on pharaonic projects, all of which have stirred great controversy.

None has been attacked so devastatingly as the Opéra Bastille, the 2,700-seat, high tech opera house designed not only to replace the beloved old Palais Garnier but also to fulfil a socialist ideal by bringing opera to the people with more performances at more affordable prices.

...

Most damning of all, the Opéra Bastille has reneged on its basic promise. The cost of the average ticket today is around $100, three times that of admission to, say, the Folies-Bergère, and the number of performances last season never rose above 135, less than half the proclaimed goal.[91]

These works were invested with the connotations of socialist/humanist politics and thus were anathema to the old forces of order. The Opéra Bastille was the last of the big presidential projects to be decided upon and proved to be the most contentious. It suffered from being volleyed between and neglected by both sides of the political spectrum. When the left conceived of building a 'Cité de la Musique', and eventually a new opera, it wanted to make an architectural and thus cultural statement. The choice of site and date for the opening ceremony, decided in 1982, both confirm this. The international competition held for the design of the building yielded, however, poor fruit and no-one was enamoured with any of the designs submitted.

In a *Sunday Times Magazine* article of 26 November 1994, 'Phantoms of the Opera', Charles Bremner wrote:

> The biggest international competition in history, entered by 1,650 architects, was launched with Mitterrand's order to 'build the biggest and most modern' opera in the world. That formula bore a strong resemblance to Napoleon III's command for the competition won by Charles Garnier in 1860: 'Build the biggest and most beautiful opera in the world.'
>
> ... seats that, despite a budget running at £59 million a year – four times Covent Garden's – still cost up to £70 a time.[92]

Thus the actual concept of 'an opera' was betrayed from the very first. The cultural minister Jack Lang and the President hardly disguised their disappointment and in a sense the project lost the very essence of its meaning as official enthusiasm waned. Saint Pulgent wrote of the realisation that the Opéra Bastille, because of its less than visionary design, could not rival the Palais Garnier:

> The initial mediocrity of his project couldn't be amended and the Opéra Bastille today contains, in addition to other handicaps, the disgrace of having exchanged for 3 million francs the carriage of Charles Garnier for the pumpkin of Carlos Ott.[93]

To the old guard the building of a new opera was an attempt to efface a powerful symbolic representation of their order. Proposed by a government which used terms such as power and democracy to describe the new house, the Opéra Bastille was to them nothing more than a very painful thorn in their side. The attempts which they made to stop the project during the cohabitation are very well documented. And it seems that these attempts were not successful only because of in-fighting within their own ranks.

> Under the new regime the opera will move partially back to Garnier for Mozart and other smaller-scale *oeuvres*, while the ballet will pull in the crowds with its golden oldies at the Bastille. The home of all that gold and plush velvet, so reviled by the apostles of *opéra populaire*, is finally undergoing an expensive renovation. The Bastille, with its vast cavern of black, grey and wood, will be left with the Wagner and Verdi and other grand mega-shows.[94]

Thus, the Opéra Bastille became a much unloved building and an acceptable battleground for the right and left of French politics. On the one hand, it was to disappoint those who conceived of it initially yet retain, through its site and size, powerful symbols of a leftist political regime, and on the other it served to remind the right of a diminution of their power. Thus it was not surprising that during each political cohabitation of right and left, projects emerged whereby opera could be returned to the Palais Garnier, for smaller works, leaving the operas with greater mass appeal to the public in the larger, more impersonal hall.

Michael Dittman, one of the early instigators of the project, bitterly describes the reluctance with which the Opéra Bastille project was received:

> An important part of the opposition to the Opéra Bastille was linked to the refusal to abandon the Palais Garnier to the nostalgia which inspired the idea to devote to this very beautiful theatre, charged with history, activities other than opera.[95]

And Michèle Audon believed that the project had become a pretext for the right and left of government to vaunt their political standards. 'Thus the Opéra Bastille became a pretext for the struggles between ministers and the undercurrents of the new government, which sought to exercise their respective powers.'[96]

The project was, however, realised and the opening of the house bore many more similarities to that of the Palais Garnier than those who created it would have liked to acknowledge. Furthermore, in choosing to open the house on the symbolic occasion of the bicentennial of the French Republic, they were choosing to invest the house with the dignity, prestige and precepts of the regime. The Opéra Bastille was to be an emblem of the new democratic popular order to which access was a byword. The dichotomy between the language used to describe the opera and its intrinsic meaning was never more evident. Audon asks the question: did the socialist politicians understand what they had asked for?:

> In hindsight, I believe that the performance of the 13th July exactly reflected the situation. It was an 'apparat' more than a fete, a well-organised demonstration but without the joy nor the creation nor the breath that we had dreamt of for this theatre. It is a good illustration of a misunderstanding of this opera. Francois Mitterrand and Jack Lang 'ordered' in 1982 a modern and popular opera. That is exactly what was delivered. But did they really understand what they had ordered?[97]

Dittman reflects on the arguments by officials that the opening of the opera could not take place among 'popular festivities':

> They told us that the 14th July was a bad choice of dates as the Bastille would be filled with firecrackers and a popular ball. I acknowledge that

precisely the challenge would have been to manage to make the opening of the opera at the centre of the popular activities.[98]

And Saint Pulgent pinpoints the irony that the audience to whom the opera house was opened was far from one which could be described as popular. There were many Heads of State present and in particular those attending the Annual Summit of the Industrialised Countries.

> To celebrate the bicentennial Jacques Attali organised the Annual Summit of Industrialised Countries to coincide with that date and take place in Paris mid-July. In order to have not only rich countries at his table, the President of the Republic had also invited all the heads of state from the Third World. That made a lot of presidents, ministers, diplomats and especially police. For his part Jacques Chirac made it known that the Parisians had the right, like every year, to popular balls, of which the most popular is that at the Place de la Bastille. There was a conflict between two popular cultures: should the people go to 'the concert of the voices' of the Opéra Bastille, or should they dance with Yvette Horner and her accordion?
>
> But the conflict was purely theoretical. The presence of 36 heads of state, both rich and poor, at the inauguration excluded of course the people, who would be represented, as in the inauguration of the Palais Garnier, by a large concentration of stuffed heads. The only difference with that of 1875 is that then the happy, elected few paid for their places at a high price and the evening gave a fabulous profit to the concessionaire of the opera. This time the spectators were invited at the expense of the contributors.[99]

Some of the left's ambiguity is perhaps demonstrated by the nomination of certain officials in the Bastille saga. Michèle Audon, for example, was head of a state housing company in Avignon before being transported to Paris for this task. Jean-Pierre Agrémy, writer, former cultural attaché and opera-buff, and an early supporter of the project, was excluded from the team asked to set up the opera, his political allegiances not being exactly in accord with the government of the time. Perhaps the most remarkable appointment of all was that of Pierre Bergé, head of the Yves Saint Laurent empire, home of French fashion and haute couture and in a sense commercial cultural policy, certainly image building, as head of the opera in 1989. Head of a great business empire and personal friend of the president of the Republic, Bergé was not, however, experienced in the requirements of running an opera, although he did own and manage a small bijoux theatre, which gave emphasis to prestigious lyrical evenings and was located not far from the Palais Garnier. Bergé acknowledged that: 'In France everything is political. The Right was always against the Bastille, so when they came back I had to go because I was a friend of the President.'[100]

Patronage, privilege and power, linked overtly, remind us of Lully's relationship with Louis XIV at the very beginning of opera's long and chequered history and the relationship with the interests of the French state. Today no leader can say openly, as could Louis XIV, '*L'état c'est moi*', but this message can be disseminated by the symbolic means of opera.

More simply, the first work performed at the Opéra Bastille, and at the Sydney Opera House, the reopening of Covent Garden in 1945 and the Palais Garnier, was not operatic at all. In other words, it was an opera house without an opera, but 'opera' nonetheless.

4

THE DISUNITED KINGDOM

London's Operatic Battles

> Britain deserves to have an opera house in the first rank of inter-
> national excellence. The Royal Opera House has established a
> justifiably respected international reputation, and the newly rede-
> veloped building should help to maintain and enhance that
> position.
> Sir Richard Eyre, *Report on the Future of Lyric Opera in London*, 1998.

In the wake of an extremely public debate about the Royal Opera House in
Covent Garden, where we have been delighted by in-house fly-on-the-wall
videos, kiss-and-tell stories from three past executive officers and a general free-
for-all about the meaning of the opera house, one wonders what remains to be
said about opera in England. Indeed, to some that august institution had become
nothing more than another grand symbol signifying the grandeur of a long lost
empire. Certainly, if one is to believe the sentiments expressed in the *Report on the
Future of Lyric Opera in London*, written by Sir Richard Eyre at the behest of a
Labour government, the Royal Opera House Covent Garden's 'international
excellence' and 'reputation' are an important part of what Britain by right
'deserves'.

To some it was a national disgrace when England chose in 1999 to look
towards America to provide it with a manager to put its 'house' in order.
Furthermore, Michael Kaiser, the American general manager, ambitiously
avowed that he would 'ignore the past' when he took office shortly after the
submission of Sir Richard Eyre's report to parliament. But when he
resigned from his short tenure, he made it clear that he had not found
himself able to work with the presiding power brokers, some of whom were
elected to public office and some of whom, in this democratic age, were not.
Michael Kaiser learnt a lesson from the past which he had thought he could
ignore and, even though he had been put in place ostensibly to realise the
Cultural Minister's ambition of making the Royal Opera House more
'accessible', it had plainly become, as Rodney Milne stated in *The Times* of
21 June 2000, 'a much more elitist place' and access had in fact got worse.[1]
Michael Kaiser may have succeeded in putting the finances and management

systems of the house in order, but he did not so much as dent the image of the opera house, which has remained in the same social position for 250 years. A successor has, after much consideration, now been found, yet again from within the ranks of the British establishment, Mr Tony Hall, an 'Oxford' man, a BBC chief, and so the house itself is now firmly back in the hands of the British power brokers.

It would seem, if one follows the news media closely, that the public of Britain care very deeply about the Opera House and that there is a genuine public debate about its function and importance. After all, the last few years have been littered with government reports, official statements and plans for the Royal Opera House; but does all this noise really denote interest in the house or what is performed there? Certainly Philip Hensher in *The Independent* is convinced that all would be well in Covent Garden if 'an annual beanfest' were held in which the power brokers could display themselves:

> If I were Mr Hall, rather than wasting time deploring the snobbery surrounding the opera house, I would immediately exploit it by putting on an annual beanfeast. If the first night of the new season were as grand an occasion as La Scala's, with compulsory black tie, the attendance of the Queen, the Prime Minister and Mrs Guy Ritchie, and tickets at a thousand pounds each, who could doubt that it would be absolutely full?[2]

He is absolutely unconcerned about the artistic criteria of this first night, acknowledging, however, that the new power brokers are identified amongst pop stars, film-makers, politicians and royalty, all bedecked in the traditional vestments of grand attire. This perhaps facetious journalistic comment should be taken seriously in the light of findings of the House of Commons Culture, Media and Sport Committee, led by the very critical Gerald Kaufman, which clearly stated in its report that:

> We would prefer to see the house run by a philistine with the requisite financial acumen than by the succession of opera and ballet lovers who have brought a great and valuable institution to its knees.[3]

The 'valuable institution' clearly is of national interest in terms of statehood and the 'opera and ballet lovers' should not be given such a valuable charge. Rather a philistine, as the committee so loudly, publicly and shamelessly howled.

When one looks at any information about what British people think about opera, one discovers that they assume that it is government business, that a lot of rich people are distracted and amused by it, but that it is nothing much to do with them. There is not the same kind of popular fervour as there was, for example, for the Tate Modern opening. The 'public debate' surrounding the British Opera House is, in fact, largely bogus. The majority of British people are not much involved, which is why the politicians and the patricians are left to argue over the plunder. In fact the British regard what goes on in the Royal Opera House in much the same way as they regard the private affairs of the royal family; they have a mild interest in the participants, whom they assume are corrupt nobs. The television series on *The House* reinforced the popular view that the opera is sustained vigorously and ruthlessly by the ruling class.[4]

It is assumed that there is an élite of power brokers to whom membership is always available. This élite changes, but when one is powerful and at the heart of the state then one attends the opera.

Opera in England does have a considerable history, antedating that in France (something acknowledged by Louis XIV). It has continued to remain acknowledged by those in power both in the UK and abroad since that time. More significantly, whatever the squabbles, today so public, about whether or not to support the Royal Opera House, and how, it will clearly remain. In a society fast losing the ceremonial institutions which gave it pomp, ceremony and grandeur, the opera represents a haven of symbolic references, a place in which the feasts once reserved for renaissance courts are played out to the princes and statesmen of today. Indeed opera has in Britain, as on the continent, often been associated with the political forces in power, although its actual funding has been carried out at arm's-length from power, except when the institution has been deemed to be in immediate jeopardy and the king, government or chancellor of the exchequer has directly intervened to save it.[5]

A charge brought against opera throughout its history in Britain has been that it is very much an art designed to satisfy the 'happy few', but opera gains importance precisely because it *is* the entertainment of the élite. It has grown as an institution distinct from popular culture, a symbol of establishment culture,[6] a national showcase in which state ceremonies are performed with political consequences. Furthermore, it symbolises the continuity of governments, both as an institution constantly supported by them but also through the content of the works themselves and the iconography contained within the state opera houses.

The claim that it is foreign has also been a charge against opera in England. The aristocracy, the bourgeoisie and corporations, for example, often have foreign origins or are amalgamated with foreign interests, and opera has reflected such foreign interests in the same way as these influential groups have done. Their foreign sources are very often the strengths of these socio-political groups, which are to all intents and purposes national symbols. The élite has generally been more 'international' throughout modern history than those serving them, and thus nationalism in terms of opera has to be understood in this broader context.

This paradoxical situation fuelled a debate led by two eminent English critics at the beginning of the eighteenth century, Addison and Steele, who used the operatic stage as a vehicle from which to denounce the fact that there were very much two cultures in existence within one nation. Opera to them, as it was performed on the British stage, denied popular culture a voice and was a hybrid form. They therefore campaigned for 'English Opera'. By this they meant opera performed and written in English. It was not so much that they held particularly strong views about the nature of 'Englishness' in opera, but rather that as social critics they took exception to the manner in which the alliances between political power and the operatic stage were seen to be evolving.

Sir Richard Steele in *The Tatler* in 1709 highlighted the double standards of social demands and actual content of the performance of Italian opera:

> Letters from the *Hay-market* inform us, That on *Saturday* Night last the Opera of *Pyrrhus* and *Demetrius* was performed with great Applause. ... That the Understanding has no Part in the Pleasure is evident, from what these Letters very positively assert, to wit, That a great Part of the Performance was done in *Italian*: And a great Critick fell into Fits in the Gallery, at seeing, not only Time and Place, but Languages and Nations confused in the most incorrigible manner ...[7]

Here Steele developed his major arguments by suggesting that the presentation of opera in England had reached farcical proportions, for the manner in which the performance is described was intended to incite scorn directed at the audience, and thus by extension the nation. His argument is based on a defence requiring that the content of the work be well constructed in traditional theatrical terms. His description of it is designed to demonstrate how farcical the results of this form of pasticcio performance were. It would appear, however, that the major focus or objection in his argument is devoted to the fact that the work was sung in Italian.

Addison rises to the argument with his inimitable style when commenting on opera sung in Italian on English stages, as well as the audience's (or critic's) attitude to this, in his essay published in *The Spectator* on 21 March 1711. There is occasion to reflect here on whether the wrath which Addison directed towards Italian opera was not occasioned by the reception of his libretto *Rosamund* in 1707. Although in the vernacular and written for English audiences in an attempt to create a national opera, it proved to be 'a dismal failure'.[8] Nonetheless, the following lively description of the state of opera in England in the early eighteenth century sets out a very clear notion of his position, highlighting his literary and linguistic concerns and transposing them into the domain of the political, social and cultural relationship between England and its European counterparts.

> It is my Design in this Paper to deliver down to Posterity a faithful Account of the *Italian* Opera, and of the gradual Progress which it has made upon the *English* Stage: For there is no question but our great Grand-children will be very curious to know the Reason why their

Forefathers used to sit together like an Audience of Foreigners in their own Country, and to hear whole Plays acted before them in a Tongue which they did not understand ...

...In the meantime I cannot forebear thinking how naturally a Historian who writes two or three hundred years hence and does not know the Taste of his wise Forefathers will make the following Reflection, 'In the beginning of the eighteenth century the Italian tongue was so well understood in England, that operas were acted on the public stage in that language.'

One scarce knows how to be serious in the Confutation of an Absurdity that shows itself at first Sight. It does not want any great measure of sense to see the Ridicule of this monstrous Practice: but what makes it the more astonishing, it is not the taste of the rabble but of the persons of the greatest politeness, which has established it. ...

At present our Notions of musick are so very uncertain, that we do not know what it is we like; only, in general, we are transported with anything that is not **English** – so it be of foreign growth, let it be **Italian**, **French** or **High-Dutch**, it is the same thing. In short, our English music is quite rooted out, and nothing yet planted in its stead.[9]

Addison's comment makes mention of all the major issues concerning opera in England. Firstly, he remarked upon the exclusivity of the audience, pointing out that there is a general lack of communication between the performers and the public. He suggested that the reasons for frequenting such a venue have little to do with the work performed, and his derision of the practice of singing in foreign tongues has two elements associated with it. He concludes that because the audience is left without comprehension it serves little purpose to perform and also that it leaves the English as a nation open to ridicule, not only from its contemporaries but also from future generations who would view it with the critical hindsight of historical comment.

In fact, performances of opera in England had become so disparate as to be quite ludicrous. After 1710 the King's Theatre and Drury Lane both staged operas. Both their managements, motivated by a need to captivate the largest and most exclusive public, embarked upon a number of operatic experiments. Nalbach, a scholar of the King's Theatre, sums up the situation:

And what polyglot experiments in opera – Italian opera in Italian, Italian operas in English, Italian arias with English recitative, and, most strange of all, Italian and English singers both singing in their respective languages in the same production![10]

Whatever the critiques led by Addison and Steele, opera was enjoying considerable popularity and had a tacit link to the court. By 1711 John Jacob Heidegger, manager of the Queen's Theatre and Master of the Revels for George II, was keeping 'the "image" of the house as an institution of glamour in the eyes of its noble patrons'.[11]

More specifically, in England when what was known as 'Italian Opera' was first performed,[12] it was considered to be allied with nobility and grandness. From the eighteenth century to the early twentieth century 'Italian Opera' was commonly understood to be opera. Unlike other musical forms, which have roots in English theatre, the notion of 'Italian Opera' represented a specific musical and theatrical form and was considered to be exclusive. All this is clearly demonstrated by the fact that it was not until 1892 that 'Italian' was deleted from the official title of the Royal Opera in England.[13]

The nature and form of a state institution, however, varied markedly between the kingdoms of England and France, although the notion of the meaning and value of a state institution did not. This again is well demonstrated by opera's singular relationship with the state. In England discussion focused upon the need to establish an English opera and the apparent absurdity of the maintenance of an art whose relationship with the state was not formalised and, even more significantly it was argued, which did not have indigenous roots. The ambiguity of this relationship spurred argument over which language was appropriate for operatic declamation. Italian opera in England also served as a metaphor for a deeper social malaise, for it was to represent unspecified but powerful forces that were linked to notions of social distinction and exclusivity, but these could not be directly singled out as their unique symbolic function.

Opera in England had thus gained the reputation of being a foreign and 'unpopular' art, whereas we have seen that in France, since its inception, opera was sung often in the vernacular and integrated into the heart of the state's symbolic language. This difference between the two countries is significant. Their separate notions of an opera derive from this. 'An opera' in France could be French or of other origin, whereas 'an opera' in England was commonly understood to be synonymous with Italian opera. 'The opera' in both countries also took on these meanings, in England emphasising foreignness and in France integrated with the language and state.

Other differences are in part due to the development of different kinds of political regime in these countries during the latter part of the seventeenth century. E.J. Dent suggests that it was the existence of the relatively stable economic conditions of court life in Paris which made it possible for steady progress in opera to be made there, whereas in England, where such conditions did not apply, opera occurred only in spasmodic fits and starts.[14] Nonetheless, the major difference between opera in England and France during this period is that opera in France was overtly used by Louis XIV and his successors as a ceremonial arm of state, whereas in England, where the monarchy was less stable, opera evolved outside the court but acted as an institution which paid homage to the monarchy.

In England there were attempts to institutionalise opera after the French fashion between 1719 and 1737 by Handel, and it was for this opera that most of his work was created. This Academy of Music is important in that it 'marked the first serious attempt to launch opera in England on a grand scale'.[15] Perhaps an even more significant reason for its importance can be advanced here. George II (1727–60), as Heidegger's patron, paid £1,000 per annum 'to meet the extraordinary expenses of the opera'.[16] This overt association with, and subvention from, the monarchy displays the institution's significance to the state and the importance of ensuring its continuity. Hitherto financial patronage was clearly the domain of the nobility but in this instance the intervention of the monarch signified the opera's importance.

The nineteenth century theatrical historian George Hogarth comments upon the fact that the opera had come to mean simply a place where the fashionable congregated:

> The public, too, had begun to grow weary of an entertainment, the character and beauties of which were, as yet, but little understood in England, and which had been supported exclusively by the aristocracy, more for the sake of fashion than from any real taste for Italian music drama.[17]

By 1733 there were four predominant musical venues in London: Drury Lane, Covent Garden, Lincoln's Inn Fields and the Little Theatre in the Haymarket.[18] In 1734 the Opera of the Nobility was created, an Italian opera organised by the Neapolitan impresario Porpora and starring the famous castrato Farinelli, which played in opposition to Handel, who had created an opposing theatre at Lincoln's Inn Fields. Heidegger soon became manager of this company, which he brought to the King's Theatre, and Handel was forced out to Covent Garden. Significantly, George II and the Prince of Wales patronised both these theatres.[19] These institutions were the ones that Addison, and later on Johnson, used as their benchmark for opera. They were venues in which Italian was the language used and, due to the composition of their patronage, they had a very distinctive social position. Thus they represented more than an opera and contained a complex iconography which could be extended to symbolise connections with the corridors of power. The works performed reflected scenes of courtly love and noble values, reconciliation of love and glory, both moral and spiritual, and musical intervention of the spirits.

In 1737 both companies went bankrupt and the Licensing Act made The King's the only theatre in which opera could be presented. Periodic performances occurred at the King's Theatre between 1737 and 1741. By 1741 a new syndicate of '30 gentlemen' tried to refound an opera company. This too was oppressed by debt and closed in 1744 and for a short period there was no formal operatic presence identifiable in England. Burney describes the difficulty in remounting such a project in the prevailing political climate:

> The rebellion (1745) broke out; all foreigners were regarded as dangerous to the State; the opera-house was shut up by order of the Lord

Chamberlain; and it was with great difficulty and address that Lord Middlesex obtained permission to open it again.[20]

However, by the season of 1745–6 Gluck had been contracted 'as resident composer for the King's',[21] and Handel's oratorios were revived in the Haymarket in 1747. This is Burney's appraisal of the difficult situation, based on fear and suspicion of foreigners, which Gluck was to find himself in:

> Gluck worked … with fear and trembling, not only on account of the few friends he had in England, but from an apprehension of riot and popular fury at the opening of a theatre, in which none but papists and foreigners were employed.[22]

It is evident, however, that despite very brief interludes it had always been possible to attend, and even have a choice of, operatic performances in the early eighteenth century. This continuity and choice rather demonstrate the fallacy of the argument that opera has little or no place in English cultural history.

Indeed 'society' after half a century of operatic attendance was requiring increasingly inventive modes of operatic distraction and during the early 1750s Italian opera's popularity amongst its previous benefactors waned. It was also blighted with frequently changing management and impresarios, who only occasionally displayed the brilliance of earlier times.[23] The fortunes of the King's Theatre thus declined, whilst other venues began to house and attract significant audiences to opera in London.

Samuel Johnson sets the tone of the debate for the mid-century with his frequently cited remark that Italian opera (in England) was 'an exotic and irrational entertainment'.[24] White, Fiske and James Johnson, amongst others, have pointed out that this statement has often been quoted out of context and taken to mean opera in general and not Italian opera in the early part of the eighteenth century, which was very clearly Johnson's intention.[25] This is important, as the misquotation of this phrase has been used by detractors of opera in general to demonstrate its short-comings. Samuel Johnson did, however, set forth a view which will be endorsed by almost all parties, whichever side of the debate they support. Both adjectives are in fact being used in unusual, specialised senses. Firstly, 'exotic' suggests something deriving from foreign climes, thus setting the stage for the arguments of future generations. Secondly, the use of 'irrational' suggests something lurking below the conscious mind, uncontrollable, Dionysian and therefore perhaps dangerous.

Samuel Johnson was not the only critic to be publicly engaged in the opera debate. Lord Chesterfield highlights the continued social correctness of going to the opera when, in a letter to his son, he unequivocally states his view of the social usefulness of opera – as paraphrased by Henry Raynor in *Music in England*:

if art had any intellectual or spiritual value, that was nothing to the 'man of fashion' who attended the opera or listened to other music for no more than pleasant relaxation and because his position in society demanded that he attend.[26]

Thus there was participation by more than simply the aristocracy in musical representation in England. The popularity of English opera can be viewed in this light, along with the success of such composers as Thomas Arne and Dibden. It is interesting that, as soon as Arne was assured of his popular success, he tried to transform his work into a product for the King's Theatre.

A most eloquent connection between opera and the state is commented on by the nineteenth century French opera historian Castil-Blaze. He describes the night of 22 February 1781, when the two highly acclaimed performers the Vestris were in London. That very day Edmund Burke was due to present his economic bill. Lord Nugent, however, preferred an evening at the opera to the affairs of state and annulled the passage of the bill on that day.[27]

It can be seen that throughout the first part of the eighteenth century opera was consistently performed in London. The opera was sometimes represented by two companies, and there was a choice of venues, restricted only by royal decree. The opera was supported by the monarch, nobility and a merchant class. Opera took various forms and was most often thought of as Italian, although that did not always mean a work sung entirely in Italian or by Italian singers. Perhaps most significantly, opera was not a rare fruit but an everyday part of theatrical life – at least for a certain social class in English society.

Thus by the end of the eighteenth century opera was popular in London and no longer associated exclusively with one venue. The schisms of thought concerning opera, in the domains of language, nationality and the associated attitudes of social behaviour linked with class and connotations of high and low culture, had been declared. It was out of this climate that the nineteenth century drew upon its past in order to create new theatres and introduce innovations in all aspects of opera. Most importantly, however, opera was still to be dominated by the unresolved debates dating from opera's beginnings, which now incorporated a tradition of criticism and thought developed by the foremost critics of the century.

Operatic life in England in the early nineteenth century diversified. There was a proliferation of venues and forms of operatic spectacle, ranging from Italian opera and Pasticcio to English opera. Notions of prestige dictated which kind of venue and what kind of performance one attended. The monarchy and aristocracy continued to frequent the Italian opera, and their ranks were swelled by the upper echelons of middle-class society. This created a source of considerable rivalry between theatres for the privilege of mounting opera and profiting from the associations between the venue and its public. Indeed the glamour of these events increased due to the injection of new blood, which supported the old values, displaying them whenever possible. Fashion was dictated from the top of the social pecking order, described by Hobsbawm as 'the picture of Royal or Imperial Majesties graciously attending opera or ball, surmounting expanses of jewelled, but strictly well-born gallantry and beauty'.[28]

As in the eighteenth century, the satirical strain of the English intellectual class continued to deride opera in journals and yet at the same time it was acknowledged by them to be an important part of its cultural composition. The rivalry between England and the continent continued in the form of the traditional debate about the relative merits of English opera. The following article from the *Morning Chronicle* of 1802 exemplifies this:

> The united world could not display such a body of talent as was combined in the King's Theatre last night; and it was almost all English. The first woman was an Englishwoman. The leader of the band was an Englishman. An Englishman was at the harpsichord. The bassoons (the best in the world) were English. The French horns (also the first in the world) were English. It showed that if the people of fashion would resolve to give their united protection to the Opera, and not divert their patronage to triflings, that can only serve to reduce London to the contemptible state of a mere colony, instead of being a metropolitan seat of the arts, there is no splendour to which we might not bring this as a national theatre.[29]

The critic William Hazlitt also contributed to the debate, questioning opera's utility in England:

> The Opera is a fine thing: the only question is, whether it is not too fine. It is the most fascinating, and at the same time the most tantalising of all places. It is not the *too little*, but the *too much*, that offends us.[30]

This critique demonstrates that perceptions of opera had not greatly changed since the early eighteenth century when Addison and Steele criticised the Italian opera on similar grounds and in a similar fashion. Furthermore, Hazlitt introduced a tone of moral aestheticism, the notion of its separateness from the other arts:

> When the Opera first made its appearance in this country, there were strong prejudices entertained against it, and it was ridiculed as a species of the *mock heroic*. The prejudices have worn out within time, and the ridicule has ceased; but the grounds for both remain the same in the nature of the thing itself.[31]

Hazlitt in fact seems to suggest that this is a fundamental dilemma in the treatment of opera. It would appear that what he means by opera, however, is an entity which is aristocratic, exclusive and Italian.

It was prestige and the maintenance of exclusivity which distinguished opera from other musical activities, which reinforced its position and ensured continued success. The paradox remains, however, that, in a society increasingly inclined to follow the paths of the politics and theories of economic rationalism, a cultural institution based on entirely other precepts was plainly maintained by a social class prepared to support an institution which signified its order, conservatism and ceremonial purpose.

As the demand for entertainment increased and tastes diversified in the early part of the nineteenth century, the English theatrical scene reflected these changes and the venues themselves were accommodated to the requirements of the time by expanding in size and configuration for new audiences. The traditional operatic venues of the Italian opera were also affected and underwent, over a thirty-year period, a restructuring not only of capacity, but also to include technical innovations which in themselves were harbingers of the new industrial age. The Haymarket was razed by fire in 1789; Covent Garden suffered the same fate and was reconstructed in 1792; Drury Lane was rebuilt in 1794. In a five-month period between September 1808 and January 1809 first Covent Garden and then Drury Lane were destroyed by fire. Covent Garden was reconstructed within a year and Drury Lane was reopened in 1812 and presented a serious challenge to the former. This constant razing and reconstruction of theatres allowed for the technical innovations of the era to be incorporated into the newly constructed venues. Innovations such as gas lighting became an important element in these new auditoria. The technology was now available with which to undertake the construction of buildings which would cater for a greater audience capacity. So the larger audience, taken from a larger sector of society, could now effectively regard itself with increased ease and became an even greater part of the operatic spectacle.

The diversification of venues encompassing larger audiences of more disparate tastes led to the serious development of more forms of opera than simply 'Italian'. By the 1820s three non-Italian venues (Covent Garden, Drury Lane, and The Lyceum) were vying for ascendance in the non-traditional but newly awakened operatic climate.[32] This popularity created an increased demand for English opera and resulted in the investigation of modes of financing it by increasing audience sizes and changing the structure of the auditorium. Managers and exponents of this movement also began actively to seek government subvention.[33] Moves towards the creation of an operatic venue with the express purpose of the promotion of national composers, singers and musicians were gaining ground by the 1830s.

1843 is an important year in British theatre history for in that year the Act for Regulating Theatres was passed. This Act finally broke the monopoly of 'royal theatres', and the last barrier was thus removed between the legalistic and formal restriction of theatrical and operatic representation. It did not challenge, however, the Lord Chamberlain's role as censor, and the holder of this office continued to maintain and exercise significant power in that respect. This situation was not changed until 1968, when the Theatres Act finally revoked these powers.[34] White suggests that the effects of this Act on Italian opera were also substantial:

> If the two patent theatres lost their monopoly of spoken drama, then Her Majesty's (formerly the King's Theatre), which for about a hundred and forty years had enjoyed a special licence to present Italian opera and *ballets d'action*, lost that monopoly too. The almost immediate result was that ... Covent Garden Theatre decided to turn itself into an opera house ... and in the course of time the success of Covent Garden in its new role led to the decline and eclipse of the older theatre.[35]

Audiences well understood the distinction between 'English' and 'Italian' opera. English opera was thought of as being a barometer of popularity and intermingled with nationalist sentiment, but the notion of it being a 'low-brow' activity remained substantially unchallenged.[36]

Italian opera continued to be regarded as being absolutely the exclusive domain of fashion and the conveyor of 'high art'. Its role was certainly not threatened by the national and aesthetic tone of English opera's exponents. In 1847 Covent Garden burnt down again, and the theatre raised on the site in 1856 is substantially the theatre in existence today. It has been called the Theatre Royal, the Royal Italian Theatre, Covent Garden and latterly the Royal Opera House.

A Noah's ark of Victorian ideology, the Great Exhibition of 1851 comprised many of the elements that were new and unique to the century and the Western world, displaying them on one site. It reflected the spirit of the new era, and also served to give importance to all those who created the Exhibition, both the individual and the mass, which was personified by the concept of the nation. It finally brought to England's shores a sense of greatness which hitherto had been displayed almost exclusively on the battlefield.

The Great Exhibition also demonstrated to Englishmen and foreigners alike the fact that all kinds of musical entertainment were available and well frequented in London.[37] Opera, however, was rarely linked with other musical activities during the period of the Great Exhibition, as it did not share an audience, a reason for being or a 'musical' popularity. It played to its traditional audience and in fact did rather well because of the number of foreigners in the city. Such visitors were always a factor in creating large opera audiences. As has been noted, at the beginning of the eighteenth century Addison specifically cited opera as a barometer with which the foreigner would judge English society, as did Dr Johnson later in the century. Ten years after the Great Exhibition this continued to be true. Mapleson, director of the Italian Opera at the Haymarket in 1852, comments on the direct result which it produced for his business:

I had got together a magnificent company, and as the public found that the performances given merited their support and confidence, the receipts gradually began to justify all expectations, and within a short time I found myself with a very handsome balance at my bankers. This may be accounted for by the very large influx of strangers who came to London to visit the Exhibition of 1851.[38]

Thus Mapleson directly relates his success not only to his 'magnificent company', but also to the influx of visiting strangers who were already opera lovers.

One of the most notable aspects of Victorian society by the mid-century was that religious sentiment had become intermingled with the new doctrines of the times and had taken on moral and ethical dimensions that influenced activities in many domains. Fiscal success was deemed to be a social and moral virtue. Captains of industry epitomised the image of the new patriarchs, and yet the outward manifestations of success, steeped as they were in religious and moral connotations, had not changed significantly with the times. These new successful leaders symbolised the achievements of Victorian society and were emulated throughout it. Although they represented only the pinnacle of the economic triangle, their moral tone was imitated down to the codes which the family breadwinner imposed on the structure and nature of the family. A consequence of this was to promote constructs endorsing justifications for meretricious financial dealings through the creation of a national religious language. The platform which served as the meeting house for this revival was the state church. Principles virtually unseen since the Commonwealth were revived and became emblems of an age represented by an ever increasing new middle class which had few antecedents in the hereditary aristocracy of yore.[39]

Sanctimonious sentiments were used to support the quasi religious morality which served to justify the new found wealth. Papism represented a foreign and unsettled world where the precepts of financial achievement were constantly attacked by revolution and penury. Thus the sanctimonious foundation of Victorian well-being was defended at all costs.[40] Opera (and what it represented) was thus denigrated, as it could only disturb the newly found social ethic of the middle class, which could not legitimately enter the 'old order'.

The irony inherent in this perspective is that, whilst the middle-class exponents of the era were indeed adverse to the concept of opera, those who had surmounted the barriers represented by great economic achievement and political power joined the aristocracy as supporters of 'Italian opera' and upholders of its traditions.

The opera can be seen to be a classic example or symbol of the Victorian era. Through its very architectural form, the ceremonies held within it and the vestments worn by its audience, it exuded prosperity. The opera was frequented by, and associated with, those holding the reins of national security. As an institution it was seen to represent a continuum of purpose and was increasingly to become overtly associated with the state. It upheld a moral code through the works which it represented and which could be displayed proudly to foreign observers.

The history of opera in England since the 1850s, and the establishment of Covent Garden as the first opera house, can be interpreted as associating the symbolic meaning of opera with a specific venue. This was important as it would be seen to represent the institutionalisation of opera in England, aligned with the state, and create a nexus which had historically been lacking. The alignment of these forces enabled the crucial transformation from a general perception of opera as an exclusive art form devoted to the province of particular and anachronistic interest groups, to its becoming part of the recognised fabric of the state and functioning as a significant symbol of it. Indeed the Royal Italian Opera, Covent Garden, was quickly to become distinctly identified as a singular state institution. Other companies performing Italian opera were not perceived as having the same meaning or fulfilling the same function by the English public in general. Mapleson, indomitable manager of Italian Opera at the Haymarket and rival of Gye, the Manager of the Royal Italian Opera, recounts an amusing anecdote which clearly serves to demonstrate this point:

> (Mdlle. Albani) told the cabman to take her to the manager's office at the Italian Opera. She was conveyed to the Royal Italian Opera, and, sending in her card to Mr. Gye, who had doubtless heard of her, was at once received. ...
>
> He explained to her that there was a manager named Mapleson who rented an establishment somewhere round the corner where operas and other things were from time to time played; but *the* opera, the permanent institution known as such, was the one he had the honour of directing.[41]

On the strength of this most important information, Albani broke her contract with Mapleson and remained in London to sing at the Royal Italian Opera.

Since gaining Covent Garden in 1856, the opera's relationship with monarchy in particular had become more visible. This was partly due to the fact that Queen Victoria did not have the political difficulties which some of her eighteenth-century predecessors had in establishing the acceptance of the monarchy. She could ostensibly integrate crown and legitimacy and thus define through the varied ceremonial mechanisms of her power base, such as paraphernalia so important to the transmission of greatness and thus power, the tone of her era.

> One of the most splendid sights that human magnificence could present to the eye was to be seen at Her Majesty's Theatre on this occasion (June 8 1844). The presence of our gracious Sovereign and Consort Prince alone has often shed a lustre upon this aristocratic and noble *salon*; but appearing as they did, attended by two such stars as his

Imperial Highness the Emperor of Russia, and His Majesty (Frederick Augustus, King of Saxony), the spectacle was dazzling in the extreme. No theatre in the world could afford such a *coup d'oeil* of majesty, nobility, beauty, rank – fashion – wealth – power – in short, all that can make a nation great and interesting, as was to be seen and wondered at on last Saturday night at the Opera.

At the end of the first act the National Anthem was sung with admirable effect; for then a beloved sovereign was receiving the heart-felt homage of her people, and the potentates of other lands were congratulating her upon their sincere and ardent affection. Afterwards followed the Russian National Hymn, which was admirably executed by the band. The house was crammed from the floor to the ceiling. The opera 'Il Barbiere', and other entertainments were but heedlessly attended to – his Imperial Majesty's eyes seeming to *basilisk* everybody.

By the way, we pitied many anxious beings in those side boxes which were ingeniously contrived to enable the would-be spectators to look at their *vis-à-vis* neighbours instead of the stage. They stretched and stretched their necks, but they were as far from seeing the 'grand sight' as they were from the centre of the earth. When will our theatrical architects gain a *little* knowledge of their business?[42]

As can be seen from this *Illustrated London News* article, it was all important to the Victorians that the performance of monarchy was put before the requisites of theatrical performance and, as the writer clearly suggests, the architects had to understand this singularly important meaning of the house. Victoria's reign epit-omised stability and the importance of mercantile assets, and the Victorians cherished the symbols of these things. The opera continued to serve as a venue in which the forces of influence within society could be displayed to the greater world through the structure of the audience, its dress, behaviour, taste, and the public occasions which took place within the house took advantage of all these factors.

Despite the abundance of new venues, the association with the Italian language became even more firmly entrenched during the mid-nineteenth century. Throughout the century there had been numerous attempts to intro-duce 'English opera' as an equally acceptable form as 'Italian opera'. In 1849 a committee was set up and a prospectus published in which an explanation of the need for such an institution was furnished. The following text by Richard Northcott reminds us of Louis XIV's first *privilège*, and elaborates the arguments first used by Addison and Steele, as well as adding new social arguments peculiar to the industrialised age of education and the masses.

The present depressed condition of the national lyric drama in this country is a matter of deep regret to every patriotic lover of the art … there should be no theatre exclusively appropriated to the performance of opera in our own language. The taste and fondness for the lyric drama are more strongly evinced every year, but it is reserved for London, with its enormous population, to be the only European capital which is without a lyric establishment, fostered and sustained by the nation. In other countries the national opera houses are supported by large annual grants of money, as well as by the liberal private subscriptions, but individual speculation has been hitherto the sole and precarious chance of support for an English Opera House. ...

There is likewise every reason to expect that a great dramatic school of instruction will arise from the existence of an English Opera House. The musical masses must derive benefit from hearing lyric works in their own language, and its tendency will also be to create and form good singers. ...

The great national establishments in France, Italy, or Germany are never closed on the plea of a scarcity of leading vocalists, ...

It is confidently believed that a National Opera may be called into existence worthy of ranking with the great continental theatres. ... The time has arrived when an earnest and energetic appeal may be made for public support of an undertaking having for its object the formation, on a permanent basis, of a Royal English Opera House.[43]

This great demonstration of faith, however, did not come to fruition. What has remained are the basic notions which have been employed to structure the arguments furnished in support of the concept of 'English opera'; these remain extant to the present day.

The *Illustrated London News* critic demonstrated in 1862 that the major themes concerning English opera highlighted by Addison, Steele and Hazlitt were far from forgotten. Indeed, it seems that in the nineteenth century these themes had become more ingrained and accepted in England, as critics lamented their countrymen's incapacity to emulate the great national operas of Europe:

Now and then a feeble attempt to set going an English Opera made by some person without experience or means, struggled a little while and was abandoned. How times are altered we need not describe, English opera has now the occupation, not exclusive indeed, but regular and permanent – of the largest and noblest theatre in London, with all its rich appurtenances; she has a musical director of the highest eminence, with an orchestral and choral establishment, not surpassed in any theatre in Europe; she gives our most distinguished composers an amount of employment which she was never able to give them before and stimulates their exertions by holding out the rewards due to genius. ...

Much has been done, but much still remains to do, for it can never be said that the musical drama holds its due place among the entertainments of the English metropolis, till it is established in a dwelling of its own, and till the phrase 'the opera' shall be applied, as in Paris, to the national Opera, and not, as at present in London, to an entertainment which, however splendid and beautiful is only an exotic.[44]

This article stresses the importance placed on the role of the opera. It is interesting that opera is described in such terms as 'noblest theatre' and the musical director as of 'highest eminence … not surpassed in any theatre in Europe'. The debate which has hitherto contented itself with social and linguistic difficulties has now broadened to that of the role of opera and the state. This article is very much an antecedent to the debate to be led by the exponents of the 'Opera in English debate', E.J. Dent, Professor of Drama at Cambridge University between 1926 and 1941, and Tyrone Guthrie, celebrated director at Sadler's Wells Theatre during and after the Second World War.

The arguments supporting state subsidisation of national opera contributed to the popularity of this concept. The mid-century is viewed by Dent, for example, as the moment when the modern notion of the subsidisation of English opera out of nationalistic sentiment was first mooted. However, as early as 1828 John Ebers, manager of the King's Theatre, detailed in his memoirs some ideas which are clearly antecedents to this modern notion, linking the state's responsibility to opera's continuation:

> As a security against the fluctuation in receipts … the Continental plan should be adopted, by the King's Theatre being taken under the immediate protection of the Government, and aided by its support and guarantee.[45]

He went on later to suggest that another method of sustaining opera might be:

> an incorporated body of proprietors, having their powers and responsibilities regulated by Act of Parliament. This plan would probably be found to remove the chief difficulties attached to others which have been tried or proposed, as tending to effect the permanency and security of the management, the main object in view. Or, if the obtaining of the act should be found impracticable, a guarantee fund might be raised on a principle similar to that on which the musical festivals, given in the country are secured.[46]

If the opera were to have been subsidised, surely it would have been simplistic to speculate that this would have occurred essentially due to a recognition of English opera's supposed musical popularity or its intrinsic merit to the state. In reality its association with the royal insignia was the basis of its purported claim. It is evident that the support of English opera at Covent Garden depended upon royal patronage, which alone could bestow higher significance upon the art.

Royal patronage could, however, be contentious, as William Charles Macready observes:

> London, September 24 (1831). Robertson told me that Sir H. Wheatley had, on the part of the Queen, expressed a wish that the price of her box should be reduced from £400 to £350. If this be Royal Patronage commend me to popular favour! Patronage to a declining art![47]

Theatre managers could not afford such a policy and sought to develop projects through which the opera could profit from its association with the crown and parliament. Mapleson went so far as to gain the active support of the Prince of Wales for the creation of a project which literally was to be physically, and thus inextricably and incontestably, linked to parliament, and thus would be well placed to gain its overt support through pecuniary subsidy.

This project is an excellent illustration of the prevailing relationship between opera, society and the state in the 1870s and, as such, its aims merit close investigation. In his conception of this project, Mapleson eloquently united the competing forces behind the dilemma inherent in the meaning of opera. He succinctly associated the spirit of an age with an acknowledgment for a continuum of opera's national meaning and its socio-political role:

> In designing this, I intended it to be the leading Opera-house in the world; every provision had been made. The building was entirely isolated; and a station had been built beneath the house in connection with the District Railway, so that the audience on leaving had merely to descend the stairs and enter the train. In the sub-basement dressing rooms, containing lockers, were provided for suburban visitors who might wish to attend the opera. A subterranean passage, moreover, led into the Houses of Parliament; and I had made arrangements by which silent members, after listening to beautiful music instead of dull debates, might return to the House on hearing the division-bell. The Parliamentary support thus secured would alone have given an ample source of revenue.[48]

In particular Mapleson acknowledged the structural changes of urban life. He accommodated the need for facilities for use by the new suburban mass, but still clearly expected them to possess and use vestments which would distinguish this activity from the outside world, by making provision for a place to disrobe before entering the house in the correct attire. Furthermore, his scheme to connect the Houses of Parliament with the national opera is a forceful demonstration of the importance of the symbolic relationship between the two. Members of parliament are seen as those who, sensitive to aesthetic arguments and surrounded by cultural philistinism, would uphold the notion of opera and could thus be looked upon to support it. This notion encapsulates some of the earliest steps towards active government subvention and the methods employed in political lobbies with respect to opera. The concept, already nascent in the placement of the very first stone of this house, was that a government needed to maintain close and overt ties with the national opera house. In the context of the late nineteenth century, dominated by capitalist sentiment, it would then be incumbent upon government to pay for the maintenance of opera in order for it to perform the ceremonial services which the state would, in turn, require of it.

In 1875 Mapleson announced his aims for the new 'National Opera House' at the ceremony to mark the placement of its foundation stone. One can make no mistake about his order of priorities. He stressed unequivocally that the National Opera House would be 'devoted firstly' to 'Italian opera'. Mapleson cleverly accommodated the cries for 'English opera' and expressions of nationalist sentiment but made certain they were seen as of secondary importance. Furthermore, as a final concession, and having first acknowledged the challenge represented by the influx in the 1850s of highly proficient European musicians educated in the conservatories of their countries, Mapleson paid lip service to the inspirations and fashionable new trends concerning national musical education. To appease popular nationalist sentiments he suggested that the National Opera House should serve as a training ground for British musicians.

Mapleson's manifesto is steeped in nationalist rhetoric. Its language uses conventions similar to those which have been examined previously, linking nationalist sentiment with cultural hegemony. Mapleson's aims stress that national opera is important in order to ensure that England could at least keep up with, if not surpass, foreign competitors.

The ceremony of the placement of the foundation stone was designed to mark the creation of a 'Grand' and 'National' Opera House, a title which vividly encapsulates the preoccupations of the time, for opera was not deemed to be opera if it was not invested with 'grand' and 'national' connotations. Implications of patriotic support formed part of the material, albeit symbolic, contained in the foundation stone, and the monarchy was thus required to place a symbolic blessing on this unison of spirits:

> The National Opera-House is to be devoted firstly to the representation of Italian Opera, which will be confined as heretofore to the spring and summer months; and, secondly, to the production of the works of English composers, represented by English performers, both vocal and instrumental.
>
> It is intended, as far as possible to connect the Grand National Opera-house with the Royal Academy of Music, the National Training School for Music and other kindred institutions in the United Kingdom, by affording to duly qualified students a field for the exercise of their profession in all its branches. ...
>
> In Paris, when sufficiently advanced, the students can make a short step from the Conservatoire to the Grand Opera; so it is hoped that

English students will use the legitimate means now offered and afforded for the first time in this country of perfecting their general training, whether as singers, instrumentalists, or composers, according to their just claims.

In conclusion I beg leave to invite your Royal Highness to proceed with the ceremony of laying the first stone of the new Grand National Opera-House.[49]

The late nineteenth century is often described, in the phrase coined by Klein, as the Golden Age of Opera in England. Galas were held at the house for prestigious occasions, such as the welcoming of heads of state and foreign dignitaries or even musicians, who in this century had gained the stature of cultural ambassadors or living icons. Because 'society' was assured a role, and those who attended were more likely to be accepted by it, subscriptions grew. Incidentally, Covent Garden was also to become home to some of the greatest singers in Europe. When it finally became assured of its position, the need to maintain the word 'Italian' in the title of the house became obsolete.[50] The significance of this change in title is witnessed by the fact that there was no longer a need for linguistic reinforcement and justification of Covent Garden's international predominance. Consequently, the support of a qualifying adjective to opera was rendered redundant. The term opera alone was understood as a place where 'society' congregated to indulge in high, privileged culture. Thus it is not surprising that 'Opera' took its place alongside 'Royal' without need for qualification. This implied as well that state endorsement through the adjective 'Italian' (which for so long had been intimately connected with the legitimacy of the institution) was no longer essential.

It is true in both England and France that the separation of the notions and social significance of 'high' and 'low' culture became the arbiter of what was, and what was not, accepted as opera during the latter half of the nineteenth century. In London this was particularly evident, given the intermingled debates concerning notions of nationality, language, grand and common, juxtaposed against the Victorian ideology and rhetoric of the new industrial era. The problem was how, in effect, to define what was, and what was not, opera, as opposed to something rather similar to it in strictly musical or theatrical but not social terms. The proliferation of works performed in English, the abundance of theatres housing performances of these, and the growing audience which attended them, were evidence that something did very much exist and, far from going away, was occupying a considerable place on the cultural map.

Thus the argument could no longer plausibly be sustained that 'English opera' did not exist within the fabric of operatic performance and convention, and yet this argument is precisely what had been maintained by many commentators and historians who accepted the notions in which English cultural language had hitherto been schooled. There would appear to be a perverse relationship between the desire for national opera and a deprecating sentiment that, if the product were English, then it could not have serious merit musically, nor could it qualify for representation on the national platform, as 'English opera' breached national etiquette and the notion of opera and the significance of 'high art'. The plain refusal on the part of eminent critics and those with social and political influence to address these issues is one of the essential factors leading to the schism between language and interpretation which came very much to light during the twentieth century, when there were many attempts to create an opera company and redefine the meaning of the term.

Opera in England was revived at the beginning of the twentieth century by grand patrons who, despite their idiosyncrasies, brought a continuum to opera throughout the war years. Sir Thomas Beecham ruined himself financially in his undaunted quest to provide opera at Covent Garden, and John Christie created the prestigious Glyndebourne festival. Opera was to remain within the nine-teenth-century tradition until after the Second World War, when the state took over as patron, largely ignoring the contributions which both Beecham and Christie had made. The new notion of opera was very much that of a state event, financed and produced by the new bureaucratic classes aided by the aristocracy.

As early as 1946 it can be observed in the manifesto by the music publishers Boosey and Hawkes, who had taken over the house, that Covent Garden was to act as a beacon of national culture, preserving traditions and national pride:

> We hope to re-establish Covent Garden as a centre of opera and ballet worthy of the highest musical traditions. The main purpose will be to ensure for Covent Garden an independent position as an international opera house with sufficient funds at its disposal to enable it to devote itself to a long-term programme, giving to London throughout the year the best in English opera and ballet, together with the best from all over the world. If this ambition can be realised it is felt that it will prove to be a great incentive to artists and composers, since it will offer to them an opportunity for experience in the performing and writing of operas on a scale equal to that which has prevailed so long on the Continent but has been lacking so long in our musical life here in London.[51]

This manifesto represents a significant shift from the past in that it acknowledges the new ethos of society, and yet it clearly calls upon the language of tradition and English glory so familiar in operatic debates since the eighteenth century.

The national malaise brought about by the awareness that the days of the Empire were numbered and the interests of the mass, so inculcated in the concept of the Welfare State, were to change the structure of British society. In such a context, holding on to deeply embedded national traditions would be vital if the traditional emblems of power were to survive.

Democratisation was the byword of post-war language. Dent named his book in support of English opera *A Theatre for Everybody*, clearly calling upon the new notions of democratisation and culture. As one of the great exponents of the popularisation of opera, he helped create a new tradition employing the new terminology and ideology:

> But it does not seem to me unreasonable to suppose that the war has awakened in many hundreds of thousands of people a realisation that many things which formerly they had considered to be too high-brow or too grand for them are now easily within their imaginative and financial grasp; and that many things which used to be considered the pleasant amenities of a fortunate few, should more rightly be regarded as universal necessities.[52]

Yet Dent calls upon the traditional language of national pride to support his 'modern' views and interprets state support of the arts as a cultural policy which will enhance the national image that had previously been displayed on battle-fields or in the realms of economic ascendance:

> Britannia, waging her most desperate war, has decided that the pen, the harp, and the buskin must be added to shield and trident. In practical terms the State, carefully protected against undesirable exploitation, is prepared to spend a little money on opera.[53]

Randolph Churchill describes the reopening of Covent Garden after the war in much the same language as one would have expected before it. He laments the fact that this was an 'austerity opening', not because of the 'pen, the harp, and the buskin' but because, even though the monarchy was in attendance, the splendour could not live up to that of his 'grandmother's Edwardian days':

> a marking event in Britain's tardy post-war revival. In my grand-mother's Edwardian days the Opera House admittedly presented as brilliant a spectacle as could be found in Europe – two tiers of boxes running all round it, replete with beauty and fashion. The women wore tiaras, the men white kid gloves, while on the stage were all the most famous cosmopolitan singers, who were supposed to appear there for lower fees than in some other capitals because, for some reason which can hardly have been purely artistic, they looked on the applause of London as the surest seal on their reputations. …
>
> The change and decay set in. Milton tells us how best things get perverted 'to worse abuse, or to their meanest use', but no doubt the quotation is too severe, for Covent Garden never became anything worse than a *palais de danse*. Still, it was a come-down. Now the new management has restored the beautiful auditorium almost to its old splendour – not quite, for though the gold and crimson have returned, the boxes have shrunk to a mere dozen or so on one tier only; and

though the audience, headed by the king and queen and the prime minister, contained figures of every known form of distinction, they were not on the whole much to look at; for nowadays nobody has any clothes worthy of the name. It was an 'austerity' opening.[54]

Not once in this mournful reminiscence does he describe the performance. Indeed, great events at the opera house were often determined more by who was in attendance, and what the occasion was, than by the performance itself. Naturally, the post-war opening of the opera house (to a performance of ballet, not opera) required the blessing of the highest orders in the land. *The Times* of course did not fail to cover this important event in its social pages and editorial:

> The King and Queen, Princess Elizabeth and Princess Mary were present last night at the reopening of the Royal Opera House, Covent Garden. ... The distinguished audience included the Prime Minister and Mrs Attlee and many members of the Cabinet and their ladies, as well as members of the Diplomatic Corps.[55]

or to draw allusions based on ancient civilisations, the references to which could be seen in the ceremony surrounding the event and the building itself:

> We do not nowadays consult auspices and look for omens before embarking on a new enterprise, as the Romans did. If we did we might not find the omens encouraging. But we can on an occasion like last night, when the great curtain went up again at last at the Royal Opera, sense whether the start is auspicious even for so chronically precarious an art as English opera. It was more than auspicious, it was festive and it symbolised the rolling back of some of our oppressions from our minds, for the King had come with his family and his Ministers to give their blessing and we the audience had done what we could to respond, longissimo intervallo, of course, in a sartorial sense to Mr. Oliver Messel's brave and beautiful spectacle on stage.
>
> It has proved to be a sound policy not, in making a new start, to have everything brand new ...
>
> ... last night's auspicious beginning of a new and difficult but very exciting adventure.[56]

The Times then went on to give considerable coverage to the dress of the royal party, noting that the King appeared in his naval uniform and the Queen with her tiara.[57]

The great champion of accessibility of opera for the English people, Professor Dent, believed that a new ethos and the democratisation of the country would be translated into the social configuration of the national opera house. He was not the only one to espouse such a philosophy. Accessibility to a hitherto restricted experience was to be a keyword for a new generation. In the following quotation from *The Times* it is interesting that the journalist uses phrases such as 'the right sort of audience' and 'tradition' in an attempt to endorse the creation of the Sadler's Wells company. It is as if an attempt to establish a new meaning in opera attendance borrows so heavily from the past that the new experience can only be deemed successful if it has components which minutely simulate the old experience.

> In short, this was the right sort of audience for the right sort of performance; one which proves that the tradition of Sadler's Wells has so far established itself that even the unfavourable conditions of the present time cannot shake it.[58]

Post-war Britain was, however, seeing some changes to the bureaucratic nature of the arts. The House of Commons was informed by the chancellor of the exchequer that the 'Arts Council would be incorporated as an autonomous body' and the economist J.M. Keynes was appointed as its chairman. Keynes, who in fact barely survived the transitional period, was according to many 'unabashedly elitist',[59] favouring the 'high arts' over the bucolic. Many attribute the modern relationship of the state to opera as stemming from Keynes' influence over the Arts Council and therefore the opera house. In spite of Keynes' powers, he could not overthrow the cumulative impact of centuries. As we have seen, the relationship between opera and the state had been the product of many centuries. We witness, for example, the following letter, written on 1 August 1946 (the same day as the king granted a royal charter to the Arts Council)[60] by the Chancellor of the Exchequer to Sir John Anderson, which effectively illustrates the importance of opera to the state. Thus opera could be assured that it would not be 'let down'.

> This is in reply to your letter of the 26th July, in which you ask me to review my attitude to the Covent Garden Trust as expressed in my letter to Pooley of the 15th July.
>
> The assistance which the Covent Garden Trust receives from the Exchequer will, of course, come to it through the Arts Council. You will understand that in general I should wish the Council to feel themselves responsible for the allocation of the funds which Parliament puts at their disposal, and to plan their work ahead in the expectation of an assured but limited grant.
>
> I recognise, however, that the magnitude of the Covent Garden undertaking and the difficulty in present circumstances of estimating its future needs places it in a special position, and that the State will be assuming a definite obligation to see to it that, subject to others playing their part, Opera is not let down. I do not therefore rule out the possibility that the fulfilment of this obligation might in certain

circumstances make it necessary to increase the Treasury grant to the Arts Council still further than I undertook in my letter of the 15th July.[61]

This letter clearly indicates the intention of government. It speaks of potentially increasing the grant to the Arts Council, but clearly states that it means that the grant to Covent Garden will be increased.

In 1991 *Opera Now* highlighted the dichotomy between support for opera and democratisation:

> The art (opera) continues to grow more expensive. The root cause, ironically, is democratization. On the one hand opera is labour-intensive, and while orchestras and choruses and stage staffs are not paid fortunes, the days of cheap labour have gone. On the other hand the audience for opera has broadened but because most opera runs at a loss, meeting the demand costs more than resisting it.[62]

The paradox is clear yet whatever the public outcry may appear to be, opera will continue to be supported by the state. In the light of the new interventionist thought it is hardly surprising that Britain would save the jewel in its cultural crown, as Russia had saved its national opera, the Bolshoi.

It has been noted that the twentieth century is plainly a century of monumental social and technological change. It should be thought remarkable that opera and opera-going have remained consistent in form throughout major events such as social revolution in Russia, two world wars involving the United Kingdom, France, Italy and Germany, and the vast changes in communication media. Such continuity is evident, for example, in the following passage written by White, which draws upon the traditional meaning of opera.

> In 1953 H.M. Queen Elizabeth II gave Britten permission to compose an opera to mark the occasion of her Coronation, and *Gloriana* was produced at a gala performance in the presence of the Queen and members of the Royal Family.[63]

One would scarcely think that he was writing of a period only eight years after the Second World War, nor that mass media had totally altered the face of society, for such a description would hardly have altered since the times of the first Elizabeth.

The destruction of the Second World War was displayed in the external scars on the great European opera houses, but their essential meaning and function were hardly scathed. Frank Howes describes the condition in which these great houses were to be found at the end of the war:

In 1945 the Vienna Opera was a heap of rubble; the Hamburg Opera, having lost its auditorium, converted its stage into a theatre; La Scala at Milan was repairing its bomb damage; Covent Garden, physically intact, was a dance-hall run by a catering firm.[64]

Yet these houses were rebuilt, or 'saved' from other functions. Howes suggests that this was due to an enlightened popularism:

> But war damage to opera was offset by an unexpected war gain – British armies discovered opera as an entertainment worthy of civilian patronage. CEMA and ENSA had accustomed timid politicians to the idea of subsidy, and private initiative set out to restore the Royal Opera House to its proper use.[65]

Furthermore, opera is supported uniformly by modern states, whatever their political allegiance. Littlejohn notes that:

> On the other side of the now-melted Iron Curtain, every communist government in Europe has subsidised at least one opera company, often lavishly. (One of the collateral losses of a 'reunified Germany' and of a decommunised Eastern Europe is likely to be the loss or reduction of many of these subsidies.) The Sydney Opera House, the Opera-Bastille, recent visits of opera companies to Japan and Hong Kong (which are very costly to the host country), and the more than 200 new opera companies started in the United States in recent decades are all evidence of the symbolic importance, the political prestige, and the public relations value of opera, and hence its probable survival.[66]

This illustrates the very important motives of the modern state in supporting an essentially nineteenth century institution.

The desire to artificially impose a change in the traditional social structure of the opera audience was not to be fulfilled, as Lord Harewood discovered. He presumed that the bastions of the old order would relinquish their positions to the new. He was betrayed not only by their refusal to give up their seats but also unwittingly by the constraints of their dress standards.

> My idea was that the premiere would bring together the arts community in a tribute to the Queen, not the sort of people who had attended the Coronation. But the reality was that Covent Garden was full of official big-wigs who thought that they should be there. Totally the wrong audience. Apart from anything else, everyone was wearing gloves. As you can imagine, the sound of people either clapping or not clapping in gloved hands is feeble. The piece wrongly gained the reputation of being an insult to the young Queen.[67]

In this instance, an attempt at social engineering was clearly thwarted by those who knew and upheld their relationship to opera. When the Queen was in attendance at the opera house for *Gloriana*, an opera composed in her honour, their duty was to splendidly represent their order. It seems naïve of Lord Harewood, himself cousin to the Queen, to have failed to recognise such a call to arms.

The critic Ian Bevan comments on the same event and is apparently unperturbed by Lord Harewood's designs, for he appears convinced of the real reasons for royal patronage:

> At the gala performance of *Gloriana*, the royal party did not sit in the usual royal box on one side but in a box made for the night in the centre of the grand tier – as has been the custom at Covent Garden for royal galas since 1948. Although this involves a lot of work ... it is willingly done because it gives the audience a much better view of the royal party.
>
> One of the important points at a royal gala is that the presence of royalty should be emphasised and, in a sense, made part of the performance.[68]

By 1956 no more experiments of the Harewood sort were made. Attention was directed to more traditional forms of operatic presentation and the development of its quintessential function through the art of the gala. The gala performance as described here represents the ultimate separation of the house and audience from the art and emphasises the disinterest of royal parties in operatic performance as distinguished from the importance of the event as part of state ceremonial function. The opera was indeed a magnificent stage designed to show off the brilliance of what remained of the empire and a focal point of national pride, as suggested by Joan Sutherland's biographer:

> It was probably, in fact, the need to entertain Royalty that had prompted Covent Garden to offer Sutherland the Amina role in *Sonnambula*. The King and Queen of Nepal were on a State Visit to London and Her Majesty's Government were anxious to entertain these distinguished guests. Since none of Britain's Royal Highnesses are supposed to enjoy Grand Opera, and the Nepalese Royal Family no doubt could understand it not at all, a gala performance at the Royal Opera House had inevitably been chosen by the Government as the means of such entertaining. ...
>
> Lord Home, the Foreign Secretary, received his long-suffering Royal guests in the foyer of the Opera House. Queen Elizabeth II, Prince Philip and the King and Queen of Nepal were then escorted up to the Royal Box with its gold and crimson chairs and the two gilded demi-thrones presented to the Opera House by Queen Victoria and her Consort after the Crystal Palace Exhibition of 1851.

To-night a specially constructed Royal Box in the centre of the Grand Tier was canopied in watered silk of pale yellow, white and silver. Above the box were the crowns of Britain and Nepal. Queen Elizabeth and Prince Philip wore Nepalese Orders – and lights blazed from the diamond tiara and necklace which had been South Africa's twenty-first birthday present to the then Princess Elizabeth. Prince Philip wore knee-breeches and the Order of the Garter. Men in the audience wore white ties and tails, orders and decorations; women wore gowns and jewels. The whole of the crimson and gold auditorium was hung with chains of magnolia. As the trumpeters played their fanfare, and the performance began, who cared, on this splendid occasion, that outside it poured with rain and that Madame Sutherland, as she entered the stage door, had got wet?[69]

Indeed, in the twentieth century as in the nineteenth, the gala performance is a significant indicator of many of the aspects of opera-going. Writing on these performances in the catalogue of a retrospective exhibition on Covent Garden, Michael Wood distinguishes between the roles which galas serve, stating that 'there are, at the Opera House, two kinds of Galas'. The first kind:

> are informal gay affairs with a small Royal Box arranged in the middle of the Grand Tier and are nearly always graced by the presence of HM Queen Elizabeth the Queen Mother. The audience is made up of followers of either the opera or ballet and the occasion is usually a world premiere or the premiere of a new production. A large part of the audience are 'regulars' and a great many are friends of each other so that they have the atmosphere of a large party.[70]

The notion of the audience knowing each other, and consciously participating in an off-stage performance, is clearly his idea of the event. The second kind of gala is one of political significance:

> Then there is the less frequent but much greater State Performance, which is arranged as part of the entertainment for a visiting Head of State. There have been seven since the War, the first being for the French President in 1950.

> On these occasions a large part of the theatre is taken over by Government Hospitality for the Government, the various diplomatic missions – leaders from all the various walks of life and other distinguished people.[71]

Not only are the people in attendance at such events distinguished in their role as state emissaries, but in traditional venues the theatre itself is transformed to perform its function:

> A very large Royal Box, seating between thirty and forty people, is set up
> in the centre of the Grand Tier. The theatre is specially decorated, the
> Crush Bar is closed to the ordinary public and decorated in its turn, and
> in place of the Long Bar a beautiful silken tent is set up for the Royal
> party, furnished with priceless pictures, chandeliers and furniture from
> the museums. The Entrance Hall and Grand Staircase are also decorated
> and Yeoman Warders in their red and gold Tudor uniforms are on duty.

> The normal seats and boxes are taken out from the Grand Tier and the
> Stalls Circle, and rows of small excessively hard gilt chairs are put in
> their place – on which those who are invited have to sit for a very
> uncomfortable evening.[72]

And, of course, the audience decks itself in full regalia, not to be outdone by the
performances of the state, and the house.

> The most important, as connected with the fortunes and reputation of
> the theatre, was unquestionably the visit of the Queen 'in state'.
> Friendly agencies were employed to procure this desired result, but
> fortune seemed determined to smile upon me just now in every way,
> and my task was not difficult. Several of the leading men of the day
> smoothed the path for the manager, and even strewed it in some sort
> with roses. The 'state visit' was fixed for Thursday 20th July, and there
> was considerable excitement existing on the occasion, not only as this
> was the first state visit since Her Majesty's accession, but for more than
> ten years no monarch had appeared in state at the opera-house. As may
> be supposed, considerable care and boundless expense were bestowed
> upon the decoration of royal boxes and in spite of some carpings and
> cavillings at what were considered the exorbitant prices demanded, the
> evening passed over with *éclat*, not to say with triumph.[73]

The undeniable symbols of glamour and importance are displayed in the dress,
the adornments, the decorations and spatial configurations. The gala night was a
great state celebration.

> State Performances are in a way almost glimpses of fairyland – the
> whole theatre decorated by some great designer like Oliver Messel,
> Cecil Beaton or Dennis Lennon, the huge Royal Box, the ladies in their
> beautiful dresses, jewels and tiaras, and the men in full evening dress
> with orders and decorations. For a brief moment one is transported
> back to those pictures of the pre-First World War period when people
> lived and looked like that most of the time.[74]

Harold Rosenthal cleverly managed to combine concepts of both social and musical tradition, which slowly became incorporated into the generally accepted terminology of the state and critics alike:

> Before 1939 Covent Garden can be said to have had a glorious operatic history, but little in the way of a permanent tradition. The post-war Royal Opera on the other hand has not only added to that history, but has helped to establish the first real operatic traditions in that great house.[75]

Thus the attempt to institutionalise grandeur was incorporated into the new language of opera's supporters. This is demonstrated in post-war journalism, which focused on nationalist language and symbolism:

> In a statement of policy accompanying Mr Rankl's appointment, the C.G.O.T. points out that it has as its aim not merely the organisation of occasional opera seasons but the foundation at Covent Garden of a permanent national institution which will give opportunity and training to British artists.[76]

Furthermore, the demand for anglicisation of operatic language stirs arguments frequently heard since Addison and Steele first ridiculed opera. Now, with the help of government subvention, and popularisation of the concepts of entertainment and culture, their aim was close to being realised:

> The immediate purpose of the Trust, however, is to establish at the Royal Opera House a resident opera company and a residential ballet company of the highest standard mainly of British artists. ...

BRITISH ARTISTS

> The associate conductors, the musical staff, the singers and producers, with extremely few exceptions will be British. The soloists will be chosen almost entirely from among singers already known in this country and from unknown singers discovered in the auditions which are still being held in London and the provinces.
>
> The trust, it is stated, believes that the development of opera in England – and, indeed, the formation of a style of performance – depends to a large extent on the use of English. The performances of the resident company will therefore be given in English. The trust intends to do everything in its power to secure a high standard of English translation where none exists at present, and to attempt, in

collaboration, to secure the adoption of standard English versions by schools, teachers and opera companies throughout the English speaking world.[77]

This policy, however, did not outlast the early 1960s. It was out of harmony with the British operatic tradition. Opera in English would exist as it always had done but in another place. The Royal Opera needed a broader space which a strict nationalist and linguistic policy would thwart. The language of accessibility and equality would dominate official declamations but yet again opera's essential meaning remained unchallenged. An example of duplicitous language designed to make today's public believe that they have access to the real experience of opera is demonstrated by Michael Wood's description of royal galas:

> Galas are survivals of a bygone and almost forgotten age – when it was normal for men to wear white ties and women their best clothes and jewels if they went to the opera. The audience then was drawn from a very small select group of the well-to-do. *Now all can, and do, go and wear whatever clothes they like.*[78] (my italics)

Nowadays the idea of the opera house is debated once more. It has become fashionable in some quarters to deny the fact that the opera is any longer an élitist institution. Those responsible for the Royal Opera today are at pains to stress that, in order to justify its existence, it needs to be perceived, in terms of contemporary arts terminology, as being 'accessible' to the general public.[79] The argument most commonly used to justify this is that the opera's extramural following is as important to the notion of opera as those who partake of the total experience. This is essentially a fragile if not fraudulent justification. Opera means the total experience in the minds of the public in general and no 'State speak' will shift such opinion. Theodor Adorno illustrated this point well when he wrote that: 'Opera, more than any other form, represents traditional bourgeois culture'.[80] Certainly the Royal Opera House and its audience could not be described as being representative of contemporary British society. According to Crispian Palmer: 'The government, which blames bad management, is worried that Britain's flagship arts organization has become too elitist.'[81] Yet that is precisely the nature of a flagship institution!

This debate about what the opera house should represent, i.e. 'accessibility' or 'élitism', is well documented in a rather venomous and public exchange of correspondence between the recently knighted (June 1996) Jeremy Isaacs and *Sunday Times* reporter Hugh Canning:

> Hugh Canning (October 23), rather intemperately I thought, denounced the Royal Opera House as unpopular and its prices as too high. Unpopular with whom? Not with the half million who enjoy our

performances each season, nor the millions who watch them on radio and television, nor with the schools, hospitals and community centres that benefit from our educational and outreach work.

Our prices are high, it is true, but as Canning once briefly appeared to have grasped, our grant from the Arts Council is low. The Royal Opera House has to earn a high proportion – 60% – of its income. If the grant were ever to be raised (it would have to be trebled) to levels available to comparable houses in Europe, patrons would find our prices cut dramatically.

Even a modest increase in grant, beyond RPI, could enable us to cut some prices. Every little helps. At the moment, though, we are promised a standstill, a cut in real terms.[82]

Hugh Canning replied:

Jeremy Isaacs misses my point. Many pastimes – fox-hunting, boxing – are popular with those who participate and attend, but 'unpopular' with the general public. *The Royal Opera House has an image of privilege and inaccessibility.*[83] (my italics)

The Canning–Isaacs controversy recalls the vexed definitions of 'popular'.

And yet the Royal Opera House is extremely keen to demonstrate just how broad its base is. In the 1985/86 Annual Report of the Royal Opera House, Sir Claus Moser, the House's Chairman, wrote:

Those who choose to characterise us simply as a House for Grand Opera must be reminded of the range of opera and ballet performances, of tours at home and abroad, of the educational programmes, performances in the Tent, the Proms, the Schools Matinees, the Hamlyn Week, TV and radio, and the manifold activities of the Friends of Covent Garden. Of course we want to do much more to widen audiences, and above all, if finances allow, to bring seat prices down.[84]

As if this broadening of familiarity with the house and repertoire somehow broadened the meaning of opera.

In recent years the Royal Opera House seems to have reversed some of its democratic state-speak. In 1995, the day after receiving a considerable grant towards its building fund from the proceeds of the lottery, the Royal Opera closed down its schools programme. It argued that although it had just received a large injection of funding, this was only available for the refurbishment of the building and was not to be used on special programmes.

Robert Maycock highlights how far the situation has moved since 1945 in terms of propaganda at least:

The ROH seems to be able to keep the stalls filled no matter how much it charges for them. Unfortunately there is a social price, in that a growing proportion of the potential audience becomes unable to afford a ticket. Not only does that reverse the democratizing process, it contradicts the duty of the Arts Council, whose charter required it 'in particular to increase the accessibility of the fine arts to the public'.[85]

Thus we see that the notions of the meaning of opera have become less indigenous to each nation and therefore more international. It is the way in which the state or those in power choose to support opera which changes nationally; however, its meaning in the twentieth century context does not. The French cultural attaché, writer and early designer of the Opéra Bastille, Pierre-Jean Rémy, describes the opera-going public of London in the 1980s as being deeply entrenched in the class system, although certain eccentricities of dress may initially appear deceptive. He also draws comparisons between the rigidity of the English ceremonial caste system and that of the USSR. These analogies have been made more than once in the context of opera in totalitarian states:

> The Covent Garden audience is quite unusual for a national opera, where evening dresses and dinner suits mix easily with turtle-neck sweaters of the intellectuals from Hampstead and Highgate. We cross paths, acknowledge each other on occasion, as they are in fact often of the same family, those who hold the reins of England, where one gains one's place as a right in a hierarchical system second only to Indian castes and perhaps the Soviets, which know the same social barriers.[86]

There did emerge, however, a new opera-going public in the latter twentieth century. The following extract, taken from an advertisement for a book published in the early 1990s, clearly sets out some of the functions which the successful businessman's wife must perform:

> The new lady in the life of a successful man ... can afford to pay for herself, and instead of pottering in the back garden attends Covent Garden on opening nights. She's the ultimate accessory.[87]

It highlights the social role of the new ascendant class which supports the opera. Royalty has had to share its partnerships with a wider public than before. Its role has changed; the royal family now fawns to its public and makes us ask who really personifies power today.

David Mellor MP, former Arts Minister, asserts that a barrier to going to the opera is still the cost:

Cost is the final straw. The most expensive tickets at the Royal Opera House in Covent Garden are now 112 pounds. It charges those prices, greedily swallows a subsidy of more than 7 million a year and yet has still managed to show a deficit of 4.5 million for 1990/91. Impressive. You can pay as little as 3 of course, but that will get you a restricted view.[88]

Furthermore Mellor asserts that there is no 'tradition of opera' in Britain. It has been demonstrated so far in this book that in fact the only indisputable tradition is the British insistence that there is no tradition of opera. Interestingly, Mellor goes on to use the new public language of the operatic democrat, insisting that the opera-lover is the traditional opera-goer:

> Privately, I may deplore the way opera houses have become the exclusive preserve of the fat cats, as seat prices year on year soar into the stratosphere, leaving the ordinary music lover on the outside looking in, or confined to the rafters, but one has to accept that today opera is inevitably expensive.[89]

It always was, in Mellor's unlovely phrase, a preserve for 'fat cats'! It would, in fact, have been more plausible for Mellor simply to state what he must surely have known from his experience in his former position as Minister for the Arts, that the opera house is maintained with relatively high seat prices in order that the traditional audience could participate in a time-honoured social ritual.

Opera in England in the latter part of the twentieth century still potently contains the rite, ceremony, majesty and pomp of previous eras. The Church of England, the state and the monarchy are, in the following article, equated with the significance of a fictitious operatic scene and, despite the obvious imaginary relationship, this does best sum up the inauguration of George Carey, Archbishop of Canterbury, not operatic in intention but operatic, in the greatest sense of the word, in nature:

> This lavish ceremony was as perfectly predictable as only the British establishment can manage. ...
>
> Yet the audience in the nave loved it ...
>
> The rest of the ceremony owed more to high drama and opera.
>
> Enter fanfare of trumpeters from right, in brilliant red, moving across to left. A procession of several hundred ... From the rear enter two princesses, Diana in white, Margaret hard to see in a black hat.
>
> Then Dr Carey, offstage, appears on the BBC's monitors, approaching from the south behind his cross, his buttermilk-coloured stole billowing in a high wind, his hood decorated with crimson and gold flames.

He seizes a staff, takes careful aim, and knocks resoundingly three times on the oak door. Thus knocked the ghost in *Don Giovanni*.[90]

It is useful to point out that the present British establishment running the opera house promulgates two conflicting ideas about the opera house. The first is that the present opera house in Covent Garden exists for the people as a benevolent gift from the cognoscenti or connoisseurs to ordinary people and, secondly, that it is the *same* opera house that it has always been.

Of course governments will, from time to time, request reports on the state of opera in Britain, as has been witnessed periodically in the 1980s and latterly with the arrival of a Labour government into power. The Eyre Report responded to a political need for enquiry about a symbol of prestige so linked to the outgoing Tory Party. Needless to say, the report, for all its many words, did not recommend the destruction of so integral an institution, whatever the fashionable rhetoric of the day may have led the public to believe.

Thus, in Britain debate about opera has seemed to be a debate about public provision and yet it is actually a private argument between small groups of privileged people. The opera house will 'not be let down' today for the same reasons Hugh Dalton would not let it down in the 1950s. It is a place for England's power brokers to repair to, dressed in their black ties, a kind of exclusive club which hides behind a veiled wall of democratic rhetoric. The closing plea by *Daily Telegraph* journalist Norman Lebrecht, in his recent book *Covent Garden: The Untold Story*, that 'those who care for English culture must demand that Covent Garden be put on a stable footing and spared the tortures of uncertainty as it resumes the quest for excellence' sounds impressive but is based on a false perception.[91] His final claim, that 'It is an opera house, no more, no less. Its future should have no bearing on the state of the nation', is clearly untrue in the light of the weighty evidence that Covent Garden and opera in England are inextricably linked with the state of the nation.

5

ALONG THE DANUBE AND THE RHINE

Playthings of the Austro-Hungarian and Prussian Empires

Opera in Vienna has been intimately aligned with the political destiny of the great European powers. Whatever the regime, absolute monarchy, constitutional monarchy, republic, dictatorship, democracy, the opera has been used as a symbolic platform of the state or to capture the hearts and minds of the Austrian people. We have seen in recent times how the rebuilding of the opera house was to unite the nation and inspire critics world-wide. With the opera house resurrected from the ashes in 1955, perhaps Austria too could be seen to be cleansed of its recent past. The opera historian Marcel Prawy commented that it was perhaps symbolic that the last opera to be performed before the air raid of 12 March 1945 was *Götterdämmerung* and 'that it was equally symbolic that the house should re-open in 1995 when the Austrian state treaty was signed'.[1] Spike Hughes suggests that it was certainly 'appropriate and ironic', when Wagner's *Götterdämmerung* was performed on 30 June 1944 on the last day of the season, that 'when the curtain fell on the twilight of Wagner's gods that night, it fell for the last time'.[2] This was the house created by an outgoing emperor to crown his imperial city in the latter part of the previous century and then bedecked by swastikas only twenty years earlier, when the *Völkischer Beobachter* commented that: 'lavishly decorated with swastika flags and brilliantly lit, the Opera presents a more magnificent and festive picture than ever in its history upon the opening of the house on 27 March 1938 in the presence of Fieldmarshal Göring'.[3]

The history of opera in Austria changes with each era. Even Austria's geography is difficult to determine. At its greatest the Austro-Hungarian empire dominated the map of Europe in much the same way as the pink-coloured British territories dominated the world map in the early twentieth century. Begun by dominant monarchs with autocratic designs, who needed to have opera houses as emblematic symbols of state, democratised in the revolutionary year of 1848, the symbol of modernity in the early 1860s and made popular in the bel canto era of the 1890s, the Vienna Opera came to symbolise all that was great about the Austrian Empire, albeit that the monarchy was fading and power disintegrating.

Presentation of opera in the country known as Austria today is virtually a continuous story spanning more than three centuries and, as in so many other

European countries, its sources can be found in sixteenth-century Italy, when powerful princes were influenced so greatly by the Italian renaissance courts and their musical performances.[4] When the seat of power moved from Graz to Vienna with the Habsburg ruler Ferdinand II, so too did the musical influence in his court. His son Ferdinand III composed music and was 'a generous patron of opera'.[5]

The first accounts of operatic performance at the Viennese court date from the late 1630s, but it was Emperor Leopold I (1658–1705) who regularly and ostentatiously held operatic performances at his court for important occasions, such as weddings and birthdays.[6] Leopold's own wedding was celebrated by a vast operatic spectacle for which he contributed music; a theatre of 2,000 seats was constructed within the main square of the imperial palace and liberally incorporated 'machines' for effect, making a magnificent entertainment. According to Spike Hughes, 'the cost of the decor alone ... amounted to £50,000'.[7] The very positioning of such an event, within the heart of the imperial palace, combined with the royal support of the entertainment, shows opera to have been a significant, if not extravagant, art to the Habsburg court. That it was a state art is demonstrated also by the frequency of performances. During Leopold I's forty-seven year rule, more than 400 operas were performed in Vienna, many of which were composed for the emperor.[8] In 1697 Leopold decreed that Vienna should have its first permanent opera house, again demonstrating opera's importance to his court, which hitherto had viewed operatic spectacles in temporary theatres and pavilions within the palace. This plan, however, was never to be fulfilled, for in 1699 a fire razed the uncompleted theatre.

In the same year as opera was granted its first 'privilège' in France by Louis XIV, operatic performances were given for the celebration of name days. Unlike the policy of the French monarch, opera was, as in Britain, considered to be an affair for the Italian language. As the Gonzagan influence was still felt deeply within the Austrian courts, this is not surprising. These highly prestigious and extravagant events invoked displeasure from the Habsburg court of Spain and Venetian ambassadors, but they served to focus eyes on the importance of Leopold's court. The imperial opera was an exclusive event reserved for members of the court, foreign ambassadors and high-ranking visitors.[9] According to Bruce Alan Brown, 'Italian opera in Vienna was an instrument of state, celebrating Habsburg victories, marriages and anniversaries, and allowing (in occasional *gratis* performances) the general populace to view its monarchs in full splendour'.[10]

There were operatic performances in other theatres, and the German language was used for more popular musical entertainment. But it was at the imperial opera (and in the Italian language) that public displays reached their high point.

Joseph I (1705–11), the first of the enlightened monarchs, was admired as much for his statecraft as for his sensitivity towards the arts, and in particular music. On his accession to power, he not only increased the size of the orchestra to 107 players, but he also started construction work on two new permanent theatres for comic operas and opera seria, situated between the imperial library and the Riding School.

Charles VI (1711–40) continued to use opera in the same way as his predecessors, producing marvels to amaze and please his court and their international observers. Known as a musician and given to great displays, he actively supported the opera at the centre of his court. The theatre could indeed be known as magnificent, and it is not surprising that Lady Mary Worley Montague wrote to Alexander Pope in 1716 that 'nothing like it was to be found in Europe'. She saw stage machinery of the like never before seen: a stage built above water which, when moved, gave way to 'flotillas of gold-painted ships'.[11] The Viennese imperial court was demonstrating its might, which spanned from Spain across the continent, through a method which today would be called 'cultural diplomacy'. Their aim was to impress and they succeeded.

In fact, Charles VI would not countenance that the splendid court opera have any rival within his city. A Viennese municipal theatre had been in existence, and partly funded by the state, since 1708 but opera was not granted a licence for performance there. The production of opera was to be restricted to the domain of the court.

Maria-Theresa's reign (1740–80), like Catherine of Russia's, brought with it a French influence to the court. But like the increasingly embattled French monarchs, her personal taste had to be restrained as she had internal battles of another order to fight. The grand operatic debates so vehemently being played out at the French courts were followed in Vienna, and Gluck's operas gained imperial approval. She did, however, fete the marriage of her sister in January 1744 within her court with a work of Italian/Austrian provenance, Metastasio and Johan Adolf Hasse's *Impermestra*.[12] Maria-Theresa did construct a small theatre in Schönbrunn Palace in 1747, where, later in the century, special revivals of Gluck's works were performed for the visit of the Russian Archduke Paul and his wife, the emperor and Chancellor Kaunitz. Opera was to retain its primary purpose and to remain an affair of state, performed within the great opera houses linked to the palace and used to entertain the aristocracy and foreign dignitaries.

Maria-Theresa could not afford the frequent extravagances of her predecessors in retaining the use of opera for diplomatic affairs, so she allowed for the performance of opera to be financed and therefore undertaken outside of her court. On 14 May 1748 the Burgtheater, situated within the city of Vienna, was inaugurated with an opera in celebration of Maria-Theresa's birthday, Gluck's *Semiramide riconosciuta*. The success of this theatre was cut short by the monarch herself as, under the pretext of religious fervour, she ordered that theatres be closed for many religious festivals, thus decreasing performances by 20%. Her motivation for this may not have been primarily religious, as it wrested this popular entertainment from the populace and impoverished it through lack of receipts, thus assuring that its magnificence be confined to her courts. It is interesting to note that the theatres did not close their doors as a public lottery called 'Lotto di Genova' managed to raise enough funds to cut much of the deficit. This is not the first time (and nor will it be the last) that we have seen the use of lotteries to support the arts, in particular in states which profess gambling to be a nefarious activity. There is a certain irony in the pretext of closing theatres for religious reasons only to have them financed by very temporal urges.

The opera house burnt to the ground on 3 November 1761 and the court immediately began to build a grander opera house for the city on the same site. This theatre remained for over one hundred years. According to Hughes:

> In order to do this, part of the neighbouring church of the Holy Ghost had to be demolished – a situation which will be seen to occur with remarkable frequency in the History of the Opera House. Churches or religious institutions were knocked down to make way for the Hofoper in Munich, for La Scala, The Carlo Felice in Genoa and Covent Garden, to name only four of the more famous theatres standing on formerly holy ground.[13]

This argument would suggest that in such cases the temporal power brokers had more significance than the guardians of spirituality, whether state endorsed or not, and that the opera house was more important and significant to these states than the religious guardians. Monuments traditionally have been designed to represent spiritual and temporal powers. They have served as temporal evocations of religious symbolism, which is evidenced largely by their capacity to provide a structure of consequent dimensions and grandiose allegory which in turn is used to imitate much of the ritual of religious congregation. Monuments did not only fulfil civic functions but were also designed to evoke the ecclesiastical symbolism of a temple. What better monument than a theatre in which to act out the ritualistic performance of rites, accompanied with the paraphernalia of ceremonies swelled with chant, percussion, draperies and procession? Riemer firmly equates the two in this detailed description:

> Vienna's churches echo with memories of the opera. Even the interiors of venerable gothic piles underwent thorough modernisation in the seventeenth and eighteenth centuries to transform them into God's theatres. The churches constructed in that epoch are often indistinguishable from the court theatres of the age. The Karlskirche ... reveals its essentially theatrical design from the moment you set foot inside the porch. It is a miniature foyer – your eyes scan its wall and corners in search of the cloakroom and buffet. The church itself is embellished with every variety of coloured, veined and patterned marble. The high altar is displayed behind an ample proscenium arch, its curtain raised to

reveal a stunning spectacle of marble, gold and bronze. The organ gallery, protected by an elaborately carved balustrade, occupies the position of a royal box.[14]

The war of the Austrian succession meant that, as events went badly externally, German opera was to take precedence over Italian, but as fortunes improved Italian opera was performed again. The question of financing the theatre, which could no longer rely on resources from state coffers, was addressed once more. The Italian opera manager Durazzo convinced Maria-Theresa that the enterprise could succeed if gaming rooms were incorporated on the premises. This may appear far-fetched but one need only consider the existing arrangement between the Opera and Casino of Monte Carlo today. Thus, yet again, this noble art was financed, like so many others, from sources which now many would scoff at. Given that the monarchy had relinquished its role as paymaster, it was up to the entrepreneurs to obtain money from the classes which wished to attend it, that is the 'nobility and the gentry'. The Burgtheater finally relinquished its position to the grander Kärthnertor Theatre, which had taken the name 'Court Opera'. The Court Opera was such in name only, in much the same way as the Royal Opera House is today. It was a title bestowed like a privilege but the theatre had to make its way through independent management. The ensuing years were difficult for all operatic ventures in Vienna, as instrumental music had gained favour temporarily.

It was, however, an international event which yet again turned eyes to opera. The Congress of Vienna took place in 1814 and Beethoven's revolutionary opera *Fidelio* was performed highly successfully to this new public. Yet again it was the international and public visage of opera which was to influence its importance. Methods of funding, now exhausted yet again for this extravagant art, were again ingeniously sought. This time a raffle was announced; the winning entry could take over ownership of the theatre or a vast cash sum. In the event the winner chose the cash, but the financial problems were not altogether resolved and by 1820 the court had cancelled the lessee's contract.

The next manager of opera in Vienna was to have an even more illustrious connection with gambling. Barbaia arrived in Vienna in 1821 from Italy, where he had run the San Carlo in Naples, which was largely financed by the gaming house he ran from it. His genius lay in the ability to marry popular tastes and the emperor's needs. Barbaia produced Weber's *Der Freischütz* and immediately, upon its success, commissioned *Euryanthe* specially for the court theatre, which was performed in 1823. In the years until 1848 performances were sparse but continued to be held.

Early in the nineteenth century, and after social upheavals which had rocked much of Europe, legislation was introduced to separate performances of theatre and of music, and the middle classes, who throughout Europe had gained access to corridors of power, joined the ranks of those in attendance. Not surprisingly, this changed the nature of the operatic institutions and allowed an increased audience to make the opera house its ceremonial performance venue.

As the century progressed on its tumultuous path, various kinds of opera management were experimented with, as in France. So too were operatic themes, with the politicised and highly charged 'rescue' operas coming into vogue during the second quarter of the century. In a 'collaborative' venture in the decade preceding 1848 La Scala of Milan and the Vienna Opera were linked artistically and economically by one manager, who installed gaming rooms on the premises. Another scheme was proposed a few years later by a Milanese architect, but it was rejected not only because of cost but 'because it was considered unseemly that a foreigner should *design what was intended as a national monument*' (my italics).[15] The significance of the Austrian opera house was always clear to Austrians and, if it had to relegate the German language to minor houses, its architects could not be seen to bow to those of a subject state.

Connections between the management of the Italian and Austrian operas were not surprising, given that they were part of the same empire with a significant history of cross-fertilisation between Naples, Milan, Florence and Vienna. In 1857 'the Austrian Minister of the Interior instructed the Governors of Venice and Milan to examine the possibility of three month's spring seasons of Italian opera in Milan, Vienna, Venice, Verona and Trieste, all run by a single director, "an Italian of course", who was to have at his disposal all the subsidies granted to these five cities, all of which in those days belonged to Austria.'[16] This scheme never came to fruition because Austria lost its Italian states.

In the same year the Emperor Franz Joseph (1848–1916) gave his approval for an ambitious scheme to glorify the city of Vienna through a monumental construction programme, the crowning glory of which would be the new opera house. Prawy comments that the 'imposing edifice reflects the splendour of the Habsburg Empire which had by then recovered from its losses in Italy and its defeat by the Prussians in 1866'.

An open competition was held to design the new theatre in 1860, although such competitions had been held often before, for example the international competition of 1789 in Venice resulting in the construction of La Fenice. Construction of this opera house began in 1861, at roughly the same time as the Palais Garnier in Paris and, amid similar controversy, opened after almost eight years under construction.

Instructions to architects for the construction and design of opera houses reveal much about the intentions of the governments that write them. In this case, the opera was very much to demarcate the levels of exclusivity and separation within the great Austrian empire.

The 'Regulations for the construction of a new Imperial Opera House in Vienna' included some clear stipulations for the architects. There were to be 2,500 seats and tiers of boxes, and the theatre should cater for opera, ballet and the Opera Ball. Even though the opera house was a public venue, the architects were required to build into their designs an imperial box, antechamber and salon and two separate approaches for the emperor and the court.[17]

The building's construction was keenly watched and appropriate moments were duly celebrated. The foundation stone was laid in a grand ceremony on 20 May 1863. In the same year, after facing much public criticism, Eduard van de Null, one of the two architects, committed suicide. His death was closely followed by that of his partner, who died of a stroke at the age of 32. The architects were small spokes in this national machine. The significance of the opera house, which caused so many to deride their work, was precisely due to the fact that so many eyes invested a sense of meaning and honour in the building. (The tale is not dissimilar to that of the dismissal of Joern Utzon in 1966 by the NSW Minister for Works, who, as Utzon admitted in a rare interview in 1999,[18] loved the opera house but needed to mould it into his own vision and not be subservient to the views of the architect.) Thus for the commemoration ceremony it is not surprising that: 'The whole area was flagged, emblazoned and decorated with pine-sprigs, while the onlookers included Ministers, leading citizens from various walks of life, and all the workmen engaged on the site, amongst whom 4,000 guilders were distributed.'[19] The ceremonial opening on 25 May 1869 was made not by an opera singer but the actress Charlotte Wolter, who delivered a prologue. This was followed by Mozart's *Don Giovanni*, sung in German, and the occasion was marked by the fact that all the leading dress shops were sold out. The gala opening was presided over from the imperial box by the Emperor Franz Joseph, members of his family and the King of Hanover.

The opera also became a professional activity and under Hans Richter's direction (1875–97) gained musical accolades to augment its monumental ones. Opera-going was not considered to be a frivolous pastime, as some of these regulations from 1897 demonstrate:

Rules for Visitors to the Court Opera

(regulations pursuant to the law forbidding late arrival)

1. A canon will be fired in the Imperial & Royal Arsenal at 5 p.m. daily as a signal to visitors to the Court Opera, that they should begin their preparations at home. On days when the performances commence at 6.30 p.m. the signal will be given at 4.30.

2. At 6 p.m. or 5.30, respectively, a second shot will give warning to ticket-holders who are resident in the outer suburbs that their journey to the Court Opera should now start. It has been arranged with Viennese householders that the concierges shall inform such tenants as intend to visit the Opera on that day as soon as the 6 p.m. or 5.30 p.m. shot has been fired, and shall urge the said tenants to leave the house immediately.

3. As the tramway and omnibus system, particularly during the current pipe-laying operations, is exceptionally prone to involvement in traffic blocks and thus may cause ticket-holders in vast numbers to arrive late, all owners of season-tickets and ticket holders are obliged *on their word of honour* never to board one of the said vehicles to travel to the Opera once the above mentioned signal has sounded.[20]

On 12 December 1877 the first 'Imperial Opera Soirée' was held. According to Klein, it was 'the precursor of today's annual Opera ball',[21] which remains the highlight of the Viennese social calendar. It is interesting to note that in 1892 the opera club at the Met was formed and the theatre turned over for spectacular galas. Such a trend seems to be supra-national and have its roots in the social world of late nineteenth century society, whether it be of the old or new world. The opera house was where society repaired to see and be seen and not necessarily to listen to that art form called 'opera'. For example, in 1879 the Emperor and Empress Franz Joseph and Elisabeth celebrated their silver wedding anniversary at a gala performance.[22]

Hans Richter was replaced by Gustav Mahler with much acrimony in 1897, and Bruno Walter joined as Mahler's assistant in 1901. So the new century was heralded with a grand opera house, within which the values and etiquette of the great Habsburg Empire were clearly maintained and a new musical professionalism was also ascribed to. The audience not only had to look the part but also appear to play the part as respectable musical amateurs. The actual construction of the opera house took place as the empire was crumbling. Lombardy was lost in 1859, the Veneto in 1866 and the Prussians were advancing their interests steadily. The creation of the Austro-Hungarian monarchy coincided with the completion of the new house, and their fortunes were intimately linked until the monarchy's disintegration in 1918. According to Prawy, 'the Austrians, though keenly aware of the decline of their political prestige, had no inkling of the far greater prestige their new Opera House was to bring them.'[23]

During the First World War the opera was still the place to be seen and Anthony Gishford notes that the war years 'seem to have passed almost unnoticed'.[24] But he does comment that the audience changed, as 'by the beginning of 1916 a new generation of opera-goers was in being – the war profiteers. Most of them cared nothing about music but a great deal about being seen in the right place. Not surprisingly the price of seats rocketed.'[25] As one person observed: 'People go to the Opera without even looking to see what's on.'[26] From the death of the Emperor Franz Joseph in November 1916 until the end of the year the Opera was closed, but in 1917 the normal routine was resumed and the new emperor offered Richard Strauss the intendantship.

In November 1918 the Emperor renounced all participation in state affairs and a republic was proclaimed. It was to be a decisive moment in Viennese operatic history. The opera house, so aligned with the empire, now had no court to house it and was to be purely a place for musical congregation. The new Austrian Republic acquired one of its very first state institutions: the 'Staatsoper' (the Vienna State Opera), as the former court opera was to be called henceforth. 'The double-headed eagle and the designation *k. k.* (imperial and royal) disappeared from the Opera's posters'[27] but 'notwithstanding all that had occurred, still preserved high up on the famous French Renaissance façade of the theatre' was 'the commemorative legend 'Kaiser Franz Joseph I, 1868'.[28]

By 1933 other powers were to be ascendant in Vienna and the opera house was to become one of their principal venues for the display of their might. The free state of Austria was overtaken during the 'Anschluss' of March 1938 and the opera remained closed for a fortnight, to be re-opened in the presence of Field Marshal Göring to a performance of *Fidelio*, significantly the same choice as in 1814 at the Congress of Vienna. The 'Anschluss' and consequent political results meant that the Nazi Party now held greater power in Austria than the courts of Leopold or Maria-Theresa ever had. The opera house was used in not dissimilar ways. For example, like every other institution the Staatsoper became part of the national Nazi apparatus and was subjected to the race laws and other ceremonial components of the new regime. The Jewish artistic adviser Bruno Walter, already barred from Germany, was locked out of the Austrian opera house, which was to become an important venue for the new power brokers. On 27 March 1938 Field Marshal Göring attended a gala performance of *Fidelio* and 'Hitler's first birthday in the new "Gross-Deutschland" era was celebrated by the Vienna Opera on 20 April 1938 with a performance ... of Wagner's *Die Meistersinger*, conducted by Furtwängler', who had to account for his actions to many, amongst them the CIA, at the end of the Second World War.[29]

The notion of cultural exchange which we saw being used in the early 1830s by the Austrian empire was to be exploited again under the so-called unity of the new 'Gross-Deutschland'. Exchange schemes among various opera houses demonstrated this concept. The Berlin Opera brought its production of Wagner's *Lohengrin* to Vienna, which was augmented by the Viennese chorus.

Furthermore, the use of the operatic stage to fly the state flag high was not underestimated by the Nazis. 'On the "Grossdeutsche Reich Day", after the incorporation of Czechoslovakia in 1939, the Vienna Opera performed in Prague and Bonn, and in later years there were visits to the Netherlands, Zagreb and Bucharest after German troops had occupied these territories. The Rome Opera sent its ballet to Vienna, and the Teatro Communale of Florence gave *Falstaff* in Vienna with Mariano Stabile, who was also the producer. The whole area of Europe under Hitler's domination was criss-crossed by visiting operatic companies.'[30] This kind of cultural diplomacy is in many ways not dissimilar to the international tours of the Stalinist regime's ballet companies, or even the international tour of the *Mona Lisa* from France to the United States at the height of the Cuban Crisis.[31]

The opera continued to maintain full houses and the composition of the audience reflected the on-going war and political situation. The imperial box was occupied by Nazi VIPs and the audience was largely dressed in uniform. This kind of display in war-time is not unusual. One need only remember the public displays of Napoleon Bonaparte, who admittedly was not particularly interested in operatic performance but appeared at the opera flanked by his generals and who rewarded soldiers with seats at the house. Similarly, the Nazis rewarded their own injured soldiers with the 'Bayreuth' experience.[32]

In the final stages of the Second World War, on 12 March 1945, the opera house was bombed during an Allied air raid. The building was almost entirely razed except for its façade, the loggia and the great staircase.

In a sense the bombing was a symbolic end to this period in history. The Allies had struck the visible, monumental certainty of the Austrian regime. The opera house, centre of musical activity and shrine for those who upheld the ceremonial grandeur of this and past regimes, was destroyed and Austria was metaphoricaly reduced to rubble by such an event. It is therefore not surprising that the rebuilding of such a house took priority in the post-war period, even though materials were not easily found and austerity was supposed to be the order of the day.

Spike Hughes views the destruction of the old house and reconstruction of the new as 'the best thing that could have happened to the city'. He suggests that it was the first time since the outbreak of the First World War that Austrians could unite in a vision of something positive to look forward to, as the city's great past was a vital part of its present heritage. 'The Opera was something they owed to the past and they were always conscious of it.'[33] In fact, the reconstruction was very much that: as many monumental and architectural elements as possible of the old house were retained and built into the new one.

The reopening of the house in 1955 was a grand state occasion. There was a solemn ceremony, which began on the morning of 5 November. The invited guests comprised those in power in the new regime, the President of the Republic, government officials, international representatives and former artists. The streets outside were packed with onlookers as the nation participated in this resonant occasion. This event, even more than a performance, signified much to those present. 'Mme (Lotte) Lehmann seems to have been even more moved by the ceremony in the morning than at the first performance (*Fidelio*) that night':

> 'It was an unforgettable moment when the iron curtain rose,' she says of the morning. 'Even now in memory, it chokes me. This wonderful old house which has served only beauty, which has given joy and uplift to thousands of music-loving people, had been mute for so long. Now it lives again. Now the old times will come back again; and I am sure of that. I don't belong to those people who always sigh for the past. Nobody is irreplaceable. Wherever some beauty dies, some new beauty

is being born. Much glory lies ahead of this beloved house. If I would not believe this, I would think, "There never will be a time as we have lived through in the past", it would make me very unhappy. Today the house is yet echoing with voices of the past. But soon those voices will fade away in the glory of new voices, as beautiful as ours were. Oh, I am sure of that!'[34]

It is interesting to examine the use of the Vienna Opera House from 1938 to 1945 and the opening in 1955 of the newly rebuilt opera house. Like so many other opera houses in other countries, guest lists look remarkably similar. The evening's audience was a gathering of the great and the good of the new order, the new power brokers. Mr Henry Ford was present and so too were members of the occupying forces and those Austrians who had been cleansed by the Allies. In the words of one commentator: 'In the boxes as well as in the house as a whole a glance at the audience was enough to confirm that the ten years of austerity since the end of the war were now really over.'[35]

Hughes' comments about the nature of the internal fittings are revealing, as they clearly let his readers know what the meaning of an opera house was as opposed to other venues for popular entertainment:

> Inside, on the other hand, everything is new and of a quite remarkable splendour. The auditorium has been reconstructed to look like an opera house, not like a concert hall or a cinema. There are still three tiers of boxes, with a central 'royal' box, and two top galleries. The colour scheme is red plush, white and gold; there are a crystal chandelier and numerous welcome improvements.[36]

There is some irony here as no more royalty remained in this once illustrious empire. One can only imagine that the significance of retaining such a venue was so that heads of state could maintain an understandable iconography for state ceremonial occasions.

Much has been written about this 'auspicious' event. Andrew Riemer emphasises that the opera house was rebuilt with the intention of replicating the old house. He describes an opera house as a temporal monument, likening it to a cathedral in both form and function.

> Cathedral and opera house were both meticulously rebuilt after the disaster of the Second World War. ... Yet both are restorations, nostalgic reconstructions, not so much of the physical buildings that stood on these sites, as of the dreams and aspirations of a sentimentalised past.[37]

Littlejohn regarded the reopening of the Vienna Opera House as 'the single most important symbol of Austrian recovery'.[38] Klein suggested that: 'The re-opening of the Opera House was the first great cultural occasion since Austria recovered her political freedom with the departure of the last remnants of the occupying forces a week or two previously.'[39]

This fervour for the opera house has remained, as it has, like many opera houses around the world, openly been seen as a source of 'national pride'. In 1967, on the occasion of its bicentennial, the Minister of Education Dr. Theodor Piffl-Percevic waxed eloquently about its importance:

> Two centenaries of Viennese operatic culture have found a centre which promised further existence when in 1869 the Opera House on the Ring was inaugurated. In the following hundred years this centre has become an object of national pride and international recognition. The hundred year old history of the House is the history of its spirit, for which the walls are the symbol of its consistency and continuity. The present and the future both rest on this strong foundation.[40]

In the same year Rudolf Klein could confidently write of the opera's importance to the Austrian state as evidenced by the funding procedures. There is no space here for arguments such as accountability and democratisation; the tax payer clearly gains in national glory that which he does not gain necessarily by a seat at the opera:

> The Vienna State Opera is the musical heart of this city of music, of the whole country in fact; and it is by the whole country that it is financed. Its income derives from the tax payer, is voted by Parliament, and apportioned by the Ministry of Education. There has never been a question in Parliament about the Vienna Opera being financed by the Austrian people as a whole, although many Austrians never get a chance of enjoying the operas they contribute to.[41]

This view is not only expounded by proud Austrians. The English opera historian Charles Osborne writes:

> As almost everyone with any interest in opera knows, there is no city where the Opera House is more important, more integral a part of civic life than Vienna. The Viennese are proud of their opera, they argue over it, grumble about it, boast of it, and through the years have appeared to be more concerned for its future than for the stability of their Government.[42]

This is indeed a heavy legacy for a place of entertainment to carry.

From the Austro-Hungarian Empire to Prussia, Germany and the GDR. Today, when people speak of opera in the modern state of Germany, they usually speak of the proliferation of theatres and the generous funding of opera and state opera houses in that country, but this is only a partial view of the German operatic heritage. That also includes the nineteenth century festival of Bayreuth and the operatic legacy of Wagner or the follies of Ludwig. It also includes the legacy of Voltaire's much-loved monarch, Frederick II, who invested so much in his musical kingdom. The fact that there are many centres for operatic performance in modern Germany is, to a large part, attributable to the system of arts funding in the country. There is no centralised arts body disbursing funds. Instead, each city, much like the famous 'Bunds' in previous times, is responsible for the maintenance of its cultural life. What could be more natural, then, than the maintenance of the symbolic seats of power of each of these states? These theatres, founded by princely courts in the seventeenth century, have been maintained throughout the centuries by their individual states.[43] That Munich, Stuttgart, Bonn, Berlin and Dresden have well-endowed theatres is not surprising under such circumstances, nor is the fact that so many conductors lead the opera houses and are paid some of the highest salaries in the world.

The modern republic of Germany, arising from the ashes of the Second World War and re-emerging after the annexation of the Cold War, rather resembles Italy in that it is made up of newly amalgamated territories from the great seventeenth and eighteenth century empires.

Opera was found at the heart of power, wheresoever that power resided, and it is to these places, the courts, the republics, the centres of government and the state vehicles for display, that we must go. Rather than tracing the history of the numerous smaller princely opera houses of the German state, we will focus, by way of example, upon Berlin, powerhouse of the Prussian empire, which was so intimately aligned with the great Austro-Hungarian empire, and upon the emergence of the modern nation state and events of the twentieth century. The music historian Thomas Bauman suggests that Berlin is a 'true cosmopolitan capital' and therefore certainly warrants such examination.[44] Horst Koegler views the Staatsoper in Berlin as the 'summit of opera in Germany', succinctly stating his view that:

> whatever political regime its general administrators had to bow to – Hohenzollern imperialists, Prussian republicans or Nazi maniacs – it was this house which represented the summit of opera in Germany – though Munich and Dresden may boast of a prouder record of first performances.[45]

The history of opera in Berlin can be traced back to Queen Sophie Charlotte in the 1690s,[46] but it was Frederick the Great (1740–86), that enlightened despot who it was claimed in his princely days was so influenced by Voltaire, like Catherine the Great of Russia and Joseph I of Austria, who did in fact bring music and in particular opera into the heart of his kingdom. It is claimed that he 'controlled it as carefully as his most important administrative measures, diplomatic manoeuvres and military exploits'.[47] On accession to the throne he 'set about creating an operatic establishment' in his capital.[48] Frederick acted as chief critic for the content and music on display. Frederick's court, like all European courts, watched carefully over rival regal displays. Frederick's greatest competition in those days came from the Spanish court of Ferdinand VI. Therefore, he 'cultivated opera on an even larger scale' and, on becoming King of Prussia, he appointed Karl Heinrich Graun as his court composer and sent him to Italy to bring singers to his kingdom. According to Horst Koegler, 'the building of an opera house became a political declaration of independence when Frederick the Great ascended the throne in 1740'.[49] Like his Austrian counterparts, he constructed a temporary theatre within the royal palace, the 'Comodiensaal auf dem Schlosse', which remained there until 1805.[50]

In the space of only two years he established a more permanent structure, the Berlin Opera House, whose architect would also design his magnificent palace of 'Sans Souci' near Potsdam, completed in 1747.[51] And 'one of his very first commands was to Baron von Knobelsdorff, supervisor of all royal buildings, for an opera house to be erected on the grounds of the former fortifications',[52] even though money was lacking due to the Silesian War. Opera was soon to become of national importance, with Frederick personally supervising many aspects of performance and selecting librettos and by 1749 devising plots in French prose.

The opera house, the Lindenoper, was a great extravagance, with space 'for no less than a thousand carriages'.[53] The opera was an extension of Frederick's court and admission, free to those entitled to attend, was open only to certain strata of society, including army officers; it was devoted to the performance of Italian opera. This is significant because Italian opera was understood to be synonymous with court opera; opera in the vernacular was not to grace the imperially sanctioned stages. It was important to be seen at the opera in order to demonstrate one's intimacy with the inner circle. The presence of army officers at the opera is not unusual in a militaristic state. One need only think of the early nineteenth century in France, when the Salle Peletier in Paris was resplendent with the uniforms of officers, or Visconti's film *Senso*, which so well shows the Austrian uniforms in La Fenice in occupied Venice, or the German soldiers at the Vienna Opera or Bayreuth.

The opera suffered as a result of Prussian defeat. During the Seven Years War (1756–63) most of the opera personnel were dismissed and the king contented himself with intermezzos at Potsdam.

In 1772 the English musical diarist Burney stressed the importance of the opera house in Berlin, noting the classical references in the building and commenting on its magnificence in terms of architecture and morphology:

> From hence we went to the great opera house; this theatre is insulated in a large square, in which there are more magnificent buildings than ever I saw, at one glance, in any city of Europe. It was constructed by his present majesty soon after his coming to the crown. The principal

front has two entrances; one level with the ground, and the other by a grand double escalier; this front is decorated with six corinthian pillars, with their entablature entire, supporting a pediment ornamented with reliefs, and with this inscription on it *Fri clericus Rex, Apollini et Musis*. This front is decorated with a considerable number of statues of poets, and dramatic actors, which are placed in niches. The two sides are constructed in the same manner, except that there are a number of pillars.[54]

He further comments upon the ceremony surrounding the empress's entrances and egresses:

Her Majesty is saluted at her entrance into the theatre, and at her departure thence, by two bands of trumpets and kettle drums, placed one on each side of the house in the upper row of boxes.[55]

Another musical traveller, the composer Reichardt, also comments upon the opera house of this era:

I hastened immediately to the opera house …. It was almost two hours before the opera was to begin, but these I by no means lost, devoting them to an inspection of the inner arrangements of the beautiful and lofty building. *Solemn majesty* is the character of this model of the noblest taste in architecture.[56] (my italics)

The war of the Bavarian Succession (1778) brought another cessation to operatic activity in Berlin. Like Louis XIV at the end of his reign, the embattled king was no longer attending the opera by 1785. All theatres were closed for two months to mark his death on 17 August 1786.

Whereas Frederick's tastes had been distinctly European with a tendency for appreciation of the Italian and French arts, Friedrich Wilhelm II (1786–97), who succeeded him, was a firm supporter of a more distinctly German opera, setting up the Nationaltheater in Berlin. At the beginning of his reign in 1787, renovations were undertaken at the Royal Opera House (Königliches Theater) and new singers were contracted. The reopening of the house on 11 January 1788 was a grand event. And in the revolutionary year of 1789 Reichardt's Italian opera was performed there. It is significant that, although the Nationaltheater was an exponent of the German language, supported strongly by the king, open to the public and with work by the German composer Reichardt, the Royal Opera House was to perform works by the same composer but in the Italian language. As Italian opera was the gateway to that which was universally accepted as cultivated in music, it would not have done for performances to take place there in the coarser German tongue.

When Friedrich Wilhelm II died on 16 November 1797, the normal mourning period was respected and a measure of uncertainty about the future of the operatic tradition set in. However, his successor Friedrich Wilhelm III (1797–1840), who was not known for a deep interest in the arts, actually permitted both the opera houses of his predecessors to continue, acknowledging that Italian and German productions had a place in his kingdom.

These were the tumultuous years of the French Revolution and the great wars with the French nation. Napoleon's troops were throughout Europe and artistic interests in vanquished kingdoms were not important unless needed for special ceremonial duties, as we have seen in the case of La Scala, San Carlo and La Fenice. The politics of ceremonial display in the period certainly did not spread to the German lands when the French forces occupied Berlin in 1806. The opera house by then was empty and used to store bread.[57]

Berlin was occupied from 1806 to 1807 and the nature of artistic subsidy was irrevocably changed as the monarchy was no longer capable of financing the arts. The opera house closed its doors. In 1807 the Royal Opera and theatre companies merged to form the Königliche Schauspiel and performances were opened to the general public.[58]

Fire destroyed the Royal Opera House on 18 August 1843 but Berlin was not without an opera for long. On 7 December 1844 a new and infinitely more splendid opera house, which accommodated such innovations as gas lighting, opened its doors. Throughout the century, as the population grew in Berlin so too did the demand for opera, and renovations were undertaken. In 1919 the Royal Opera House became the Staatsoper, or State Opera, and its name was finally separated from that of the monarchy. Completely renovated in 1926, it suffered badly from the economic crisis in the 1930s and, as that decade progressed, most of the Jewish and anti-Nazi artists left the house, which became an adornment of the Third Reich.

Much has been written about the importance of opera to the Third Reich. This importance extended not only to the Festival of Bayreuth and the connection between Adolf Hitler and the English Cosima Wagner, but also through the Minister of Culture, Göring. The Third Reich exploited the cultural artefacts of German heritage to the maximum and accommodated them for their own use. Thus the opera house was to be a significant emblem at which state ceremony was to be displayed. In 1935 the Nazi Party commissioned a redecoration of the vestibule and foyer of the Staatsoper 'in a manner becoming the Third Reich'.[59]

The singer Lotte Lehman provides a most illustrative anecdotal account of Göring's decision to bring what he wanted to his opera house in 1933.

> One day, I received a telephone call from Berlin: it was the Director of the Berlin State Opera. 'Frau Kammersängerin, would you be interested in coming to Berlin for a few guest appearances? His Excellency, the Minister of Education, Herr Göring, is personally inviting you.'

'Thank you, Herr Generalintendant. But I am so happy here in Vienna that I'd leave only if it were made worth my while. Berlin doesn't pay higher salaries than Vienna, so why should I come and incur extra expenses?'

'Let's forget the question of salary, Frau Kammersängerin!. ... I mean we can forget about the amount of salary. That's all taken care of. Off the record, I can tell you you will get whatever you ask.'

'Really, since when is that?'

'Since this moment, Frau Kammersängerin'. ...

A few weeks later I was giving recitals in Germany. ... During my recital, in the middle of a song, I suddenly sensed a curious unrest in the audience. ... I opened my eyes, and saw, right in front of me, a man, an official of some kind, who was desperately trying to interrupt me in mid-song. ...

He looked at me with pleading eyes, and I noticed with astonishment that he was shaking with nerves from head to foot. 'His excellency, the Minister of Education (Göring), is on the telephone. He wishes to speak to you.'

I finished the group of songs. No applause. The audience sat paralysed. ...

Lotte Lehman was whisked off by private plane to Berlin and met at the aerodrome by the director of the opera who informed her of her imminent meeting with Göring, the Minister of Education and proffered the following advice:

'His Excellency is very interested in you. He wants you for the Berlin Opera, not only as a guest artist, but as a permanent member of the company.' ...

We drove to the Ministry of Education. Soldiers everywhere. Swastikas everywhere. The 'Heil Hitler' greeting everywhere. It all seemed to me like rather third-rate theatre. ...

Göring came straight to the point. 'I read about your success in America' ... 'You had earned a good deal of money, and are likely to pay it into a bank in Vienna, where the Jews will deprive you of it.'

Göring then offered Lehman a contract in Berlin with some explicit demands attached to it:

Of course Göring had a few wishes: he expected me, as a matter of course, never to sing outside Germany again. 'You should not go out into the world,' he said dramatically, 'the world should come to us, if it wants to hear you.' .... 'And in Berlin you will never get bad notices!' [60]

This rare account of an artist and a power broker merited being quoted at length. The operatic prize is held dearly and is understood by those seeking legit-imisation of their power to be one of the rare jewels which soften their iron fists. This account is attested to in part by MacDonogh, who claims that:

> After 1933 it (the Berlin Opera) was a fief of Hermann Göring, who, among his many other titles, held that of Minister President of Prussia. Apart from making full use of the ex-royal box, Goring used the building for his parties. Klaus Mann in his novel *Mephisto*, a fairly vicious attack on his former brother-in-law, the actor and director Gustav Grundgens, imagines the scene of the Minister President's 43rd birthday party:

> 'The well-groomed crowd milled around the extensive foyers, corridors and vestibules. Corks popped in the boxes, the parapets of which were hung with gorgeous draperies; there was dancing in the stalls from which the rows of seats had been taken away. The orchestra took its seats on the whole expanse of empty stage. ... It was playing a cheeky medley of military marches and that jazz music which, though it was frowned upon for its niggerish indecency in the Reich, its grandees couldn't do without on their birthdays.'[61]

Hitler, a very few years earlier, according to Carey, cited the opera house as an illustration of Germany's ascendance over American culture and thus implied that cultural politics were at the heart of national ascendance:

> The Americans, Hitler conceded, possessed cars, clothes and refrigera-tors, but the German Reich could boast 270 opera houses and a standard of culture of which America could have no conception.[62]

When the grandest opera house, the Staatsoper, was bombed and destroyed on 9 April 1941, it was therefore not surprising that reconstruction work should commence immediately. As the Reich's foremost theatre, it had to be rebuilt at once,[63] and on 7 December of the same year the reconstructed Staatsoper was reopened. Horst Koegler put it in the following terms:

> Even those wretched dictators valued the Staatsoper so highly as the national symbol of German art, that they immediately rebuilt it on an even more splendid scale after it had first been bombed.[64]

Towards the end of the war the opera house suffered in a further bombing raid on 3 February 1945. With the Third Reich on its knees and an uncertain centre of government, it took another ten years before the new house could open its doors as the Deutsche Staatsoper on 4 September 1955. Significantly, the design of the new house originated from Prussia's glorious past, as the original plans of Knobelsdorff's theatre of 1742 were its source. However, the inscription on the façade was updated to display the new title of 'Deutsche Staatsoper'. One might argue that this visible link to another era of Prussian greatness, albeit accommodating the new lexicography, was an architectural reference that no one in the crippled state could forget.

The Second World War over and the Cold War just beginning, Germany was not only decimated but soon to be split asunder. Hans Busch wrote in 1954:

> In the ruins of 1945 there was and there still is today a widespread and genuine need for 'Kultur' and artistic expression which in most instances is still promoted and subsidised, as it was in the days of royalty and the Weimar Republic, but no more propagated by the state. Apart from its purpose of entertainment, the theatre is still considered a 'moralische Anstalt', a moral institution without which the Germans refuse to live.[65]

Within the space of less than a decade, Busch could claim that:

> Most of the important theatres and opera houses in Western Germany have been repaired or rebuilt with enormous sums allotted by the cities and/or the government.[66]

Post-war Germany was to be a divided country and there was significant 'internal political manoeuvering'; however, by 1957 the rebuilt house once again housed an opera company. Even more remarkably, the newly reconstructed German state held on to the essential meaning of opera. According to Karl Ruppel:

> So, insofar as general intellectual and stylistic tendencies of our time have not brought about a change in the very essence of opera and its formal realisation on the stage, the creation of countless new theatres has not altered the nature of German operatic life, nor uprooted its traditions. In the new buildings as in the old the same laws that have governed the various regional and local preferences since the beginning of German operatic history are still responsible for the angle from which opera is viewed. Irrespective of the complex and fundamental inner development to which opera is being subjected today, in that it testifies to the creative spirit, it has remained unchanged for two hundred years as a theatrical institution and in its effect on the public. It appeals to the emotions of its audience more than any other type of art; it is in fact one of the few phenomena by which people allow themselves to be emotionally touched in this overcivilized, highly technical and intellectual age.[67]

If we are to accept Carey's hypothesis, such a description is not surprising, incorporating as it does a traditional view of opera endorsed as much by Germany's recent totalitarian past as by its modern democratic principles. For Carey opera contains all the references which he suggests traditionally involve continuity and high art:

> The superiority of 'high' art, the eternal glory of Greek sculpture and architecture, the transcendent value of the old masters and of classical music, the supremacy of Shakespeare and Goethe and other authors acknowledged by intellectuals as great, the divine spark that animates all productions of genius and distinguishes them from the low amusements of the mass – these were among Hitler's most dearly held beliefs.[68]

On 13 August 1961 the Berlin Wall was constructed and the Staatsoper soon became the operatic flagship of East Germany and as such was to act as a home for communist ceremonial display. Many prominent artists had left the East and moved to the Deutsche Oper in West Berlin, which became an increasingly important theatre. This opera house of 1,885 seats in the Bismarckstrasse, designed by Fritze Bornemann, opened on 24 September 1961 with Mozart's *Don Giovanni*. It became known as the Deutsche Oper Berlin. The Staatsoper company soon became the flagship of East Germany and as such was to act as a home for communist interests, whilst in Western Germany the different municipalities vied for importance by creating and financing opera houses throughout the state.

The French critic Michel Leiris describes the audience at the opera in Berlin in the 1960s with thinly veiled contempt, suggesting that it had lost its rarefied role and become just another 'necessity of life', the amateur now more of a 'glutton' than a 'gourmet'. Leiris, a product of the beginning of the century, reveals to us that this change in the audience also means a change in opera, as if for him, in this instance, opera is no more as it is given over to a vulgarisation of interest.

> Situated behind the stalls of the Staatsoper, there is a corridor where a crowd forms, mainly comprised of young people equipped with binoculars. Here, opera seems to be amongst the necessities of life. But that doesn't necessarily mean that the public are real connoisseurs. They are gluttons rather than gourmets; they fill the theatre irrespective of the programme and give themselves over to ovations and other exclamations and applaud indiscriminately a singer who sings off key.[69]

When the Berlin Wall fell in 1989, there was great uncertainty as the Staatsoper very much needed to be reintegrated into the cultural framework of the new state. The decision was made in 1991 by the Berlin Senate to appoint the controversial but world-renowned conductor Daniel Barenboim as its music director (from 1993) in order to 'transform ... the Staatsoper once again into a glittering international house employing the world's leading directors and singers',[70] and with *Parsifal* as the inaugural work.

It is interesting to compare the choice of inaugural works for the German opera houses since the war, as the re-unification of Germany called for the grand Wagnerian piece to be performed. For the humbler Deutsche Oper, which had first opened its doors to greater Berlin with Beethoven's *Fidelio* on 7 November 1912 under the title of a 'people's opera', Mozart was to be the musical choice. Given the great Wagnerian debates of the nineteenth and twentieth centuries the symbolism of such a choice cannot be lost on us.

6

THE JEWEL IN THE CROWN –
STRONGER AND MORE
PERMANENT THAN
IDEOLOGIES

Why Opera was Retained by the Bolsheviks

> For a time the stablest thing in Russian culture was the theatre.
> There stood the theatres, and nobody wanted to loot them, or
> destroy them; ... the tradition of official subsidies held good. So
> quite amazingly the Russian dramatic and operatic life kept on
> through the extremest storms of violence, and keeps on to this day.
> H.G. Wells, *Russia in the Shadows*, p. 45

Continuity is the key word when referring to the history of opera and its institutions in Russia. Such continuity in the face of the enormous social and political upheaval of the past 150 years might seem remarkable, but in Russia opera has always been an 'affair of state'. Performance and ceremony were as important to the great Russian Tsars as they were to their communist successors, Lenin, Stalin and Khrushchev, who saw to it that, whilst institutions with tsarist legacies came crashing to the ground, the opera was preserved, a vestige of cultural omnipotence, seen by the new power brokers as a jewel in the crown of the Soviet state. As Commissar of Public Education and the key exponent of the Communists' cultural policy, Anatoly Lunacharsky said, at the opening of Glinka's *Ruslan and Ludmilla*, to his new and chosen audience at the Maryinsky Theatre in St Petersburg, former home of imperial opulence:

> To you, workers, will be shown one of the greatest creations, one of the
> most cherished diamonds in the wondrous crown of Russian art. On a
> valuable tray you are presented with a goblet of beautiful sparkling
> wine – drink it and enjoy it.[1]

This left no doubt as to opera's significance in the newly formed communist state. Opera was a jewel in the crown, a cup of luxury, and the Soviet state supported it. Today's leaders have inherited the legacy of this past.

The history of opera in Russia is also one of the tussle for cultural eminence between the great cities of St Petersburg and Moscow to serve as the emblematic cultural crown of the state. The Bolshoi and the Maryinsky theatres have witnessed many events of social upheaval and for the most part have kept their doors open to audiences from the tsarist aristocracy to the Bolshevik and communist power brokers and eventually to the new democratically enfranchised public of the modern post-communist state.

During the October Revolution the Maryinsky Opera, which was the former tsarist court theatre, stayed open every night, leading the musical historian Boris Schwarz to comment that :

> Nothing seems so reassuring to an unnerved population as the continuance of theatrical and musical events. This proved to be as true in revolutionary Petrograd in 1917 as in besieged Leningrad of 1941–1943.[2]

Such an analysis does not go far enough, however. If everything we have mentioned in previous chapters is true, then keeping the opera house open means more than simply being a pacifier of the people. It is a deliberate symbol of continuity. The Bolsheviks, who took over the running of the theatres as early as 22 October in the heady days of the 1917 revolution, understood clearly that they were shaking their society to the core. Arrangements were made to protect some vital institutions and these included the opera houses of Moscow (the Bolshoi) and Petrograd (the Maryinsky). This was no accident. All the state theatres had been reorganised under the Theatre Division of the People's Commissariat of Public Education (NARKOMPROS) but its head, the musician Anatoly Lunacharsky, refused to give them jurisdiction over these great theatres. His unsurprising explanation was that the newly appointed bureaucrats 'do not have the premises for correctly evaluating the importance of preserving the tradition of an already established culture'.[3] Lunacharsky's explanation can be understood only when set against the operatic institution's history of permanence through changing regimes and the need for the state, to use his own words, to preserve 'the tradition of an already established culture'. This culture is the language which is understood world-wide by power brokers and, although Lenin could believe that the Bolshoi, for example, represented 'a piece of pure landlord culture' and objected to the 'pompous court style' of the opera,[4] he effectively allowed his Commissar Lunacharsky, who recognised the need to retain symbols which outlasted ideologies, to shape the cultural visage of the new Bolshevik state.[5] The great singer Chaliapin, in his memoirs told through Maxim Gorky, also recounts how he visited Lenin in order to make a plea for the Maryinsky Theatre, which Lenin agreed to and immediately honoured by announcing 'Don't worry, don't *worry*. I understand everything, perfectly.'[6]

The genesis of the Russian operatic traditions, which appear to resemble those of Western Europe, lies in the seventeenth century. When in 1703 Peter the Great (1682–1725) created a city in the marshes of northern Russia, he did more than create an isolated administrative state, he set the foundations for what has arguably been the cultural bridge between Russia and the West. He also laid the foundations for a battle for ascendancy between two cities, Moscow and St Petersburg. This battle is still in evidence today. Some argue that Moscow has more often housed political power but St Petersburg has added cultural sophistication to that power, translating Russian moeurs into stylised European elegance, thus consolidating its links with the continent. And herein lies a tale of two great traditions of opera within one country. The cities may have fought long and hard for ascendancy, and we will trace this history, but the tsars knew why they had incorporated opera into their country, as they presented 'elaborate coronations and pageants' within their courts and in their capitals. Opera to the tsars was to serve the same function as it did to the kings and emperors of Europe.[7]

Peter's successor, Empress Anna, imported the first Italian operatic troupe to Russia in 1734. For her German successor, Catherine the Great (1762–96), who was known for her sweeping westernisation of Russia, opera was one of the refinements which she provided for her aristocracy.[8] It was in St Petersburg, the chocolate box of Russian sophistication, that Catherine the Great was depicted in Tchaikovsky's *The Queen of Spades* (5 December 1890) as entering the opera herself 'accompanied by the French ambassador and assorted princes as the chorus of guests, amid bows and curtsies, sings "*Slavsya sim Yekaterina, Slavsya nezhanya k nam mat! Vivat! Vivat! Vivat!*" ("Long live Catherine, long live our gentle mother! Long life to her!")'.[9] Catherine, who possessed no musical talent of her own, became undoubtedly the grand patron of opera in her empire, by importing artists and supporting the construction of opera houses and companies. Opera to her was the opera which she had seen in the German courts of her childhood and was fundamentally an Italian art form with the ceremonial trappings of statehood.[10]

About a century after opera had gained a real foothold in Western European capitals, Prince Petr Urusov determined that a theatre be built in Moscow to 'serve as the city's adornment and in which opera, ballet and drama performances and also masquerades could be held.' On 17 March 1776 Urosov received Catherine's 'privilege' to create an opera house (the Petrovsky) and opera company (called the Bolshoi) in Moscow, representing the official integration of opera into the Russian state. The house was opened on 30 December 1780 and called the Petrovsky Theatre.

By 1783 St Petersburg also had its first grand public theatre, the 'Bolshoi Theatre', described in the Maryinsky theatre programme of 1999 as the 'symbol of Russian culture' and by Julie Buckler as 'a severe-looking neoclassical structure' which 'could boast of being forty years older than the Moscow Bolshoi and only five years younger than La Scala.'[11]

At the beginning of the new century, in 1803, in a step which resembles that of Joseph II in Austria and Frederick Hohenzollern in Prussia, 'Tsar Alexander I reorganised the public theatres of Russia under an imperial monopoly and sanctioned public performances of operas by foreign troupes.'[12] This allowed the tsar greater control over performances outside of his court but also served to open

Russia up to foreign influences, leaving no doubt in anyone's mind as to which power they were serving. The tsar attended the opera both in his court and in public theatres, and these new regulations ensured a consistency of approach.

In 1805 the Petrovsky Theatre in Moscow, which housed the Bolshoi company, was destroyed by fire. In 1811 the same fate was suffered by the St Petersburg Bolshoi, closing it for a number of years. Its reconstruction in 1817 rendered the theatre more opulent and grander with columns, bas-reliefs and statues in marble as well as a grand covered entrance.[13]

But Moscow would not be outdone. The new theatre erected on the same site as the Petrovsky Theatre was named after its resident company (the Bolshoi) and opened on 6 January 1825.[14] This new theatre was a showcase: 'The spectators who arrived there in the evening were amazed by the noble architectural design and its realisation, by the unprecedented dimensions of the building and the beauty of the auditorium décor.'[15] And so, like its European neighbours, we see that the Bolshoi was intended and destined to become one of the great operas of the Western world, distinguished not only by the works presented inside its walls but also very deliberately by the nature of the building and hence the kind of audience who would attend it.

The writer Sergei Aksakov wrote of the new theatre:

> The Bolshoi Petrovski Theatre which has risen from the old charred debris ... stunned me and I admired it. ... The magnificent great building, devoted exclusively to my favourite art, made me happy and I was agitated even by the sight of it.[16]

Newspaper reports concurred with this view. On 17 January 1825, shortly after its inauguration, the *Moscow Bulletin* published the following patriotic piece, describing in terms now familiar to us the phoenix-like resurrection of the theatre.

> There are events in Russia which stun their contemporaries by their rapidity and magnificence and are viewed as miracles by distant generations. ... Such an idea naturally occurs to a Russian person whenever something happens bringing our motherland in the midst of European powers, and this comes to mind at the sight of the Bolshoi Petrovski Theatre which has risen like a phoenix from the ashes, with its walls shining in their new magnificence.[17]

This language is reminiscent of that used by Burney, Stendhal and others when writing about the great Italian opera houses. In particular the claim that it has 'risen like a phoenix from the ashes' is a direct borrowing from La Fenice in Venice, whose name and history attest to such phraseology. It is true, however, that the construction of such a theatre, designed to evoke awe, was essential to the international public image of the Russian state. Certainly, the opera house in

Moscow was a meeting place of aristocracy and foreign diplomats, and it behoved the state to house such a meeting in appropriate circumstances.[18] Buckler cites David J. Levin's view that the opera was in fact 'a cultural hand-me-down of the elite ... effecting the orderly transfer of the cultural trappings of power from one generation of the "entitled" to the next.'[19] It also allowed for easier congregation of dissenters, where so few were allowed by the state.[20]

The reopening of the Bolshoi in St Petersburg in September 1836, with the première of Glinka's opera *A Life for the Tsar*, was 'a great social affair',[21] the house having undergone significant renovations to its 'raspberry-velvet and gold interior'.[22]

This Moscow Bolshoi Theatre was virtually razed by fire on 11 March 1853. Reconstruction work began at once, and it was reopened on 20 August 1856, retaining its original façade. This theatre is the one we know today as 'the Bolshoi' of Moscow. The opening ceremony, true to form, was a great event 'attended by the royal family and the representatives of all the states'. The architect Alberto Cavos described his intention, and one wonders whether such an opera house could have influenced Napoleon III's great house, conceived in that year and opened a decade and a half later:

> I did my best to make the auditorium as magnificent as possible and also to produce a light effect, if possible, in the Renaissance style in combination with the Byzantian style. White colour, the bright crimson drapings, overstrewn with the golden interior decoration of the boxes, different on each storey, the plaster arabesques and the main effect of the auditorium – its grand chandelier with three rows of lights and candelabrums, adorned with cut-glass – all that has won universal praise.[23]

The theatre had a classic Ionic façade and a horseshoe auditorium with a capacity of 2,150 seats. As in many European theatres of this nature, the seating hierarchy denoted who the power brokers of the age and society were.[24]

Alexandre Benois is of the view that the Bolshoi was in fact 'rushed through by a special date – the coronation celebrations in 1856'. Describing the Bolshoi theatres of Moscow and St Petersburg, he writes:

> The aim of these theatres was to amaze with splendour and luxury and this aim became excessive, particularly in the Moscow Opera. ... In both theatres the decorations were red and gold, the gold covering most of the architectural part. Both auditoriums were considered to be models of elegance.[25]

In 1859, after yet another fire, construction of the Maryinsky Theatre, ostensibly as a home for Russian opera in St Petersburg, was begun. The theatre, named after Alexander II's wife Maria, opened with *A Life for the Tsar*, thus claiming its place over the old Bolshoi, which was the home of 'Italian opera' and had opened with the very same work in 1836. The Maryinsky quickly undertook its new role as the pre-eminent opera house of St Petersburg and therefore internationalised its repertoire towards the Italian.

One of the important aspects of the Maryinsky was the tsar's box, placed in the centre of the circle, which according to Buckler 'represented a modification of the ducal loggia in Renaissance Italy, when the city ruler surveyed both his subjects and the performed spectacle from a uniquely privileged, elevated seating area at the rear center of the theatre.'[26] There were other grand boxes on either side of the stage: 'Members of the imperial family or highest nobility might occupy these boxes for casual attendance, but would sit in the Tsar's box on state occasions.' There is no ostensible difference between the descriptions of this box and its use and those of other such boxes in Europe. The opera house was used for the same kind of state ceremonies as any other, and those sitting in it were from society's highest order, the power brokers.

Alexandre Benois' recollections of the Maryinsky in 1875, when he was aged five, give us a good description of the magnificence of the house:

> Avidly I examined all the details of this odd splendid space sparkling with light and gold that stretched above and below me. I was awestruck by the semi-circular auditorium built up in five tiers, each outlined with a row of little boxes. Over the blue curtains of the Tsar's boxes fat white cherubs supported golden crowns and crests of eagles, and from the domed ceiling, painted with dancing maidens, hung a huge chandelier, burning with a multitude of candles.[27]

In 1882 the imperial monopoly of theatre productions in St Petersburg was repealed,[28] but it was not until 1885 that the Maryinsky replaced the Bolshoi as the Imperial Opera and Ballet theatre.[29] According to Volkov, Alexander III 'knew that the imperial theatres ... were the mirror of the monarchy; the brilliance and opulence of their productions reflected the majesty of his reign'. He was therefore concerned that attacks by the liberal press were in fact 'veiled attacks on his regime'.[30]

Reforms were also beginning to occur in Moscow. The Bolshoi, which had hitherto been the exclusive domain of the aristocratic world, was opened by order of Tsar Alexander III to the general public in 1880.[31] The public quickly adopted this new institution.

> In 1897, Russian opera advocate N. Dmitriev asserted the importance of the Moscow Imperial Opera Theater, since, he claimed, its position 'at the centre of Russian life in the most natural fashion gives [the opera theatre] the significance of a model national institution, which ought to serve both as an artistic museum and as a guiding light to Russian art, for which an epoch of luxurious flower is coming or has already come'.[32]

This institution was necessary for a number of reasons. As in the case of the British aristocracy, the Romanovs were to be found at the public opera. The following is an account of a performance by Kchessinka, ballerina and 'mistress first of Nicholas II when he was heir to the throne, and then two grand dukes', which attracted 'le tout petersburg'. A reporter for the St Petersburg Gazette described the audience at the Maryinsky during Kchessinka's performance:

> Innumerable ball gowns in every color and shade, diamonds sparkling on shoulders, endless frock coats and tails, small talk in English and French, the heady scent of fashionable perfume ...[33]

This was a place to see and be seen for the cosmopolitan, wealthy and well connected. This situation held true until 1914 and the audiences 'remained as glittering as any in the world: probably more glittering, because Russian men were still much preoccupied with uniforms and decorations, even those whose political sympathies were liberal.'[34]

This Bolshoi company of Moscow was to represent the Russian state at the celebration of the coronation of the British King George V in 1911.

George Balanchine, in conversation with Solomon Volkov in 1981, described to him the Maryinsky theatre of 1916, where he was a child dancer in the Imperial Petrograd Theatre School. This remarkable account gives us an idea of the theatre on the eve of revolution and its special social configurations.

> Everyone thinks that the royal box at the Maryinsky is the one in the middle. Actually, the tsar's box was on the side, on the right. It had a separate entrance, a special, large stairway, and a separate foyer. When you came in, it was like entering a colossal apartment: marvellous chandeliers and the walls covered with light blue cloth. The emperor was there with his entire family. ... We all stood at attention. ...
>
> Then we received a royal gift: chocolate in silver boxes, marvellous ones! And mugs of exquisite beauty, porcelain, with light blue lyres and the imperial monogram.[35]

One could reasonably have expected that such an opulent venue, complete with the trappings of all that could reasonably be understood to represent tsarist Russia, would be destroyed, or at least left to fall into ruin during the tumultuous events which were to shake Russia at the beginning of the century. This was, however, not to be the case. Like many public buildings, the theatre was damaged somewhat during the October Revolution; for example, it lost half of its window panes due to the vibrations of nearby artillery. But these windows were quickly replaced and the building remained essentially intact.

By 1918 Moscow was restored as the capital and the Bolshoi had regained state pre-eminence.[36] Indeed it became home to the great theatre of Konstantin Stanislavski, who formed a studio within its walls and formulated some of his principles of operatic direction with the direct support of the Soviet government.[37] By the 1920s Soviet operas such as Zolotarev's *Decembrists*, Vasilenko's *The Sun's Son* and Shishov's *Tupee Painter* were being performed within its previously tsarist walls. The state had appropriated all that the opera meant.

Alexandre Benois was the grandson of the constructors of both the Moscow and St Petersburg Bolshoi theatres and tells us in his *Memoirs* that:

> It is noteworthy that even in the worst periods of Petersburg life, during the years 1919, 1920, 1921, and in spite of the distinctly proletarian appearance of the audience, the Mariinsky Theatre retained its aristocratic atmosphere and even lent a touch of elegance to the Bolshevik comrades.[38]

But artistic excellence represents not only what states hold most dear, and the new power brokers, who strove to make a new world in so many spheres, understood this inherently where the opera was concerned. From 1919 the Bolshoi Theatre became the focal point for celebrations of state importance and the Maryinsky Theatre was renamed the National Academy Theatre of Opera and Ballet. The Bolshoi became home to events such as 'sittings devoted to the celebration of revolution anniversaries, party congresses, and jubilee meetings devoted to events of national importance'.[39] Its name became synonymous with 'the centre of national culture as a whole'. It would have been tantamount to national sacrilege to intimate that the institution represented anything other than the summit of state sophistication. In 1935 the Maryinsky underwent another name change to commemorate the recently assassinated Sergei Kirov and became the Kirov Theatre. Thus this theatre of imperial elegance was to bear until 1992 the name of the former head of the Leningrad Communist Party.

The impoverishment of the Soviet state as a result of the gruelling events of the Second World War was reflected in the Bolshoi, which, like so many other operatic buildings, in time had its functions curtailed. In fact it had a more promising use than most during wartime because, unlike the Palais Garnier, which became a storeroom during the siege of Paris in 1870, or the Staatsoper, which was used as a warehouse in Berlin, or even Covent Garden, which became a music hall, the government decided that part of the company was to perform in the building of the Bolshoi during the daytime. Performances at the Bolshoi were often interrupted by air raids and the audience and performers alike had to scurry to shelters, only to return after the all-clear signal for the rest of the show.

However, by 15 April 1941 urgent repair works were required and the Bolshoi was finally closed. The government evacuated many of the Bolshoi personnel and their families on 14 October 1941 to Kuibyshev (Samara). This exile of its personnel far from Moscow lasted a total of 21 months, but they performed sporadically at the Kuibyshev Palace of Culture.

At 4 a.m. on 28 October 1941 a German bomb fell through the façade wall and exploded in the entrance hall, destroying all the stucco and decorative elements on the main façade which had survived the fire of 1853. The capitals and bases of the portico columns were almost completely destroyed. The sculptures of Muses in the niches were turned into heaps of splinters. The ceiling of the entrance hall fell through and damaged the floor. The oaken entrance doors and all the windows of the main façade and some on the side facades were torn off. The interior decoration not only of the central foyer of the dress circle but also of the auditorium was also damaged. In spite of this substantial damage and the fighting that took place close to Moscow, the theatre, which was without electricity or heating, was shrouded in camouflage meshes and restoration work undertaken almost immediately and in extraordinary circumstances. This building obviously resonated with importance to the Soviet state and its preservation was of great concern to the power brokers.

In July 1943 the Bolshoi company ended its exile and returned to Moscow. The performers of the Bolshoi were esteemed to be great patriots as a result of giving of their talent by performing for soldiers of the Red Army at the front and also giving their personal savings for the country's Defence Fund, for the construction of tanks and war planes. Some of the performers accompanied the frontline units 'all the way from the Volga to Berlin'.[40]

Thus we can see how and why in Berlin on Victory Day, 5 May 1945, a gala concert was held on the steps of the smashed Reichstag with the leading stars of the Bolshoi opera and ballet. This is, of course, a simplistic explanation of why this concert was given. In the confusion of the victory of the Allies after the Second World War and before the Cold War had frozen Europe, and Berlin in particular, the Russians were exercising their political strength through their cultural arm. The Bolshoi ('great') was indeed behaving as if it were great. The performance was a display of might and of dominance, military, artistic and cultural, and therefore political. Opera was used to convey this message on the smashed steps of the defeated order.

St Petersburg probably suffered more trials than any other city during the Second World War under the German siege and bombardment. The theatre was evacuated and the company moved to Perm. Approximately 20 shells hit the Maryinsky theatre and yet, as in the case of other grand opera houses, it was rebuilt at great speed and with the inclusion of new amenities by the autumn of 1944.

The Cold War years led to cultural exchanges and cultural diplomacy, with British and other artists visiting other countries in order to display their importance. This principle held true when Prime Minister Macmillan visited the communist rulers in 1957, at the height of the Berlin crisis, when he took his honoured position in the Royal Box at the Bolshoi Theatre, alongside the mighty Russian rulers, a political performance which could have taken place in tsarist times.

In 1966 Moscow celebrated the 190th anniversary of the Bolshoi Theatre.[41] In 1968 the Maryinsky Theatre underwent reconstruction, but it was the Bolshoi Theatre Opera which remained at the heart of Moscow's concerns since the war and throughout the post-war era. Successive Russian presidents entertained foreign emissaries there. In 1975 the grand chandelier was restored and in 1976 the stucco décor was cleaned and the silk panels repaired in the former imperial foyer, renamed the Beethoven Hall.

Not long before the fall of the iron curtain, the French critic Bernard Bovier-Lapierre remarked that the audience at the Bolshoi in Moscow was actually watching a performance of the power and authority of the USSR as an icon of the unification of the diverse cultures of the state held up as a symbol of grandeur under one roof:

> The Bolshoi theatre of Moscow welcomes the pilgrims, come from all the states of the union to Lenin's tomb. … The evening at the Bolshoi is part of the tourists' political circuit used by the many who have come to witness Russian power, the founder of socialism and the unity of the State.[42]

John Pick suggested that the Russian audience bore a remarkable similarity, in terms of clothing and behaviour, to that of Covent Garden:

> I am amused to see all around me the kind of behaviour which would-be Western revolutionaries think 'typical' of Covent Garden or of the decadent West End. There are the fur stoles, the painted faces, the long gowns, the dapper theatrical suitings; there are the noisy greetings, the forced mechanical laughter of the stiff groups intent upon their social-ising, the endless standing up in the seat to be seen, and the tell-tale roving eyes of the socialisers. All perfectly harmless, but quite different from the single-minded purpose with which citizens are said by the guide books to attend entertainments.[43]

In 1987 it was argued that this renovation was of 'vital importance and necessity, rather than a luxury'.[44] This is no different now than in any other time in which a country chose to renovate a theatre; it is invariably of 'vital importance'. Governments never justify their luxurious tastes by saying that they wish to create luxury; grandeur is by its very function a necessity of international display.

With the coming of 'perestroika' and 'glasnost', the West could finally witness the Maryinsky Theatre, this crown of the Russian state, which had so many myths surrounding it. It was once again given its former name, the crown and the lyre were restored to the cupola of the theatre, the imperial crown was restored to its gilted glory above the royal box, and the name Kirov, so aligned with the city's revolutionary past, was to become a relic of that past.

The Russians understood precisely what their grand stages represented, and when the Bolshoi Ballet visited London in May 1993 they brought with them as a stage setting the interior of their theatre. This is interesting in the context of this chapter, as it was not a reproduction of the proscenium or what an audience would normally be viewing but in fact of the 'hind view', the tsar's box and auditorium, thus serving to reconstruct the significant social spatial configurations of the house:

> An opulent 70ft-long 125ft-wide tableau, reproducing the interior of the company's theatre in Moscow, has been hung. ... It blocks off half the hall, turning an auditorium into a theatre.
>
> The magnificence of the tsar's box in the proscenium arch has been simulated in reds and golds. Crimson drapes hang alongside glittering pillars.[45]

Shortly after the visit to London, on 7 July 1993 Decree No. 529 was issued by the government of Russia for the provision of a two-part construction and renovation of the Bolshoi Theatre and a smaller adjoining theatre. This was never fully implemented.

In a ceremony held in the Beethoven Hall of the Bolshoi Theatre on 28 September 1995 an agreement concerning the construction and renovation of the Bolshoi Theatre complex was signed by the Government of Moscow, 'Mospromstroy' Closed Joint-stock Co. and the Bolshoi Theatre, which was to include two major theatres and rehabilitate the 'unique ancient residence of the XVII century "Sherbatov House" for the Friends of the Theatre':

> In accordance with the Order of 17 December 1998 'About founding the Competitive committee to select the principal project organization to renovate the Bolshoi Theatre' the following members have formed part of the Competitive committee: the leaderships of Gosstroi of Russia, the Government of Moscow city, the Ministry of Culture of Russia, Union of Architects and the leadership of the Bolshoi Theatre.[46]

In the highly volatile age of post-perestroika Russia, this project has not as yet been fully realised but at the time of writing the main Bolshoi theatre is currently undergoing extensive renovation. The cost of the project is estimated to be US$400 million for the whole complex and US$200 million for the theatre itself.[47]

A recent book produced by the Maryinsky Theatre itself and sold in its foyers in 1999 makes interesting claims for the theatre:

> Ever since the nineteenth century, the Mariinsky Theatre – a jewel in the crown of Russian Imperial theatres, which in the past enjoyed the direct patronage of the Romanov family – has been an important cultural symbol of Russian statehood.[48]

This mighty claim, made in post-communist Russia, is perhaps the most revealing of all and proves clearly that even after almost a century of purged history the opera, in this case the Maryinsky Opera in the renamed St Petersburg, has a clear symbolic meaning, unifying culture and statehood and reconciling political ideologies.

This chapter will conclude, however, in March 2000, when the British Prime Minister Tony Blair paid a visit to the soon-to-be-confirmed Russian President, Vladimir Putin, at St Petersburg's Maryinsky Theatre to watch Prokofiev's *War and Peace*. The new power brokers of the new orders are reassembling and, as the leading article in London's *Times* can happily predict:

> The afternoon at the opera will end with applause and flowers; Mr Blair can be confident that the performance was worth sitting through and the impression of his visit a good deal more long-lasting.[49]

What indeed will be 'long-lasting' is not so much the memories of Mr Blair's one-off performance as the sheer number of Heads of State who meet with Russian Heads of State, whatever their political allegiances, at that very place, the opera house.

7

MAGNIFICENCE OF THE MET –
THE COMMERCIAL FABLE

High Society, Corporations and State

One would expect the old orders of opera and opera house to be challenged, turned on their heads and turned out in a different form in the United States of America and in particular the city of New York, if anywhere. After all, it was here, early in the twentieth century, that so many new art forms flourished in a society freed of historically fixed class divisions. Large stage performances of the likes of the follies, musical comedies and dance were to fill new auditoria and radio brought the performing arts into people's living rooms.

It was to these shores in the early nineteenth century that the great adventurer, friend of Casanova and librettist to Mozart, Lorenzo da Ponte, came, becoming a grocer and avid entrepreneur of operatic ventures and teaching the Italian language at Columbia College.[1] It was P.T. Barnum, that intrepid entrepreneur of museums and circuses, who was probably best known for the presentation of exotica in the form of Asian mermaids, who first brought Jenny Lind, 'the Swedish nightingale', to New York and then on tour around the length and breadth of his vast country.[2] Later in the century the British impresario Col. James Henry Mapleson endeavoured to set new standards of operatic entertainment in New York society,[3] followed closely by America's Oscar Hammerstein. And yet the operatic experience in New York, in all its aspects, is remarkably similar to that which we have witnessed in other, much older, countries.

An opera house was built for the Academy of Music in 1853 at Fourteenth Street and Irving Place, with enough boxes to satisfy New York's power brokers, and so the city could satisfy itself with a venue to attract European visitors and to display themselves whilst watching and hearing opera. What is interesting and infinitely more satisfying for us to understand is that, whilst in Europe power brokers were content to renovate and change existing opera houses, which carried within their monumental staircases, porticos and stones the great traditions of their past, New York's power brokers had none of these inhibitions. There was no 'natural opera quarter', nor was there a stable monied power group. The United States' very nature, its enterprising, entrepreneurial, frontier-pushing democracy, meant that fortunes could be established relatively quickly and that, in the absence of great political upheaval and established behaviour such as primogeniture, the power brokers of New York could, in a sense, choose their own traditions.

It is interesting to observe that their chosen traditions were not nearly as radical as one might have imagined. We will see later in this chapter how boxes were to become bastions of family power and to be passed from one generation to the next just as they were in Europe. We will also see how the important male club, associated for example with the Paris Opéra, was also to make its significant appearance at the American opera. We will also see how, in the absence of monarchs and duchesses, the new American society ladies donned tiaras and ermine and took on the ceremonial behaviour of the European ruling establishment. It was to opera that New York society repaired and it was at the opera that they appeared in fashions virtually indistinguishable from their European counterparts.

However, the adulation of opera within this very small society could not be complete without linkage with long-established centres of operatic excellence. Established artists of all kinds were brought to the opera house from the 'old world': the great manager Gatti-Casazza of Milan, who brought with him Toscanini at the turn of the century, Enrico Caruso from Naples, the French-trained Australian Nellie Melba, the de Reszke brothers and numerous others. This competition with European culture was also an important factor in the provision of a new Metropolitan Opera House in New York in the 1880s, and once again in the 1960s.

New York built its first major opera house in 1853, tailoring its construction to the needs of contemporary society.[4] The house took the name Academy of Music because, 'as the term *opera house* countered the stigma of the theatre, the term *academy* countered the stigma of the opera house'.[5] Ahlquist argues that in this society, which was ambivalent about the European model of the opera house, the term Academy gave it 'respectability'. But respectability did not ensure fluidity and within a period of two decades the house was overstretched socially, rather than musically. New York was changing and according to Dizikes: 'Musically, it barely supported one opera house. Socially, it needed two.'[6] Within three decades this opera house proved too small to accommodate the growing numbers of well-to-do families. And so, when Mrs Vanderbilt found herself turned down after applying for a box, she and many of her set did what Americans are very good at – they simply joined together to build and finance an alternative house which would accommodate their social needs. The chronicler of the first fifty years of the Met, Irving Kolodin, supports this view, claiming that the 'complaint was architectural rather than operatic' due to the lack of boxes and desirable locations, with 'the new capitalists ... relegated to the *parquet*'.[7] On 7 April 1880 the *New York Times* announced the decision and that $600,000 had already been received in subscription.

So it was necessary to build a new opera house for 'the two Roosevelts, Iselins, Goelets, the Astors, the three Vanderbilts, the Morgans, and others'.[8] A competition was set up and one of the key requirements was for the incorporation of boxes in prominent positions. The building, whose architect had no previous experience in theatre construction, was completed in 1883 and modelled upon London's Covent Garden but incorporating features from La Scala in Milan and the Opéra in Paris. It has been described as being in 'early Italian renaissance manner',[9] possibly to evoke opera's grand beginnings in the ducal palaces of Italy. Kolodin remarks that 'with its triple band of boxes, (it) was clearly modelled on the royal theatres of Europe. However, the American aristocracy of wealth being more inclusive than an aristocracy of birth, the provisions were necessarily more elaborate.'[10] This was to be the house for the new money, a grand opera house, based on so many European architectural traditions. As society moved to this new grand house, the old Academy of Music did not long manage to challenge the new power brokers and closed the doors of its theatre.

Kolodin states clearly that because the:

> genesis of the Metropolitan was in a social situation, rather than in an artistic one, it is not surprising that the chief feature of the theatre was not the stage, or the best seating arrangements for a large number of persons, or even distribution of advantage in relation to the price charged for admission. The house was built for the boxes.[11]

The house was finally to have 122 gilded boxes of very generous proportions to house the seventy people who had so clamoured for them. Its interior would display the traditional colours of red and gold, with ivory-bedecked woodwork. The proscenium arch displayed a large painting of *Apollo and the Muses*.

The significance of this new house was clear. The novelist Edith Wharton clearly understood that the society in which she lived was changing and what the construction of a new opera house meant in terms of America's relationship to its newly powerful classes and Europe:

> Though there was already talk of the erection, in remote metropolitan distances 'above the Forties,' of a new opera house which should compete in costliness and splendour with those of the great European capitals, the world of fashion was still content to reassemble every winter in the shabby red and gold boxes of the sociable old Academy. Conservatives cherished it for being small and inconvenient, and thus keeping out the 'new people' whom New York was beginning to dread and yet be drawn to.[12]

The following could be a description of the opening of any grand opera house in the late nineteenth century, the Palais Garnier in Paris, the Staatsoper in Vienna or Covent Garden in London. However, this was the opening of an opera house in the heart of New York at Thirty-Ninth Street and Broadway on 22 October 1883. The new house was designed specifically to embrace the new power brokers.[13]

Outside the opera house, near the boxholders' porte-cochère ... crowds gathered to watch the arrival of the haut monde – the men dashing in top hats, opera capes with red velvet linings, and white ties and tail-coats, their starched shirts studded with pearls; the ladies resplendent in tiaras of emeralds and diamonds, parures to match, and ermine, sable, or chinchilla wraps. They came in shiny broughams, victories, and cabriolets with crests glistening on the doors, driven by liveried coachmen, attended by footmen, and drawn by high stepping horses that clopped daintily over the cobbles.[14]

A performance of an actual opera, Gounod's *Faust*, had been scheduled to begin at 6.45 to herald this event. The general public arrived early to view the magnificent new house but those who had paid for it, those who were to take their seats in the Golden Horseshoe, arrived tardily in order to make an entrance. The manager, Abbey, thus delayed the performance in order to give them time to take their seats. According to Merkling:

> Whether by accident or design, Abbey had hit upon an ingenious plan for the opening night. The very long opera, relieved by four intermissions, gave his sponsors maximum time for social activity, and they moved from box to box and tier to tier, exuberantly toasting the opera and one another in magnums of Dom Perignon.
>
> This extracurricular gaiety was by no means confined to intermissions (nor was it to be for some years, until a reform was effected). Champagne corks popped and glasses clinked and social calls were exchanged throughout the performance – to the delight of neck-craning wealth-watchers and the dismay of opera lovers in less exalted seats.[15]

Such activity, to the accompaniment of champagne corks, suggests the true significance of the new house. Intervals were to be used, as too was the ostentatious consumption of luxury goods. The construction of the new Metropolitan Opera thus signified not only a venue for opera, but also a monument which would symbolise New York's, i.e. the United States', uniqueness and its comparative advantages to Europe. It performed the function of a 'reflection of glories', to be pitted against 'glitter', 'grandness' and 'eccentric atmosphere' and combined with 'classicism'.

In American literature this notion of opera-going is reinforced. Edith Wharton, for example, draws a graceful analogy between going to the opera and a society wedding in *The Age of Innocence*:

> 'How like a first night at the opera!' he thought, recognising all the same faces in the same boxes (no pews), and wondering if, when the Last Trump sounded, Mrs Selfridge Merry would be there with the same towering ostrich feathers in her bonnet, and Mrs Beaufort with

the same diamond earrings and the same smile – and whether suitable proscenium seats were already prepared for them in another world.[16]

The author and critic Henry James describes the opera and its audience in a kind of apocalyptic fashion, an acting out of the American consciousness. He suggested that going to the opera in New York was the quintessence of fashion, and his description of the practices vividly evokes the schisms of rapidly changing worlds, juxtaposing images of tiaras with those of subways and tall buildings:

> Opera, which plays its part as the great vessel of social salvation, the comprehensive substitute for all other conceivable vessels; the *whole* social consciousness thus clambering into it, under stress, as the whole community crams into the other public receptacles, the desperate cars of the Subway or the vast elevators of the tall buildings. The Opera, indeed, as New York enjoys it, one promptly perceives, is worthy, musically and picturesquely, of its immense function; the effect of it is splendid, but one has none the less the oddest sense of hearing it, as an institution, groan and creak, positively almost split and crack, with the extra weight thrown upon it – the weight that in worlds otherwise arranged is artfully scattered, distributed over all the ground.[17]

He recognised the need for the power brokers to 'act out' their social status in a pantomime that was itself of operatic proportions.

> In default of a court-function our ladies of the tiaras and court-trains might have gone on to the opera-function, these occasions offering the only approach to the implication of the tiara known, so to speak, to the American law.[18]

Even the ushers wore evening dress, distinguished only by silver badges from the audience, and the administrative staff were supplied with rolltop desks instead of the usual standard desktop. Those who worked for the opera were expected to reflect the meaning of the house, effectively allowing only those who understood the social rules and possessed the paraphernalia to gain entrance.[19]

The memoirs of Frances Alda, the New Zealand soprano who was married to Gatti-Casazza, the great director of the Met in the early 1900s, provide an extremely thorough insight into the opera-going codes of American society at the turn of the century, highlighting the fact that the performance on the stage was but a secondary meaning of the opera experience. Her remarks concerning the rights to hold boxes, devoid of any social comment, reveal the accepted traditional social structures of the day. The opera house performed the same function as private clubs in the Anglo-Saxon world by restricting membership to those it deemed to be part of the privileged group:

At first sight of the Metropolitan Opera House, I gasped. Then I lau-
ghed. *That* an opera house? It looked more like a storage warehouse.
Dirty brown brick. Shabby. ...

I remembered the stately Opéra in Paris; the dignity of La Scala – a
palace dedicated to music and as noble as the palazzo of any Visconti
in Milan. I thought of the magnificent opera house in Buenos Aires
where I had sung that summer.[20]

Very soon European monarchs and American power brokers were fêted
within the opera house and the experience of 'going to the opera' in New York
differed little from that which one might find elsewhere.

Within a decade of the completion of the house, the male power brokers
founded an institution which would be set in the walls of the house and allow
them to enjoy unfettered entertainment in a socially acceptable environment. In
this context we can understand why Eugene Bonner, chronicler of the Opera
Club, could explain that 'Great Wealth was gradually changing hands, and the
need of its new possessors for a social center of their own was pressing'.[21] He, as
do other chroniclers, goes on to give a now familiar analysis:

> It was this amalgam of New Money and Old Blood, owning and
> controlling the financial sinews of the new organization, which was
> henceforth to so dominate the fashionable life of the community that
> the mere ownership of one of the coveted and jealously-guarded
> parterre boxes at the Metropolitan Opera House soon became a recog-
> nized hallmark of affluence and high social distinction ... lacking a
> Buckingham Palace, the Metropolitan Opera House might serve the
> purpose admirably ... before very long it came about that an appear-
> ance as a guest in a certain parterre box to the left of the proscenium
> became as much an accolade of social fitness as kissing the royal hand
> of Victoria R. & I, herself.[22]

Such a description differs little from those of opera houses within the very heart
of the royal households of Europe from the seventeenth century. But, according
to Bonner, there was one important part of the house that was missing, a Club,
which was not addressed until 1892:

> But the fact remains that such institutions as the exclusive Corridor
> Club in London, which had its own box at the Covent Garden Opera
> House, and the older and more famous Jockey Club of Paris, with its
> loge at the Grand Opera – both masculine organizations – were
> conspicuous by their absence in New York City.[23]

Such a situation, according to Bonner, could not be allowed to continue:
'Something had to be done about it ... Something was'. This 'something' was

advanced on 27 August 1892, when the Metropolitan Opera House was partially destroyed by fire; 'the undamaged assembly rooms and foyer of the opera-house were to be used as a temporary home by the Vaudeville Club, which came into existence on the evening of 10th January, 1893'.[24]

> This opening was one of unusual éclat from every point of view – the occasion, owing to the absence of any operatic performances that season, taking on the appearance of an opening night at the opera itself. Bohemia was conspicuous by its absence, and the list of members (some thousand in number) and their guests reads like a cross-section of fashionable New York of that period. ... Louis Keller, the founder of the Social Register, ... was among those present.[25]

The fire had another impact upon the life of the Metropolitan Opera House, for in its aftermath the Metropolitan Opera and Real Estate Company bought out the Metropolitan Opera-house Company, Limited. And its stockholders were given use of thirty-five parterre boxes within the house. These were to become known as the Diamond Horseshoe, replacing the former two-tiered Golden Horseshoe. Stock was to be jealously guarded and could not be transferred to another party without approval by its directorate. Furthermore, the stockholders could, and in later years would, exercise discretion about what should be presented. In 1906 the owners insisted that *Salomé* be taken off the programme and underwrote the costs involved. According to Kolodin: 'As long as the Metropolitan Opera House retained its position as the pinnacle of fashion, the directors thus constituted the arbiters for social acceptability in New York.'[26]

Some time after the opening of the Vaudeville Club, the refurbished and restructured Metropolitan reopened on 27 November 1893, again with a production of Gounod's *Faust* with its lengthy intervals, and this time the programme displayed the complete plan of the horseshoe and the names and numbers of the boxes.

Within a year the Vaudeville Club had changed its name and by 1899 incorporated itself as the Opera Club on 10 October 1899. Bonner writes 'that with its incorporation, it had emerged as a clearly-defined and well-established institution,' and that:

> By the autumn of 1906, when it entered upon its eighth consecutive season, the Opera Club had come to be recognized as an institution to be reckoned with in the affairs of the Metropolitan, not only in view of its unique social status, but also on account of its financial importance as a large and permanent subscribing unit.[27]

At the turn of the century the Metropolitan was clearly at its most magnificent. Not only did it proudly house its own club and have Italian management, but it also hosted crowned heads of Europe. On 25 February 1902 it held a gala evening in honour of the Kaiser's brother, Henry of Prussia. The building, shim-mering in electric lights, was crowned with a replica of the royal yacht, the *Hohenzollern*; without and inside the auditorium brightly displayed the emblems of the American flag and Prussian eagle and the seats were priced to reflect the magnificence of the event. The 'Royal Box', made up especially by removing the partitions of five boxes, was filled with dignitaries to greet the Prince, who arrived forty minutes after the beginning of the act with 'Heil dir im Siegerkranz'. Departing before the end of the performance, the Prince was accompanied by a large proportion of the audience. They had seen their event; the operatic medley performed that evening was merely a backdrop.[28] Thus the Metropolitan could rightly earn Henry James's comment that the 'Opera, indeed, as New York enjoys it, is worthy, musically and picturesquely, of its immense function'.

The new order was now complete even down to its clubs and it was, according to Frances Alda, to determine the policies of the house and the behaviour of its occupants for some time to come. It also combined the powerful of both the new and old orders:

> It had been built by and for the new rich of the late seventies and eighties, for whom the Academy of Music, at Fourteenth Street and Irving Place, which had succeeded the opera house in Astor Place and which was the resort of old Knickerbocker New York, was not adequate. The Astors, Vanderbilts, Goelets, Drexels, Mortons, Iselins, Warrens, and Havens who had figured prominently among the first directors and box-holders still swayed destinies and determined the policies of the company.[29]

Even the death of Mrs Astor, social doyenne of the house, could not break the tradition or its meaning. Society was very clearly the performance one went to see at the Yellow Brick building on Fourteenth Street and Irving Place.

> And this was New York. The richest, most modern, most progressive city in the world. ...It still seems to me extraordinary.
>
> I have never got used to the complaisant stagnation of America's *soi-disant* society. The sentiment among the Metropolitan's box-holders in 1908 seemed to be that what had been good enough for their fathers and for themselves back in 1883 was still good enough....
>
> That season of my début was the first season that Mrs Astor's box, Number Seven, was not occupied by society's Queen Dowager. She had died that year. I never witnessed what I was told was the usual proce-dure on Monday nights. It had been Mrs Astor's custom to arrive at the opera at exactly nine o'clock. And this no matter at what hour the curtain rose. As what she did was copied slavishly by the rest of society, it developed that the opera's first act was sung to a house more than empty.[30]

Obviously Alda saw the dichotomy so lost upon New York's society that the 'richest, most modern, most progressive city in the world' should be so flagrantly aping the standards of European empires and monarchies so abhorred by American society.

In 1908, after a struggle with the managing director Conried, the Metropolitan Opera Company was formed and took over the lease to the building and Gatti-Casazza took over the management, with Toscanini as conductor. Gatti displayed early that he knew how to please his audience, claiming of the auditorium at the Metropolitan that 'we have no such structure in Italy. It is indeed a noble house',[31] whilst denigrating the rest of the structure.

There followed many years of operatic productions, which continued throughout the First World War, although German works were banned in 1917. The house remained a place of congregation for society, although according to Kolodin:

> wartime conditions dimmed somewhat the lustre of the inaugural festivities, for jewels were definitely less conspicuous, the diamonds that had given the row of parterre boxes its distinctive name had been retired to the safe-keeping of vaults for the duration of hostilities.[32]

The managers of the opera house and its public clearly understood the purposes for which they had built an opera house. It was to receive power brokers, and to play to them in an environment which they could understand their cherished 'Star-spangled Banner', the musical emblem of US democratic statehood. The Prince of Wales' visit on 28 November 1919 is a good example of this. He was received into the box of American royalty, that of J. Pierpont Morgan, and escorted by the host country's assistant secretary of war. He himself was flanked by an admiral and a lord. Artistically the programme was a pot-pourri of arias but 'God Save the King' and the 'Star-spangled Banner' were sung out loudly for all to hear.[33]

The years of prosperity were to end suddenly in 1929, although remarkably the conservative trustees of the Club still managed to maintain its finances in good condition. What changed, however, was the dress of the members: 'business suits, and even sweaters, were eventually to appear in parterre boxes on a Monday night, but top-hats, white ties and tails continued to hold their own in the omnibus box during the lean and troubled years of the earlier Thirties.'[34]

Frances Alda claims that during the Great Depression of 1929 the directors of the Metropolitan enquired of her what action she would recommend they take in terms of the house. She was entirely convinced of the house's association with society, that to her was its main function, and suggested that they: 'Shut it down tight till times are better, and society can come back to it. Then open it. You'll find when the Four Hundred are in their boxes, the Four Thousand will be clamouring to get in.'[35] What worried her most was that, if it were to be regarded as a charity, it would lose its prestige and that would be a really fatal blow.

Nothing worse, to my way of thinking, could have happened to the Metropolitan than to place it in the position of a charity patient, in need of help. It was robbed of its prestige, just as more recently the Presidency has been robbed of its prestige.

To have the singers begging funds for it deprived the Metropolitan of half its glamour in the eyes of the public. And the public of America goes to the opera as much, or more, for the glamour and glitter of the show, and all that they believe it stands for, as they go for the music which is heard there.[36]

By 1932 we realise that the Metropolitan Opera has not only meaning for society but that it has gained national significance. The old Metropolitan Opera Company was dissolved, leaving the old power brokers to mend their embattled empires, and a public company, the Metropolitan Opera Association, was formed to replace it in 1933, buying the entire building from the Metropolitan Opera and Real Estate Company. Thus, Bonner laments, 'the fifty-seven-year-old opera house passed out of autocratic control to become a democratic institution and, with its transition, the glory of the famous Diamond Horseshoe ... was forever departed'.[37]

Merkling describes the change in ownership and management thus:

For the past 26 years this 2nd company, having bought out the first, has comprised both Church and State: the power has passed from an oligarchy to an enlightened croesus to the ticket-buyer.[38]

He highlights the change in the power brokers during this period:

If there were fears that the Diamond Horseshoe would promptly turn to paste, once the Opera House changed hands, they must have been allayed by the continuing presence of Mrs Cornelius Vanderbilt in Box 3 – and of an undeniable new millionaire, Thomas J. Watson, in J.P. Morgan's old Box 35.[39]

The enterprise was now public. One of its first decisions of the new company was the formation of a Committee for Saving the Metropolitan Opera in 1933. It is hard to imagine that in such straitened times, when artists were in fact being given their first state-subsidised work in Federal regeneration schemes, that the drive to save the Metropolitan Opera raised over $270,000 within a few weeks. This sum was enough to save what was now spoken of as an institution of national importance.[40]

The significance of the opera house was then to be used in an entirely novel and very American way. Opera from the Met was to be transmitted over the airwaves to the people of America. This was to be eventually sponsored by a large oil corporation, Texaco, and the concerts were to take its name. It has been argued that this represents the democratisation of opera, yet if this hypothesis is correct, what people were responding to, as much as the musical works, was the belief, however imaginary, that they were participating in a society event. Stephen Rubin describes it thus: 'with a flick of the switch, the average guy, in the privacy of his home, can journey to the Big City and partake of what was once a pastime reserved for the privileged few.'[41] It is the fact that the audience can metaphorically mingle with the 'privileged few' that lies at the basis of its success. This tradition would continue for decades, and in the 1960s it was possible to claim that Milton Cross, through the sponsorship of Texaco, reached out to a huge audience:

> A devoted, hard-core audience of 1,600,000 as well as some 6,000,000 other occasional listeners, tunes in to hear 'opera live from the stage of the Metropolitan Opera House at the Lincoln Center for the Performing Arts in New York City'.[42]

The world which Alda described was soon to be made vulnerable as the old world was attacked and changed irrevocably by two major world wars and a mighty economic depression. One might imagine that the ever more powerful and 'modern' city of New York would challenge the symbolic relics of the old world both in the shape of the places of entertainment and the vestiges of public display and ceremonial.

At the opening of the 1940 season the Diamond Horseshoe's occupants began to change. The Kavanaughs, Goelets, Whitneys and Vanderbilts were there but conspicuous by their absence were the Astors. As it was wartime, medals were in abundance and the house's composition had made its first really visible shift since the 1890s.[43]

By 1954 James Hinton Jnr. could proudly proclaim to the *English Opera Annual* of that year that the Metropolitan Opera was a 'national possession', '*the* opera company in the United States'. His argumentation boldly sets out in clear terms what other generations have tried to do by defining their boxes, or dressing up. He argues that Americans 'as a whole' believe that their 'national possession' is evidently 'the greatest opera company in the world'.

> It has been said, and in round, authoritative tones too, that the Metropolitan Opera is not really, in any complete sense, a national institution. Evidence can certainly be adduced to show that Metropolitan performances are primarily events that take place in New York, for the benefit of and supported by a smallish, select group of subscribers; to show that (tour performances and radio broadcasts aside) the company does not really have much to do with the people of the country as a whole.
>
> There is, to be sure, merit in this view – but the people of the country as a whole do not seem to agree with it. To them the

Metropolitan is a national possession. It is *the* opera company in the United States. Furthermore (since it is a national possession), it is the greatest opera company in the world.[44]

But opera displayed a remarkable permanency world-wide, and to retain positions of greatness renovations had to take place to accommodate new publics. The opera houses of Europe had been reduced to rubble in wartime, but they were now beginning to sparkle and gleam under their post-war reconstruction. Even 'down-under' in Sydney, Australia, work had begun on a new opera house. And so it was an essential prerequisite that the opera house in New York be as good as, if not better than, any European equivalent.

A significant event occurred in 1961, when the season was jeopardised by a breakdown in negotiations between the management and the Musicians' Union and an announcement was made that the season would be cancelled. The power brokers could not permit this and according to Briggs:

> Here newly inaugurated President Kennedy, in the interest *of preserving one of the nation's great cultural assets*, intervened, sending Secretary of Labor Arthur J. Goldberg to act as mediator. The season opened. (my italics)[45]

This certainly puts paid to the myth that the Metropolitan only represented a place of entertainment. Indeed it is a vivid illustration of its significance. The Metropolitan Opera House was deemed by the power brokers to be an essential part of the 'nation's great cultural assets' and therefore demanded presidential intervention when its future was shaky.

There were, of course, good and valid arguments presented for the construction of a new building: lack of storage space, the old house was dowdy and did not adequately fulfil its function, or even that society had changed and the old house was designed for the requirements of an audience which no longer existed. According to Russell Braddon it now 'lacked the glitter of La Scala, the grandeur of L'Opéra and the eccentric atmosphere of cabbages and classicism that is Covent Garden's – and amends were to be made.'[46] Very simply, however, the power brokers had changed. Those who ran New York during the nineteenth century had been swallowed up by the new power brokers who were simply exercising their strength and taste. They needed an opera house for themselves in which to see and be seen. And yet again we see that in the 1960s the same argument is used in a period when Covent Garden, the Palais Garnier, La Scala and the Staatsoper had remained either intact, or were rebuilt or modified upon their nineteenth-century plans.

And so a new house was needed and the new power brokers determined to find ways of financing and building one set to work. Since the turn of the century there had been many rumours that the Metropolitan would find a new home. Gatti complained of its inadequacy in 1908. In 1924 the press was informed of such a necessity, and in 1931 space was set aside for a new house at the Rockefeller Center and Radio City. A new house may have been a necessity for the middle classes, who were increasingly wishing to see and hear opera in good conditions, but to the old power brokers the old house, complete with its Diamond Horseshoe, continued to serve its purpose admirably and they, after all, owned the concession.[47] After over half a century of debate, the old house closed its doors on 16 April 1966 to make way for the New Metropolitan Opera House to be housed at the Lincoln Center. The initial cost estimate was much greater than anticipated at $50 million and the Metropolitan was asked to cut back its plans. Rudolph Bing, the General Manager of the Met, fought vigorously for the kind of house he was convinced the United States should have. His view was that the country 'simply could not afford to build a new opera house that looked old-fashioned and cheap next to the new theatres of Europe and Russia.'[48] In fact Bing, who had a reputation for being autocratic, had not wanted to move out of the old house, but he knew better than to argue with the Rockefellers and he is quoted as saying 'You can't fight the Royal Family'.[49]

The old house was closed with a gala attended by the great and good. Mrs Whitney wore a diamond and ruby tiara which had once belonged to Empress Elisabeth of Austria; Princess Marina of Greece, Mrs Joseph Kennedy and the Mellons of Pittsburgh were in the star-studded audience, liberally consuming the 500 bottles of champagne to bid farewell to the Diamond Horseshoe.[50] Rudolph Bing's speech to this audience was revealing. In this democratic country, where one old opera house was to be replaced by a new one, he cried: 'The Queen is dead. Long live the Queen.'[51] This language was understood by all. The new house was the pinnacle of regal ceremonial in New York, a platform for the diamond-studded monarchy. Both opera houses could only be likened to monarchic dynasties.

But the new house at the Lincoln Center was not to ignore its benefactors. Its foyer proudly boasted two large marble tablets etched in gold with the names of its contributors, leaving no doubt as to who the new power brokers were. They had their names engraved upon marble for all to see: 143 individuals and families, and 73 corporations and foundations. The new power brokers had literally inscribed their role to their age and for posterity. Anthony Bliss sets the tone in his Epilogue to *The Golden Horseshoe*:

> The monumental new Metropolitan Opera House at the Lincoln Center will be a fitting instrument for perhaps a century of performances, excitingly able to fulfil the ideals of the Metropolitan's founders, who dreamed extravagant dreams and made them come true. Their bequest to us is the finest opera company on earth.[52]

It wasn't the Metropolitan of its architect Wallace Harrison's dreams, however, according to Dizikes. Harrison 'had conceived an innovative building, a structurally independent auditorium within an arcaded shell, but the Metropolitan board resisted it'.[53] Their brief was for grandeur and by that they did not mean only monumental grandeur; they wanted grandeur to resonate within its most minute details:

> 'We couldn't have a modern house' Harrison said ruefully. 'I finally got hammered down by the opera people'. Inside, the board and patrons got what they wanted: the gilded trappings of tradition. Swags and tassels on the tops of the boxes, a gilded cheese-straw pattern around the proscenium. 'The opera people wanted those,' Harrison explained. The Metropolitan's ambitions were as conventional in the 1960s as they had been in the 1880s. The new opera house was 'a monument manqué'.[54]

It may not be a ground-shattering, modern piece of architectural sculpture, but one could disagree with Dizikes' view that it was 'manqué' in much the same way as the Opéra Bastille, also aesthetically disappointing, is not manqué. When one looks at the house in terms of the tradition of operatic convention, both in the United States and Europe, one realises that the patrons of the house needed these 'trappings' to convey to one and all the continuity of the symbolic importance of the house. They knew what they were paying for and demanded they got it, a house with almost 4,000 seats and 29 boxes which could be rented out to the richest and most powerful. It is true that opera houses built after the mid-1960s have done away in some sense with the colour schemes and the gilt, but like the Met they have made room for presidential boxes, gala openings, ceremonial staircases and grand panoramic vistas within, making them seem part of the same tradition. It is essential for an opera house in some way to incorporate such spatial and decorative connotations, for otherwise the public might mistake the house for something else and the opera house would become simply another entertainment hall.

The continuity of the meaning of opera in the United States would seem to be held in question by Rosanne Martorella's research in 1974 into opera-going habits, which demonstrated that preparation to go to the opera was perceived by Americans as an obstacle to attending. She states that: 'The NEA Study (1974) revealed that opera attendance could increase substantially if it has less "class" requiring less formal dress, and less planning and preparation for attendance.'[55] This could be true, but research undertaken in Europe by the present writer received to the question 'would you dress in the same manner if you attended the theatre or the opera house?' an overwhelming no. Martorella's analysis may simply be revealing the bias of the times. Statistical studies are notorious for receiving the answers they set out to find. If you had asked a young person in the peak of the liberalist era of the 1970s and early 1980s if they wanted to go out in formal attire, it would have taken a brave individual to admit to it. Certainly, if part of the opera experience is to dress up to go to the event, then it is unlikely that dressing up might preclude attendance. It is more likely that an audience will not come because they don't want to be seen as part of a distinctive social group and the donning of certain dress would indicate such adherence.

But the Met also includes a distinctive audience unique to it. The radio audience. And this audience is undeterred by hiccoughs of fashion. One such woman described at roughly the same time how she 'attended' the opera.

> 'I don't know what is worn in an opera house today,' says one elderly matron, 'but on Saturdays I get my black velvet dress out of its box. And I dress my hair and put a fresh flower in a vase beside me. After all, I am to spend the afternoon with dukes and duchesses.'[56]

This was preceded by the author's comment: '*Opera fans are crazy people. They're really nuts.*' – but are they? This virtual opera-goer clearly understood what opera was for, at least to her and many of her fellow greater operatic audience. It is argued by many that, as opera becomes more popular due to the larger audience brought by modern media, its subvention should increase accordingly. Maryvonne de Saint Pulgent points out that the Metropolitan Opera in New York has consistently used radio and television to promote its image as a national opera company, thus endeavouring to create the illusion that the opera is an activity which all citizens can partake in.[57] This, however, is far from the truth. The notion of opera may have been popularised through broadcasting but the experience of opera, the dressing up, going to, being there, cannot be reproduced over the airwaves and so the Met remains today the bastion of the élite. The democratisation of opera through radio may have attracted greater numbers and made it more accessible, but it would appear that it did not change its nature whatsoever.

It would seem that whatever concessions the United States make towards European standards, there will always be a critic who will suggest that the Met does not quite live up to the splendour of traditional opera houses. One of the first of the many planners of the Opéra Bastille, which was to be constructed two decades later, analysed the house, obviously musing upon how to avoid what he believed to be some errors and yet maintain its real meaning:

> An ugly space, The Met: too big and air conditioned. Errors to avoid. One dreams of the closeness of Bayreuth: there is a real communion of music! Here, one witnesses an over peopled desert. A horror of colours, of lights. How does one make modernity in a modern opera house?[58]

Whatever the NEA study may have asserted, the world of dress codes, clubs and society still predominates at the Met, as Pierre-Jean Rémy, writing in the 1980s, demonstrates:

> Evening at the Met: meeting at 5.30pm in the entrance hall with … the (French) Cultural Attaché. He invited me, through his secretary, to a

black tie dinner before the show. I discovered that we were the guests of the Metropolitan Opera Club. The dinner took place in the club's dining room which is placed right at the top of the building. It is the direct descendant of the same club which existed in the old Met. There are around 350 members, no more than that, who pay a fortune for the pleasure of remaining apart. Apart in their theatre, apart in their (bad) seats.[59]

This was very much a deliberate policy of the Met's management and endorsed by the board of directors. Rudolph Bing explained why he chose to entertain diplomats and not artists in his director's box, which had access via a corridor from the director's office, much as the San Carlo in Naples was connected to the royal palace.

It was a rather special kind of entertaining. I almost never invited to the box an active singer or conductor, and I rarely asked board members or contributors. Instead, I filled the box on most evenings with members of the diplomatic and consular communities, especially from the United Nations. As a great international house, I felt we had international obligations.[60]

This box would host such guests as the King of Morocco, Golda Meir of Israel and Emperor Heile Selassi. And Bing, the director whose rule spanned three decades, received honours from heads of state which would seem to indicate that his importance was not only that of a chief executive of a place of entertainment. He received a personal letter of congratulation from Richard Nixon, President of the United States, describing his administration of the Metropolitan as 'a brilliant chapter in our cultural history',[61] was knighted by Queen Elizabeth II, awarded the Croix de Chevalier de la Légion d'Honneur by the French, the highest honour possible for civilians from the Austrian Government, the Commander's Cross of the Order of Merit by the Federal Republic of Germany, and even a military rank of Commander as an Order of Merit from Italy.[62] Clearly the international recognition of ceremonial rewards emulates the operatic mission, the decoration of those who are of service to the state.

And so it would seem that throughout its 150 year history grand opera in New York has been a remarkably stable institution. It is clear that in its early days the opera was a place to see and be seen and a place to take foreign dignitaries. It was intended to rival the European operatic establishment in order to give to New York society yet another emblem of social respectability. The house was from the very first an institution, which was also home to one of the most powerful clubs in the city.

As power moved from one group of the wealthy and influential to another and society became more openly democratic, the opera house remained and, as is claimed by one writer, became as early as the 1950s a 'national institution'.

It reached out to many through the medium of radio and its listeners often aped what they perceived to be the social codes of the house itself by dressing up to listen to the opera. After the Second World War, Europe took to reconstructing its opera houses and the Met was starting to lose its place in the world operatic arena. It behoved this great nation to have an opera house which could be a symbol of modernity and of greatness and yet contain within it the important special and symbolic connotations which would link it to its real meaning. The outcome of this was the Metropolitan at the Lincoln Center, at which presidential boxes could be created when the occasion required and the new power brokers, who now consisted of corporations as well as individuals, could still appear in prominent positions as did their predecessors. Having an eminent opera, it would seem, is as important to this bastion of modern democracy as to the European countries with their older imperial traditions.

8

THE CHIP IN THE HARBOUR

One can think of many people to whom the task of standing atop the monumental staircase of the Sydney Opera House on that glorious spring day of 20 October 1973 might have fallen. The opening of an opera house in this relatively new country was seen as a great event. As opera houses are monuments in which opera, ballet and other major artistic events are performed, one might have imagined that a leading Australian artist such as Gladys Moncrieff, then Australia's greatest living soprano or the internationally recognised Joan Sutherland, would have radiantly taken their place on the dais. Perhaps one might even have expected an Australian politician to proudly mount the podium and claim triumphantly the fruits of their vision. But no, it was in fact Her Majesty Queen Elizabeth II who, though she had in no way participated in the vision, decision nor process of constructing the opera house, presided over the state ceremonial, eclipsing national and state government, local authorities, the church and the arts alike.

Queen Elizabeth II had a very important role that day. She represented the link between Australia's past (mired in spectres of its convict origins) and the potential future of a country adorned with minerals and produce from the fat of the sheep's back. The transformation from cultural and ultimately political servitude towards glory was in her hands. Thus the speech she read was as charged with iconographical references as were the emblems which monarchs from far-off times had embroidered into their clothing or displayed in paintings of their ceremonial victories. The Queen did not go so far as to suggest that the new opera house was a simple gift from the gods, rather she stressed the royal connection, the vital link between ceremony, monumental architecture and monarchical authority. Although she acknowledged that the development of an opera house had caused considerable ructions in Australia, she nevertheless implied that its construction was a sort of coming-of-age for the rough antipodeans, who could now take their place within the premier division of the cultural league, completing the need for civilised society to have visual references filled with connotations of history and grandeur. And so she simply formed a connection between the mysteries of the pyramids and the building she was opening:

Controversy of the most extreme kind attended the building of the pyramids, yet they stand today – 4,000 years later, acknowledged as one of the wonders of the world.

So I hope and believe it will be with the Sydney Opera House.

The form of the royal benediction – comparing the new opera house with ancient royal tombs that the general public is forbidden to enter – may have struck some of her listeners as odd, but if they or others thought so at the time they kept their counsel.[1]

Meanwhile the Australian press played along with the notion that opening the new landmark would of itself put Australia into a different and international cultural league and help to shake off the 'rough diamond' image which years of colonialisation and squatocracy had left as Australia's metaphoric legacy. On the day of the opening the *Sydney Morning Herald* published photographs of the new building alongside snaps of the Covent Garden Opera House, the Paris Opéra (then Palais Garnier), La Scala, Milan, and the Met in New York, adding breathlessly that the 'completion of the Sydney Opera House has drawn the attention of a world in which the theatre arts have been traditionally housed in elegant grandeur'. *The Sun* on 17 October 1973 headed its pictorial summary of the event with the words: 'Sydney will celebrate the Royal opening of the Opera House with pomp, majesty and ceremony.'[2]

As we have seen in earlier chapters, the elements of 'majesty and ceremony' are fundamental to an understanding of the real reasons for the state to have constructed an opera house rather than a multi-purpose concert hall and entertainment venue, even if the design structurally incorporated these elements. Sydney built for itself not just an agglomeration of theatres, it chose, as we will see later, to construct a fabulous monument for present generations to use and wonder at. Like so many opera houses before it, the design would eclipse contemporary engineering and so in itself become a monument to modernity and monumental greatness, inspiring awe and wonderment in all those who visited it. Thus it is no surprise to us that within a short space of time the opera house was to be likened to the Taj Mahal,[3] and within the space of only two decades was to have the ultimate accolade bestowed upon it when an operatic work entitled *The Eighth Wonder* paid homage to the building, likening the Opera House of Sydney to the lost monumental and quasi religious buildings of the great Maya/Aztec civilisations.

That such rhetorical language, full of awe and deference, was bestowed upon a contemporary building constructed to house an art form requires us to look at this monument more closely so that we can see why its creation really was a 'majestic' event. Indeed, why did Sydney need an opera house at all? And why did it need to be so monumental, splendid and awe inspiring if it were merely to be a venue for opera performances?

There are a number of ways in which we can look at this. We will see in this chapter why the construction of the Sydney Opera House became as important to the city of Sydney and Australia as a whole as the construction of the Palais Garnier was to the people of Paris, and ultimately France, a century before. We will see why it symbolised so much to a nation coming into itself just after the Second World War, fighting between old identities and the new, both in terms of old allegiances (the Commonwealth) and new ones, which led to utterances by, among others, Prime Minister Sir Harold Holt, who burbled with enthusiasm in 1966 'all the way with LBJ', thus announcing that Australia would blindly follow the United States into Vietnam and reminding us that within the space of only two decades an incumbent of the same position would announce to the Australian peoples that, as Britain was at war, so too was Australia.

Some have viewed these dramatic and accelerated political and economic changes romantically. In 1995 the programme for the world première of the *Eighth Wonder* describes Sydney at that time in the following manner: 'Sydney – a new city on the edge of the new world – was also unencumbered by the burdens of tradition. Few cities were better placed to embrace the new.'[4] As has been argued throughout this book, Sydney was in fact embracing *the old* by investing in an institution so representative of historical and artistic continuity of power. The well-known Australian arts critic John Cargher supports this view:

> the very name OPERA HOUSE has always loomed large in the histo-
> ries of cities and there must be hundreds all over the world which sport
> a building so named without ever having had a resident opera company.
> In the nineteenth century opera was the ultimate in theatrical entertain-
> ment and any building which implied by its name that it could be used
> to present grand opera immediately became the focus of attention.[5]

Political history tells us a lot of things. In the 1950s Australia had emerged from the battlegrounds of Europe and Asia an essentially more disparate nation than that which had followed the call from the 'mother country' less than a decade before. The post-war world now had more masters and the United States held an increasingly high importance to the economic welfare of the country. Furthermore, post-war immigration meant that the traditional population gleaned from mainly Anglo-Saxon stock was bolstered by European refugees often eager to transport, along with their earthly chattels, the important aspects of their native culture. Opera symbolised wealth and sophistication; it tran-scended the disparate nature of European culture and carried with it instantly recognised status.

Opera, moreover, was a universal symbol representing greatness and strength, an outward representation of the power of the state. Furthermore, in 1946 Sydney barely possessed a hall in which to hold an orchestral performance, let alone an operatic one! For a city wishing to demonstrate its importance in the newly emerging world order it lacked a focus denoting aesthetic sophistication. An opera house would provide a perfect symbol. This symbol was, as we shall see, to prove to be remarkably popular, as John Cargher remarked after the building was completed: 'Paris has its Eiffel Tower, New York has its Empire State Building, and Sydney has its Opera House.'[6] In such a statement we see at once that it is its symbolic significance which is so sought after, although Cargher does concede that, besides bringing international recognition to the country, it also, according to him, provokes an artistic surge. (This notion is disputable if one takes on the idea that quantity of performance does not necessarily mean that there is more art or that it is good art). 'It has caused the usual surge in theatrical activity which appears in the wake of new centres of the performing arts, but it has also put Sydney and opera in Australia on the map internationally.'[7] This apparently is a very good outcome of having an opera house, according to these enthusiastic sources. The theatrical historian Marvin Carlson also quotes the senior engineer of the project, who described the opera house as 'a focal point and civic symbol for a city which seeks to destroy once and for all the suggestion that it is a cultural backwater'. To put this more simply, cities which are perceived to be cultural backwaters may possess all the components which would give them significance on the world's political and economic stage but they will never sit at the main table, however strong they may be in other domains. To give a recent illustration of the effectiveness of such an argument, one only need look to one of Australia's close neighbour, Singapore. This highly successful 'Asian lion', which has weathered the recent economic turmoil in the region with alacrity, has recognised that for it to be a significant world player the time has come to build cultural edifices of monumental stature. Hence 2002 will witness the opening of its Theatres on the Bay, financed by government and endorsed by a board of the wealthy and influential.

In 1947 Sir Eugene Goossens, a musician from an extremely prestigious Anglo-European musical family steeped in the European musical tradition, was appointed conductor of the Sydney Symphony Orchestra and director of the New South Wales Conservatorium. He was soon to find an ally in John Cahill, Premier of the Labor Party of NSW, a fitter and turner by trade, whose power base was the trade union movement. They shared a dream that Sydney would have an opera house, and a monumental one at that, and that it should be placed on a site dominating the harbour entrance to Sydney and soon to be imbued with tremendous historical significance and renamed Bennelong Point in order to give the building a sense of historical context as well. The significance of the name is highly important and no accident, as the site had had a number of names since European colonisation. Bennelong was the first Aboriginal to act as interpreter and guide to the First Fleet. The 'Point' is where his hut stood. Now it would be the focal point for the new and the good. Instead of looking outside the continent, the country could look into itself at a great new innovative and provocative monument – *The Eighth Wonder*. This was to be a quintessential cultural image no matter what was to take place within its walls.

The story of the opera house, however, is not so simple in the telling; the verve which propelled it from fantasy to reality, and traversed its many stages, and, like so many great projects, the complexities of its construction also hold the key to the secret of its meaning. In that sense the Queen's linking of the pyramids and the mystery of their construction can be understood, along with the apparent contradiction of a Labor leader who dreamt of monumental greatness as a legacy for his city. This is in essence the dream shared by all, from the selection committees to the architect and engineers, funding bodies and the peoples of Sydney and the rest of Australia who were to participate in this vainglorious folly funded by speculative enterprises and built on the backs of so many. Today the opera crowns Sydney harbour, nestling under its famous bridge (an architectural challenge of an earlier era, the design of which won over its strict utilitarian purpose). But the creation of an opera house presents problems in a modern 'democratic' nation. How would the new powers integrate the two concepts? Well, language played a very important role here. The opera house had to be at least perceived as 'democratic', providing high art for the masses, who would also be satisfied by the wonder of its architectural presence. It had to be as accessible as Luna Park, which was cradled under the other side of the Sydney Harbour bridge, facing into the city instead of out from it. One institution represented lowbrow entertainment, theme park 'fun', and the other had to offer symbolic might with art and demonstrate to one and all that it was to coin a modern phrase 'owned by all Australians'.

Here we must return to telling the history of the opera house, returning to our 'marriage of opposites', as Goossens and Cahill by all rights were. By 1948 the use of Bennelong Point, which dominates the entrance to the hub of Sydney Harbour, had already been mooted as a potential site for such a venue. The concept of holding an international competition to find a design for such a site was generally accepted. Goossens suggested that:

> Like the San Francisco War Memorial Opera House, it must furnish a permanent home for our symphony orchestra, opera, ballet and choral festivals. The auditorium must accommodate audiences of from 3500 to 4000 – no fewer.[8]

He developed this idea of 'a great opera house' and brought it to the attention of influential people in Sydney, thereby steadily gaining support and consolidating the concept within a social and political group who had both an interest in its creation and the capacity to realise it. Yeomans, the writer who so forcefully made the connection between the Taj Mahal and the Sydney Opera House, gives a plausible explanation of how the idea became a reality and eventually took form:

> A London conductor of Belgian descent, determined to lodge the Sydney Symphony Orchestra in a good permanent home, convinced a Labor Party politician that Sydney needed a new cultural and musical centre; the politician became so obsessed with the idea that he pushed it through against all opposition from within his own party or outside it.[9]

By 1952 the concept of an opera house had become general parlance in newspapers, and on 8 November 1954 Premier John Cahill formally announced that an opera house would be constructed. Cahill employed from the outset the tone of language which would dominate the discussion about the house in the years to come, introducing notions of pride through public display and democratic political modernity. At a public meeting held in Sydney's public library on 30 November 1954 he stated that:

> The opportunities for erecting monumental buildings in Sydney are rare and I agree that while we must be practical, the Opera House must be something that the people of this city and the State can be proud of.[10]

Both civic and national pride were firmly equated from this point on as a stated aim bearing the mark of government's endorsement of the project. Therefore it can clearly be said that this opera house, like so many we have visited in previous chapters, was from its conceptual beginnings to represent something more than simply a building in which musical activities would be housed.

The site for the opera house was decided by the New South Wales Cabinet in 1955 and on 13 September of that year an international competition for the design of the building was announced. This site dominating the harbour of Sydney is one of the most important in the history of the settlement of the country. Not only is it adjacent to the area where fresh water was found, but it is also where the penal settlement eventually was founded: crops were grown and cattle raised on this site. It is, in fact, the very heart of Sydney. The use of the site just prior to the construction of the house was also surprisingly utilitarian. It was in fact a tram shed in the form of a castle. It makes the irony even heavier that a Labor government should sanction, if not endorse, the end of a traditional working-class place in order to put an opera house there. The decision was made, however, and the construction of a monument epitomising the ideals of the new post-war Australia was ensured. An opera house would crown the entrance to the harbour and put Sydney on the international map. And for the honour of designing it, international architects were invited to compete so that Sydney harbour would be recognised not only by its population but also across distant seas. The closing date of the competition was set for 3 December 1956 and the announcement of the winner made on 18 January 1957.

Australia, represented by the city of Melbourne, had been spotlit in the international arena for most of the year 1956 as the Olympic Games were held there. Sydney was also keen to gain recognition in the eyes of the world, and this is normally achieved by erecting noteworthy buildings. A healthy economy provides facilities for its population to use and others to marvel at and Sydney now had the opportunity to act.

The selection team of four, comprising two Australian architects, one British and one American, performed its task and voted for what appeared to be an inspired fantasy: drawings of a shell-like frame and structures, an architectural sculpture for which no design solutions were offered, let alone invented. This was not merely innovative but, on the face of it, a folly. Thus, naming Joern Utzon as winner of the international competition, with a project which was very much an inspired interpretation of the notion of an opera house, proved to be most controversial. In choosing a concept the judges chose not only a building, or even a monument, or indeed simply the winner of an architectural competition. They did not look at practicality, at cost, feasibility or any other practical functions. They did not even require specific designs. The judges inherently understood the social contract between a society, its governments and the opera house. They chose a monument responding to the real meaning of opera. Finance, feasibility and construction could wait in the wings for once; imagination, as operatic and allegoric as their stated aims, was allowed to take over.

In fact many of the engineering skills and actual modes of realisation of the scheme were to provide Sydney with an obsession with the creation of a vision which would dominate the entrance of the harbour for many years. In 1973 Yeomans would write of the choice:

> And no committee of distinguished (and in two cases famous) architects would award first prize in an international design competition to a handful of sketches indicating only some first thoughts about a building obviously crammed with unsolved problems of function. No celebrated firm of structural engineers would agree to work on a building which was begun before anybody knew whether it was possible to construct the roof. No hard-headed, electorally-chosen government would in its wildest moments order a start to be made upon a building when it had no idea how much it would cost or when it would be finished.[11]

And yet comments by individuals involved in those heady, early days seem to agree that this is exactly what happened. Professor Henry Ingham Ashworth, at that time Professor of Architecture at the University of Sydney and one of the committee's judges, comments in his recollections on the atmosphere of the time:

> Sometimes I think about the beginning of the story, too. When I look back on it, do you know I often think what an extraordinary beginning it had, with that first meeting in the Public Library where five men were told to go ahead and build a huge complicated thing like an Opera House? There we were, just five men with no money allocated and no plans and nobody with any idea where the funds were to come from. All we had was just an instruction to build an Opera House. There can't be too many countries where a thing like *that* could happen.[12]

> Obviously an opera house is a very special kind of building – one that may be erected but once in a century or two and which thus becomes a

landmark as it were, expressive of the architecture of its day and age. While we can appreciate the famous Paris Opera, La Scala in Milan ... what a disaster and disappointment it would have been if this challenge to Australia generally and architecture in particular had resulted in another revival of a bygone age or, even worse, in a pedestrian building, guaranteed not even to evoke criticism.[13]

We looked for a monumental work. After all, you don't go to the opera very often. It is a bit of an occasion and it's nice to go to a magnificent building. That's why we kept in mind that the Opera House design had to be an imaginative thing.[14]

Even more so when the distinguished engineers Arup and Zunz pointed out that the assessor's report stated that the plans were based on an inspired vision, a faith in the nature and meaning of an opera house:

The drawings submitted for the scheme were simple to the point of being diagrammatic. Nevertheless we have returned again and again to the study of these drawings and we are convinced that they present a concept of an opera house which is capable of becoming one of the great buildings of the world.[15]

No conceptual level to this building would be ignored. The building was to be due for completion on a significant national date, Australia Day 1963, which marked the 175th anniversary of European settlement. The construction of a monumental opera house surely would be the quintessential representation of European culture. And when the project ran well over its anticipated completion date and cost estimations leapt from 7 million dollars in 1955 to 100 million at its completion in 1973, this opera house was only following the traditional path of opera house construction. The Palais Garnier took twenty years to complete and its costs far exceeded estimates. Later in the century the Opéra Bastille overran its budget by 80 per cent in a seven-year period. In the light of these examples, the following recent comment, which tells us more about contemporary values of economic rationalism than the reality of decisions to build opera houses, and implies that this project would not have been undertaken if the fiscal and human realities were known, is curious.

Had those in charge been able to calculate in advance the final cost of the buildings in both financial and human terms, it is unlikely that even those drawn to Utzon's vision would have given it the go ahead.[16]

On the contrary, it could be argued that, because it perfectly understood opera's real significance, the Australian government deliberately turned a blind eye to the real costs. No one will forget Cahill and his vision, even more so because of the extraordinary nature of the building. In omitting to accurately cost the building or estimate the time needed for its construction, the Cahill government was doing what government has always done, making sure that the construction of monumental architecture is funded by governments whatever the long-term costs might be.

The basis of the costing was underpinned by broad assertions from politicians and supporters of the project that the money would be found, and when this became a necessity the creative ways proposed in which to fund the project were almost as remarkable as the project itself. The first solution was to generate a new source of income, a scheme later taken up by the Major administration in England from which the Royal Opera has been at the time of writing one of the major recipients. A national lottery was set up on 1 May 1957, with the winner gaining £100,000. The rationale for this was that state funds would not be seen to be diverted from projects of public necessity, although doubts about the morality of such an enterprise were raised. The Coadjutor Bishop of Sydney certainly was not in favour of this type of funding, stating that: 'It is regrettable that a government should be financing a cultural movement by the encourage-ment of social vice.'[17] The debate about national lotteries is an old and venerable one concerning the arts. Indeed, Professor John Pick and Malcolm Anderton in their recent book *Building Jerusalem: Art, Industry and the British Millennium* devote considerable attention to this issue, pointing out to their readers that far from being a new, innovative and reliable form of funding the arts, the lottery has in fact been used on many occasions in the United Kingdom with various disastrous results. What is clear is that it rarely raises the required sum and inevitably leads to all kinds of human suffering. Pick tells us of the clerk who paid his accrued debts, caused by gambling on the lottery, by taking his own life, and of the British government's conclusion that the lottery inevitably led to the promotion of vice and social degradation.[18] The Sydney Opera House lottery was to have its own particular spectre. The businessman who won first prize in one of the first lottery draws was to pay dearly for this when, in a manner similar to Lindberg in the United States, his son fell victim to a kidnapper. The money was paid over but the child was brutally murdered. The quick fix of gain and greed funding is not quite what it is made out to be and the price exacted for the spurious prizes often far too high.

The sponsorship model was also used and members of the business commu-nity approached fairly publicly for donations, although this form of funding has consistently proved unreliable as pledges made publicly and in the heat of the moment are often left unfulfilled or become unsustainable for the duration of the life of a public project.[19] A more curious funding method, calling to mind a practice at the Paris Opéra in the nineteenth century, was that people pledged large sums of money to kiss celebrities! These erratic sources of revenue and imaginative funding devices reflected in part the non-conventional manner in which the project was conceived. Politicians may have wanted an opera house but it was another thing to expect the electorate to pay for it directly.

At the Ceremony to Commemorate the Commencement of the Building of the Sydney Opera House, held on 2 March 1959, the Hon. J.J. Cahill, MLA, Premier of the State of New South Wales, made the following comments to support his government's endorsement of the project: 'The proposal to build the Sydney Opera House and the proof we have given of our determination to see the project through to finality, have focused the eyes of the world upon us.'[20] Cahill thus identified the project as the outcome of his political party's endeavours, bestowing on it, and by extension the city of Sydney, an international status. He then gave depth to this analysis through the development of an historical and cultural context in order to strengthen the image, finally linking this again with his party's political rhetoric and objectives:

> The nations of the past have each contributed something to the accumulation of those arts which spring from the soul and mind, and form such an essential part of any great civilisation.
>
> We have something to contribute also, and my Government is convinced that Australia is worthy of a building in which our contribution to the music of the world can be fittingly demonstrated.[21]

The notion of the 'Glory Model' established,[22] Cahill suggested that, as a representative of the new world, Australia should introduce these formally recognisable structures and combine them with the trappings of political and ecclesiastical symbolism to herald a new age and cultural domain:

> Such a building will be the Sydney Opera House and it will stand not merely as an outstanding example of modern architecture or even as a world famous opera house, but as a shrine in which the great artists of the world may be seen and heard and our own artists may display the flowering of Australian culture.[23]

Mr Cahill also made it clear that he was not betraying party principles. This opera house, designed to display the greatness of a nascent civilisation, was also to have a policy, steeped in his party's political traditions, of providing access for all members of society. This language is similar to the statements of François Mitterrand's socialist government when the proposal for a new opera house was first mooted in Paris in the 1980s. The term 'a people's opera' was coined and a site chosen to endorse this, even though in reality opera did not change its meaning or become more accessible to the general public. The use of such language enabled Cahill to duck the more obvious jibes of supporting 'élitism' but still allow his government to create a 'monument' which would be seen to represent the greatness of the nation and its exploits:

> The building when erected will be available to the use of every citizen, ... the average working family will be able to afford to go there just as

well as people in more favourable economic circumstances, ... there will be nothing savouring even remotely of a class conscious barrier and ... the Opera House will, in fact, be a monument to democratic nation-hood in its fullest sense.[24]

The Commencement Ceremony served the function of a mediating forum within which all members of the political community were publicly united in support for the project. The uniformity of support evidenced by the language used at this event is significant in the general context of this book. At its outset, no political representative dared verbalise opposition to the creation of a state emblem; all had to be seen to support it from the first. H.F. Jensen, the Lord Mayor of Sydney, wrote that:

> I am sure that all citizens will be proud, as I am, that in prospect a magnificent structure will soon appear to add dignity and attractiveness to the skyline, and provide another dominant feature to the Harbour Gateway of Sydney....
> The functional character of the structure, with its sculptural and utilitarian purpose, adds to the stature of the Mother City of the Commonwealth, and will provide the citizens with an incomparable venue for the appreciation of music and the arts.[25]

Thus by reinforcing notions of national pride through a monumental building, linking it to the outside world and only lastly stating its value in terms of its function, his emphasis is clear: his priorities are firstly political and only incidentally cultural. Davis Hughes, leader of the New South Wales Country Party (a conservative party which represented non-urban interests) highlighted its symbolic value over its functional significance: 'It will be not merely a striking landmark on the shores of Sydney Harbour, but also a symbol that our cultural thought is keeping pace with national expansion.'[26] P.H. Morton, Leader of the State opposition, the Liberal Party (a conservative party), concurred with this view, stating that 'it has attracted wide interest overseas and greatly enhanced our cultural standing.'[27] And finally, Charles Moses, General Manager of the Australian Broadcasting Commission, proudly linked visions of the state and culture, applauding the 'success in persuading people that an opera house was not only desirable but essential to the State's cultural growth.'[28]

National representatives of the fine arts were also enlisted to endorse the project, and there are also token representations from the 'artistic' community. In addition to the statements from Australia's political parties, intelligentsia and artistic community, comments were included from leading international papers, all of which support the project and endorse its significance.

That Sydney was to have a splendid opera house, and that it needed a visual symbol to crown its harbour, were generally accepted notions by the end of the

1950s. The question of 'what did an opera house mean to Sydney?' was the focus of so much compounded rhetoric that criticism of the concept was virtually non-existent and tantamount to temporal sacrilege. The consensus was such that before its opening the building was acclaimed by all. The following reference reflects language and symbols consistent with almost all writing about the opera house in late 1973:

> Make no mistake – this birth, this opera house, is not just a thing of stone and glass created by computers. It is a pyramid, a temple, reflecting in its multifaceted complexity the subconscious will to greater self-expression by our people at this era in our history.
>
> As a nation we come more vividly alive as this strange jewel glows complete.[29]

And almost three decades later the symbol for the Olympic Games, held in Sydney in the year 2000, was the Sydney Opera House, giving this statement unusual potency within a very short space of time.

Controversy did, however, surround the opera house on many levels, although its symbolic importance was never disputed. The change of government in 1965, from Labor (left) to Liberal (right), brought about in part by 'the issue of escalating costs of the building',[30] meant that its cost was scrutinised publicly. It was deemed to be a reflection of the folly of the Labor government's economic policy. In this context it is not surprising that the optimism concerning its funding, which had been founded on little more than inspiration, was called into question. The resignation of Utzon in 1966, provoked to a large extent by the new government's emphasis on realistic projections of cost and design, provided the opportunity for the entire project to be reassessed.

Let's return to where we began this chapter – the final magnificent opening of the Sydney Opera House. As we have seen, the new Australia of 1973 may have been nurturing democratic precepts of nationhood as expressed as early as 1954 by the NSW Premier, but its symbolic framework could not afford to openly take these on without the assurance of a progression of cultural heritage, accompanied by an expression of the cultural and social development of the modern state. The historical and cultural role which Great Britain played in the birth of the Australian nation, and its modest beginnings as a penal colony for Britain, were also stressed by the monarch in a statement which could be interpreted as a reminder to the colony that, although its economic future appeared healthy and in all probability would imply a movement towards independent nationhood, its cultural roots were drawn from a British inheritance and this would not, and could not, be forgotten or displaced. Thus we see that a seemingly simple historical reference made by the Queen is loaded with political associations and contains a reminder of the continued relationship of domination, albeit cultural and historical, of one power over another:

You have reminded us, Mr. Premier, that this site is not only the birth-place of the nation, but also where the first European dramatic performance ever to take place in Australia was started. In a mud hut.

This interest in the arts has been a characteristic of the people who settled in Australia ever since. The progression from the mud hut to soaring opera house reflects the continuing cultural development as well as the tremendous economic achievement which made it possible.[31]

The editorial of the *Sydney Morning Herald* concurs with the spirit of the Queen's speech. It endorsed the rhetoric she employed:

The Opera House ... has a national significance as an aspiration, a symbol and an achievement; and it is appropriate that it should be opened by the Queen of Australia. Her presence here today carries its own symbolic significance: in her person and her great office she reminds us of our origins and cultural heritage; the duty which she will perform at the Opera House acknowledges its importance as a measure of national growth and achievement....

From the beginning the Opera House was seen not simply as a home for indigenous arts but as a contribution to international culture, in which Australia, by right of maturity, should participate....

Today is a time for Sydney pride in a majestic ornament, a work of art in its own right, which is already, through its magnetic presence, focusing attention on the arts and stimulating support for our artists. More than that, it is a time – emphasised by the Queen's presence – for national pride in its acknowledgement that our artistic culture, while exploiting what is unique in Australian experience, nevertheless finds its importance and its aspiration as part of the international culture, with its differing traditions and cross-fertilisation. Those great sails ... are symbolic in many ways, but that is their profoundest and most exciting meaning.[32]

The *Sun Herald* on the following day (and in more graphic language) told a similar story, spelling out order, continuity, tradition, achievement and anticipa-tion of future glories:

The Royal presence symbolised the peak of recognition. Few govern-ments and peoples ever enjoy such happy triumphs devoted to celebrating the completion of a beautiful building. ...

Yesterday was unique, superbly perfect. A Royal day with longed-for blue skies.

The Opera House flashed white, a bride ready.[33]

On this same day another significant speech was made from the very sails of the opera house roof, this time in the form of a tribute to the Aboriginal cultural inheritance. A cynical interpretation of this most theatrical event might be that this 'poem' was an attempt to 'outdo the pyramids', a demonstration that 40,000 years of continuous history would certainly provide cultural longevity and outstrip claims of cultural ascendance from the rest of the world. The speech, delivered by Ben Blakeney, an Aboriginal actor, from the top of one of the Opera House's sails, epitomises the rhetoric of the cultural propaganda in terms which link the site and culture with operatic metaphors of rite, chant, dance and percussion.

> I am Bennelong
> 200 years ago fires burned on this point –
> The fires of my people –
> And into the light of the flames
> From the shadows all about –
> Our warriors danced.
>
> Here my people chanted
> Their stories of the Dreamtime – of spirit heroes
> And of earth's creation
> And our painted bodies flowed in ceremony
>
> On this point my people laughed –
> And they sang
> While the sticks clacked
> In the rhythm of the corroborees.
>
> And then came the great canoes floating
> With white clouds above them –
> Our children watched and our lubras grew large eyed –
> And our painted men danced
> Among the fires.
>
> I am Bennelong –
> And my spirit
> And the spirit of my people … lives –
> And their dance –
> Their music and their drama
> And their laughter also remains.[34]

As mentioned, the site of the opera house, now named Bennelong Point, was where Bennelong, the first Aboriginal to adopt Western culture, had lived in the early days of the colony. The irony inherent in this did not go unobserved, as only days earlier the Queen had been greeted in Canberra by Aboriginal protesters who, only recently enfranchised and politicised in a Western sense, claimed 'recognition of tribal rights to land',[35] thus marking the start of a new and important debate concerning ownership and colonisation.

One fundamental truism concerning the opening of opera houses is that the operatic event itself, the primary meaning of opera, is generally non-existent. The Sydney Opera House was opened with an extraordinary spectacle that used its shell-like walls as a backdrop; this was not an opera but rather an agglomeration of symphonic works put together for the day, which is not unusual and in itself has much historic precedent. At the opening performances of the Palais Garnier and the Opéra Bastille in Paris, and at the reopening of Covent Garden after the Second World War, no opera was performed either. This lends weight to the argument that the true meaning of opera is other than the performance of an operatic work. The opening of the Sydney Opera House proved no exception to this rule. Thus it is not fundamentally surprising that Smith wrote of the opening:

> The performance was not great but it improved as it continued. But the 2700 invitees were generally more concerned with being there to see the glitter and glamour than they were with musical excellence.[36]

This comment expresses an accepted understanding of the meaning of opera, the performance of an opera being merely an ancillary act.

In 1974 an article in the *Canberra Times* entitled 'Opening of Opera House a musical non-event' reflected upon this phenomenon.[37] It went on to describe the kind of event it really was:

> One of the surprising features of last year's opening of the Sydney Opera House was the scant attention it received in the world musical press. After the years of building and its astronomical cost, which made it the world's most expensive building devoted principally to the musical arts, one would have expected its eventual opening to have at least equalled the interest occasioned throughout the world by [other openings]. But such was not the case. ...
>
> The Sydney Opera House might be 'the greatest building of this century', but so far as the world musical press was concerned its opening was the greatest non-event in 1973.[38]

It could be argued that the writer has failed to identify the central problem. The musical world's lack of interest remains consistent with the view that the opera house represents something other than musical concerns. If the house were to produce exceptional works of high musical quality, there would certainly be no cause for complaint and this undoubtedly could be perceived as a bonus, but it is clearly not the intention of the political and social forces that this need be its major function. The performance of music can thus largely be regarded as not actually being very pertinent to the meaning of the construction and opening of an opera house.

An article in *The Bulletin* in October 1973 argued that political requirements reigned supreme at the opening:

> Culture took a back seat.
>
> The opening day of the Sydney Opera House was designed to be a people's carnival. It was also – not, perhaps by design – a political exercise. It was not a cultural one.[39]

The opening of the opera house was interpreted as being a symbolic political ceremony. There would appear to be some reluctance on the part of the journalist, who, having identified the fundamental truth of the 'exercise', does not commit himself to the theory that this outcome was the intention of the state. Having stated the case, he shies away from developing it although he had in his possession some very powerful material:

> Our Bob – NSW Premier Sir Robert Askin, who has just announced an election three weeks away – must have done very nicely out of the day. Despite the fact that back in the dreamtime when Bennelong Point was a tramshed and the Opera House a Labor Premier's vision a certain Mr Robin Askin MLA had protested against making this big outlay on culture while some of his constituents were living in chook sheds.
>
> Culture, the ostensible raison d'être of the exercise, did very shabbily out of the day. Joan Hammond, the great singing star who made one of the first contributions to the Opera House Fund back in 1957, was not invited to the celebrations. Nor was Nobel prizewinner Patrick White. Nor were dozens of actors, playwrights, singers, artists who will – have already – put breath into that beautiful inert body.
>
> But every politician was, every civic dignitary, every heavyweight from the armed services and the business community and the Boy Scouts.[40]

We have looked at the history of the Sydney Opera house and made suggestions as to why it is so. There are, however, other issues to investigate, such as are the rituals performed in this opera house the same as or similar to those of other opera houses? The works of art may be part of the internationally accepted circuit, with similar singers, but how, if at all, does an Australian public differ from any other public, especially in the early days of the house when this edifice and art form were new to Sydney's shores?

When the first acoustic test of the Concert Theatre at the Sydney Opera House was performed to an audience comprising mainly construction workers from the site, the dress the workers wore was seen as worthy of comment:

So, on the Sunday afternoon crowds of *well-dressed* workers and their sunburned husbands began arriving on the site.[41] (my italics)

Workers do not form the substantial part of a typical opera audience anywhere in the world. Yet this audience chose to imitate the behavioural standards of a typical opera audience. The implication of such a statement may be obvious in terms of an analysis of the behaviour of those who attend performances but it is well worth stating: when visiting a house of such significance, ordinary clothing is not deemed to be suitable attire in the minds of those who attend.

There is little doubt that the opening of the opera house proved an occasion for many to display finery. The notion of opera dress was identified clearly by Gary Hughes in the Melbourne *Herald*.

$1400 for an opera gown.

The big question in Sydney's high society at the moment is what to wear to the Royal opening of the Opera House later this month. ...

And some of the women have bought as many as six gowns to last them through the opening season.[42]

This article goes on to promote notions of access for all in a backhanded manner. As the opera house policy was access for all, perhaps gowns and evening dress were not to be strictly *de rigueur*. It would be up to the individual to tailor their dress according to their image of the house.

Although the royal opening will be a strictly formal affair, standards of dress at regular night performances are not so uniform.

As far as the Opera House is concerned there is no standard of dress patrons must conform to. 'As long as someone has tickets they can get in,' one attendant said.[43]

These examples illustrate that whatever fine rhetorical statements may be made by government, the way in which people related to the opera house was largely influenced by an inherited and shared set of values concerning behaviour, presentation and etiquette.

On entering the house the audience also took on the role of performers by playing out social scenarios familiar to European opera houses for many decades:

Overheard at the Opera House during intermission: 'Oh yes, they're singing very well. You can actually hear them above the conversations.'[44]

The festive atmosphere of celebration of high culture was not simply contained inside and outside the direct vicinity of the house. Social occasions were created in honour of the event, thus spreading even further the extended meaning of opera. This is an interesting phenomenon, where a created event replicates another construct. Questions of art imitating life imitating art spring at once to mind. The following article from the social pages of the *Sun Herald* illustrates the kind of event which the opening of the opera house engendered.

Grand Ball

> Opera fever became international on a grand scale, at the Opera Foundation and Opera Auditions Ball. ... the 'official party' was very glittering. Star of it was Madame Marcos, wife of the President of the Philippines – taller than expected, regal, skin like a pearl, beautiful and cool. ... Madame Pierre Schlumberger looked gorgeous ... Mrs Henry Ford II looked charming ... Princess Gaeta Pallavicini ... was a stunner ... The Duke and Duchess (in silvery salmon) of Bedford spread their always successful charm.[45]

Clearly the language of this text focuses on adjectives such as 'glittering', 'regal' and 'gorgeous' and on traditional colours associated with operatic language.

Of course, the gap between the official policy of accessibility and the reality of the tokenism of this situation did not escape all, as is evidenced by the following contribution by a reader of the *Daily Telegraph* on 25 September 1973 to Sir Asher Joel, Chairman of the Opera House Opening Committee, entitled 'An Opera House Plea'.

> Oh Sir Asher, dear Sir Asher, you really are a smasher. For offering 2000 tickets free. For the likes of humble me ... For weeks I've willed a miracle, while others have been cynical. And here it's come at last, the chance to be inside those great white shining shells; to see the Queen and all those swells. So won't you dear Sir Asher, won't you PLEASE?[46]

It is worth reiterating here elements from the speech made by Premier Cahill at the Commencement Ceremony in 1959: 'there will be nothing savouring even remotely of a class conscious barrier and ... the Opera House will, in fact, be a monument to democratic nationhood in its fullest sense'. Whatever the tone of the political rhetoric, it can clearly be seen that the Opera House remained a place where accessibility is still determined by the codes which, although not dictated, are understood, around which other events occur and where even basic requirements such as the taking of refreshments are steeped in notions of exclusivity:

It's full sail ahead at the Opera House now and everybody is looking for places nearby to eat before and after the performances.

Naturally, there's the Bennelong itself, exotic and beautiful with a high-flying menu and classical music.[47]

Finally, and perhaps most plainly, the following account of the first performance to be held at the concert hall effectively demonstrates the relationship between the opera house and the ritualistic functions of state embodied by the Queen in her dual role as Queen of Australia and Head of the Church of England:

Although only six bars of *God Save the Queen* is protocol for a governor in Australia, the whole anthem was played to open the test concert so that acousticians could record plenty of the tremendous crescendoes on the drums which, if the truth be told, most people of British ancestry in the audience found a little eye-misting.[48]

British ancestry and regal symbolism, although clearly diminishing as a result of the significant influx of post-war immigration, still provided a dominant sense of identification and meaning in the house. The fact is that musical performances, to a large extent supported by those of European backgrounds with a greater cultural relationship and affiliation with the actual performance of opera, took on only a secondary meaning in the state-led iconographic demonstration of the day. Furthermore, the connection between church and state was clearly identified by Leslie Walford:

Yesterday was Sydney's greatest day of pomp and majesty since humankind first set foot on these shores. Heaven, the Queen and the Government did all they could do to make it so.[49]

More recently, 'Heaven, the Queen and the Government' have taken second place to comparisons of mythological status. The opera house has taken on a meaning of its own, equated no longer with the Taj Mahal or even the Pyramids, but with the mysteries of Aztec sanctuaries and temples. This transformation from monumental state architecture to cultural icon is even more remarkable given the relatively short period of time it has taken to create such symbolism. The source of this thinking lies in the kind of language used by the consulting engineers. Writing in the 1960s, Ove Arup describes the project in the following terms:

The concept, design and construction of the Sydney Opera House stand as an affirmation of twentieth century man – that by his imagination and by his own hand he can shape his world to his needs.[50]

James Semple Kerr, who devised an interim plan for the conservation of the building, also sees it as much more than an agglomeration of building materials. He states that:

> The Sydney Opera House is a national icon of exceptional significance, built, maintained and adapted with public money by the Government of NSW on behalf of the people. Its continued function is subsidised directly and indirectly from both State and Commonwealth sources.[51]

He attributes the significance of the Sydney Opera House to what he identifies as being:

> its almost mythological status as a cultural icon arising from ... the high public interest in its protracted and controversial development; and from its power to attract artists, patrons and tourists of national and international significance.[52]

This argument closely resembles those arguments used by European governments to justify opera since its very beginnings. It has already been demonstrated that in France the *privilèges* of Louis XIV, the statements by Rousseau, the justifications by Le Roux and Bonet de Treiches and later Dr Véron all sought to justify opera's usefulness in terms of its power to attract the influential population within the country and act as a prestigious symbol of France to other countries. In England more recently it has been demonstrated that justifications by opera managers such as Ebers, Lumley and Beecham endorsed opera for its power of attraction to its particular audience and to foreigners, and that the Arts Council determined that 'opera should not be let down'. Now Sydney, Australia, with its new monumental opera house could compete with those great and older European powers on the same terms.

Even the interior of the opera house conformed to the traditional opera house standard. Smith quotes John Coburn, the designer of the tapestry curtains which adorn the two great theatres of the opera house. We see in his statement a remarkable similarity of approach to that expressed in the monumental and traditional meaning of opera houses and remind ourselves of Mitterrand's statement about the interior of the more recently constructed Bastille or Louis XIV's allegorical iconography (as the Sun King). 'I have often used the sun as a religious symbol and it seemed to me natural to use it in the curtains. I wanted to make the Opera Theatre curtain as rich and decorative and theatrical as possible – to give it the rich red and gold quality one associates with opera theatres.'[53]

There has been, however, a novel addition to this repertory of monumental symbolism, and that is the performance of *The Eighth Wonder*, which its programme grandly declares had its world première on 14 October 1995. This work, commissioned with funding assistance from the Sydney Opera Trust, is the first opera written about the opera house that it was to be performed in. It details the history of the house, romanticising the metaphorical themes it develops, fusing the notion of the opera house with that of Aztec temples and the political battles with a righteousness resembling religious fervour. Utzon is portrayed as a god-like mystic, misunderstood and maligned, his vision thwarted. Whatever the truth behind the story of the construction of the house, the interesting factor is that this 'opera' was written and performed at all. It could be argued that, not content with an opera house, the Opera Trust, the Australia Council for the Arts and the government wanted to get its message of cultural coming of age and ascendancy across to the world in an operatic statement.

There will, however, always be those critics who maintain that it is 'an opera' which always gives opera and opera houses their significance and meaning. The well-known arts journalist, Maria Pererauer, writing in *The Bulletin* in 1995, gives a traditional evaluation of the meaning of an opera by suggesting that the Sydney Opera House does not live up to that which it had been created to do:

> The Sydney Opera House is not an opera house; the city's one true opera house presents musicals, and the other states have opera houses and call them something else.[54]

The present writer's thesis, *contra* Pererauer, is of course that whatever is performed within the walls of the Sydney Opera House, it is first and foremost fulfilling the function of being the monumental opera house of Australia. The works performed in its auditorium have little consequence for the constructs which this vision of sheer white sails represents.

On the basis of the weighty commentary produced about the house since it was first mooted, it is undeniable that the Sydney Opera House has been identified as a building containing many elements which serve to endorse it as a powerful symbol representing the Australian nation. Yeomans comments that:

> It is fair to say that the Opera House is the only Australian building known outside Australia; the profile of its famous roofs seem to have become some new sort of national symbol overseas. No public building in the world looks like the Sydney Opera House.[55]

Its construction has made inroads into political and social elements of the Australian lifestyle by the creation of a new venue, which dictated a change of fashion, a reason for celebration and ultimately became a metaphor for achievement and modernity. This symbol has now been carried forward into the new century, as the sails of the opera house were used as the symbol for the Sydney Olympic bid for the year 2000. When the decision was announced by the Olympic Selection Committee, in Cannes, France, the sails were illuminated at 4.30 a.m. with the Olympic colours to display signs of victory. As laser images of congratulations were emblazoned on the stark shells, they shone out to the world as an image of national uniqueness. This is perhaps the most powerful meaning of all for the Sydney Opera House, an immediately identifiable image of modernity bringing together architecture, engineering and an extraordinary natural site as the pinnacle of cultural ascendancy.

This chapter has traced the reasons why Sydney sought and got an opera house and how the public reacted once she had one. In fact, rather than adding anything new to our notion of the opera, it reinforces the fact that state opera houses have extraordinary similarities. Their outer forms may differ, so too their forms of subvention, but their real meaning as a symbolic platform for the demonstration of a state image is performed time and time again to the passer-by or the opera-goer, or the tourist or the political and economic forces of government which act out their rites on the nation's and international stage. Thus Sydney Opera House can be viewed as virtually a prototype model containing all the traditional aspects of the meaning of opera.

9

OTHER OPERAS – OTHER WORLDS

Throughout this book it has been demonstrated that opera functions in modern states very much as it did in its first decades. The same repertoire is performed on the same stages of splendidly appointed monuments to the same richly dressed audiences, who have seemingly behaved in the same way from the age of Louis XIV to the age of the Brussels bureaucrats.

We can now briefly look at some opera houses in other parts of the world in order to test this theory. The Teatro Colón of Buenos Aires, for example, has a historical past in the Spanish Empire. Would opera in this country mean something else? Indeed, why did it exist there at all? Certainly since the late eighteenth century opera has consistently existed in Argentina and the now familiar battles between Italian and vernacular opera were fought out there. Towards the end of the nineteenth century a number of opera houses were built to accommodate the tastes of the population, and companies such as La Scala of Milan visited them regularly. In 1857, when the first Teatro Colón was opened in Buenos Aires, it seated:

> 2,500, with 80 boxes in three balconies, it also had a *cazuela* (gallery for single women) and a *paradiso* (men's gallery with a separate entrance). Fronting the Plaza de Mayon, the first Colon was also the first theatre to be lit by gas, and in every other respect it enjoyed all the most advanced equipment of the day.[1]

On 25 May 1908, after two decades of construction, a grand 4,000 seat opera house opened, also called the Teatro Colón,[2] effectively quashing opposition from older and less grand opera houses, which in their day were also grand affairs. The theatre itself is an eclectic mixture of European architectural styles, in part due to the lengthy construction period as well as numerous changes of architect. What is interesting, however, is that even here the vision is almost uniformly of European provenance. This opera does not represent indigenous Argentinian culture. It is to house the jewel of European civilisation, even though its architects could not decide upon its exact provenance.

As is the case with so many other theatres elsewhere, the need to maintain such a building meant that its running has passed through various hands and its title has reflected these changes. According to Harold Rosenthal, the movement for a national opera house originated almost 50 years previously as there was a perceived need to construct an opera house 'worthy of the growing importance of the city'. In 1887 a law was passed by the local council stating that:

> The Municipality of Buenos Aires is authorised to sell the National Bank the actual building of the Colon Theatre for a total amount of 950,000 Argentine pesos, which will be utilised in the construction of a new Municipal Theatre, which will carry the name 'Teatro Colon'.[3]

In 1925 the Teatro Colón duly became the municipal theatre of Buenos Aires and since that time has received state subsidy.[4]

According to Marie Pascal, writing in 1957, the theatre became the focal point for political manifestations during the dictatorship and 'the auditorium had been used more often than not for political meetings'.[5] This point is borne out by a manifesto written by the Argentinian Musicians' Union in that year, which clearly points out that the building is more than a place in which to house opera, but rather a symbolic emblem of the Argentinian state and an edifying educational beacon of culture and nobility of purpose:

> For the Teatro Colon, and this must be stated once and for all, is not only a theatre for the performance of operas. It is, or rather it should be, a cultural institution whose leaders as well as influencing its structure, act as a stimulus on the whole intellectual climate of the Argentine. It should embody a serious and influential school, where not only productions of the highest order take place, but where also our country's rising generations of artists can learn to familiarise themselves with the noblest artistic principles, which demand a degree of self-denial and an acute sense of responsibility. It is our University of the Arts of the future. Therefore it is unthinkable that we should allow such an institution to be conducted in a spirit of irresponsibility or to become, instead of an example to all, the scene of dissension, in which everything counts for more than art and its safe-keeping.[6]

Thus it is not surprising that when in 1958 it celebrated its 50th anniversary, many countries paid homage by sending their musical emissaries to its doors.

Let us now turn to another South American country, this time with a Portuguese tradition, Brazil. Opera in Brazil began early. We find that in the late eighteenth century three operas were commissioned 'in celebration of the engagement of the Royal Infantas of Portugal and Spain'.[7] The Portuguese Royal Court brought with it its own composer, Marcos Portugal, which 'added prestige to the operatic life of the city'. In 1813 the Teatro de S Joao, which was subsidised by the court, was founded, a replica of the Teatro S Carlos in Lisbon. In 1824 this house was renamed the Imperial Teatro de S Pedro Alcantara, thus leaving in no doubt the origins of its subsidy and its relationship with the power brokers. Opera in the latter part of the nineteenth century became a centrepiece for this relatively stable state, where the emperor of Brazil, Pedro II, who was a grandson of Emperor Franz I of Austria, determined to follow the traditions of the great European courts from whence he came.[8] Opera was thus fundamentally an Italian affair. This is not too strange in the light of Austrian operatic history, of which we know Pedro was a direct inheritor. The opera was not only to be a grand house but it was expected that the Academia de Musica e Opera Nacional should generate new works for this prestigious house. The institute was opened in 1857, and a national holiday was declared to mark this important event. European composers welcomed such moves and both Liszt and Wagner were known to have relationships with the emperor of Brazil. This kind of patronage was not unknown and the last legacy of a European system which both Wagner and Liszt understood and cultivated.

Opera was well supported by the rival cities of Rio de Janeiro and São Paulo at the turn of the century. There was, however, another 'curiosity' constructed in 1896 and that is the Teatro Amazonas in Manaus. According to Terri Hardin, it 'is a tribute to the wealth and perseverance of the rubber barons of that time'.[9] Whether it is a tribute or not, it certainly was an architectural aping of all that was European bijoux. This small auditorium comprised 700 seats, of which 450 could be found in 90 boxes in three tiers. The spatial hierarchies were minutely observed with a special box for dignitaries, a dazzling dome, drop curtain and noble room. Hardin observes that the rubber barons who financed the theatre were 'not to be outdone by the newly wealthy industrialists of the United States' and were keen to demonstrate this. What better way than through the splendour of an opera house?

It would seem that the love of European opera must have infected the South American continent because in Mexico City the Palacio de Bellas Artes, 'one of the most spectacular buildings devoted to the arts in the Americas',[10] appeared just after the great Depression in 1934. After almost three decades of construction this opera house was opened for all to see. The length of the construction period was due as much to civil unrest as it was to natural disasters, and when completed it was to reflect this country's political direction. The inspiration was art deco and the motifs were pre-Columbian. The Mayan influence was to be borne regally throughout. This is significant when one considers the inspiration of the Mayan civilisation on Joern Utzon in the construction of the Sydney Opera House and the opera *The Eighth Wonder*. These noble, sturdy symbols, such as the Mayan eagle and depictions of their gods, tell of a regal, mystical empire and are thoroughly operatic in their source, reminding us of the first evocation of opera in the ducal courts of Italy, which also sought to find references in the lost deities of the Ancient Greeks.

In our quest for opera houses and opera in other lands we travel now to another continent, settled neatly below the European shelf, to Africa and most importantly to another country with a great past of unknown mystical significance whose symbolic deities are ever apparent, Egypt. The first references to opera in Egypt date from 1841. Adelina Patti was to sing in Cairo in the 1860s. But it was in the year 1869, in order to mark the opening of the Suez Canal, that the Khedive decided to construct an opera house. This house, of Italian design with the now familiar spatial configuration of three tiers of boxes, opened within the year and was to house Italian and French operas. Indeed, it followed very much the policy of the Royal Opera House in London. When Wagner's *Lohengrin* was performed there, it was sung in Italian. Edward Said demonstrates that this monumental opera house serves not only as an arm of cultural imperialism but also as a measure of social control. Not only was the house itself designed to represent the quintessence of European culture, right down to the landscape around it, but it also served to 'hold back' the 'teeming quarters' of non-European culture. He demonstrates that the opera house stood as a symbol of the occidental world and acted as a bridge to its culture and civilisation in the same manner as the railway station provided a central key to communication and thus commercial interests, which were so much the source of nineteenth-century mercantile interests.

> The Opera House built by Ismail for Verdi sat right at the centre of the north–south axis, in the middle of a spacious square, facing the European city, which stretched westward to the banks of the Nile.[11]

In 1912 *Aida* received its first presentation at the foot of the pyramids.

With the dissolution of the Ottoman Empire in 1922, the Cairo opera became the Théâtre Royal as French was the language of the court. The vicissitudes of politics notwithstanding, the opera encountered great financial problems in 1927 and was saved from the brink of financial disaster by the Italian government. This, it seems, was to be the fate of opera in the Egyptian capital. The opera house was to be obviously supported by the many powers which occupied the state, whether it be militarily or politically or, as we shall see later, economically.

In 1965 the Egyptian Ministry of Culture formed the Cairo Opera Company and Verdi's *La Traviata* was performed in Arabic. But in 1971 the theatre was razed by fire and lay dormant for over a decade. Then an unusual donation saved the opera house from its charred fate. In 1983 the Egyptian president visited Japan and an announcement was made that the Japanese government were to offer, as a gift to Egypt, the construction of a new opera house. The Japanese and Egyptian states have little in common except that they share glorious histories. By the early 1980s, however, one state was wealthy and the other had been reduced to poverty, with no surplus income for sustaining its national treasures. It is probable that a search for a new kind of alliance between the states was being sought by using the gift of an opera house as a new kind of cultural cement. It is interesting that the Japanese government was concerned to give a symbolic gift to the power brokers of the Middle East, rather than to the common people, nights at the fashionable opera, rather than irrigation schemes for Egyptian farmers.

The opera house was designed by a Japanese architect Kuashiro Shikeda and completed in what he called 'modern Islamic' style. Such a cultural mélange is of great political significance. The house was opened in 1988 to the tunes of specially commissioned music and then three performances of Kabuki Theatre.

Remaining in the orient, we move to the mouth of the Bosphorus, to the city which bridges two continents and has boasted trade links with the great European capitals of the modern and ancient world, Istanbul.

Not surprisingly, the first opera house to be built in that city was constructed by an Italian and used by visiting Italian companies in 1840. Its management soon became local but the theatre was burnt down in 1846. Now seen as an important national asset, it was restored 'with the assistance of Sultan Abd al-Meijid'.[12] When that theatre burnt down, it was not reconstructed but the Sultan did build himself a private opera house for performance of Italian opera in the Domabahce Palace. That too did not survive fire. In 1889 Sultan Abd al-Hamid II constructed another theatre in Yildiz Palace where opera was performed until 1908.[13]

With the establishment of the Republic of Turkey in 1923, opera was not cast off as part of the old order. A new and this time municipal opera house had its foundations laid in 1946. It was not completed for over forty years, but in 1968 it was opened as part of the Istanbul Kultur Sarayi (Istanbul Palace of Culture). The building burnt down in 1970 and in the same year Opera subvention moved from being the responsibility of the city to that of the state. Opera was, therefore, in this modern democratic state still to be seen as something of national significance and deemed worthy of support at that level.[14] The company is now known as the Istanbul State Opera Company.

Not so far from Turkey lies the Arab nation of Iran, whose shah fled to Egypt in 1979. His father Réza Shah decided in the 1930s to 'create an Iranian Opera Company as part of his plans to modernise his country'.[15] It would seem unusual to use an art form so steeped in European cultural traditions, which draws much of its history from the eighteenth and nineteenth centuries, as part of a modernisation plan. But as part of a 'westernisation' plan it would surely be most effective, as it would provide many obvious linkages to the European power brokers, both of the past and present. And so construction commenced on a new opera house in 1937–38. But, as one has often seen in operatic history, when the country was occupied in 1941 by the Russians and the English, the unfinished building was turned into another more immediate use by the occupying forces; this time the edifice was to become a bank. Operatic performances, although sporadic, did continue after the war and in 1967 a new opera house was inaugurated as the shah had decreed that a house 'modelled on those in Munich and

Vienna' was to be built. The opera house contained, as is traditional, a private box with its own entrance and its inauguration took place during the celebrations for the shah's ceremonies.[16] The new religious government which succeeded the shah in January 1979 has not been interested in the perpetuation of Western art forms or cultural pursuits, although as recently as 1999 women were again allowed to perform on stage. The insular and religious nature of the regime are not therefore inconsistent with the absence of state support for an opera house, although it is one of the rare examples in this book of the western operatic tradition, once established, being allowed to fall into disuse.

Wherever European colonialism has travelled so too has the opera house. We see today that advertisements for the cities of Hanoi and Ho Chi Minh (Saigon) incorporate the fact that the grand hotels are built next to the grand opera house. No mention is made of the opera houses' musical tradition, only that they, like many other vestiges of the French colonial era, have survived the war and continue as powerful symbols of cultural traditions.

In Hanoi the house itself, constructed by the French at the beginning of the twentieth century, is a replica of the Palais Garnier. The liberation of the city on 12 December 1946 was proclaimed from its terrace. The opera house has recently been renovated by the French and Italian governments and the bullet holes made during the liberation are proudly preserved alongside latterday sculptures donated by the Australian government. The new national flag adorns the building, which was attended on the evening I visited it, by an almost entirely foreign diplomatic and business crowd. I heard French, Italian, German, English but virtually no Vietnamese and witnessed the staircases heavily laden with flowered garlands to mark the occasion of the centenary of a grand hotel. The following day I had little difficulty purchasing a ticket for the evening as the $10 price was well above what could be afforded by the local population. (Even the ticket itself was designed to resemble tickets from the Paris opera.) And so I again revisited this house, floodlit and proud, cradled by a newly constructed Hilton Hotel and warmed by French lamp posts, vaguely reminded by the fluttering flag of Ho Chi Minh's symbolic attempt at independence half a decade previously. But gone were the French troops whose mission it had been to restore colonial rule and the Americans fighting an interminable war; today they were welcomed guests of the house.

Even in Hong Kong, which has recently been returned to China, the recent articles about the mooted construction of an opera house only raise a cynical eyebrow. One could argue that the city state is fighting to retain its independence and does so by using as many symbols on the cultural front as possible. In March 2000 the *South China Morning Post* reported that:

A Sydney-style opera house that could accommodate up to 60,000 spectators is among several options being considered for arts development on the West Kowloon reclamation.[17]

Yet all this is understandable and easily explained. What is less easily explained, unless one concurs with this book's hypothesis, is the movement in the past year to realise a plan which was first mooted in 1958 by Zhou Enlai to build a national theatre but which to this day remains unconstructed. To further humiliate Beijing in its role as capital of China, a new opera house was built in Shanghai in 1998, and 'Beijing's leadership suddenly realized that the southern upstart was going to upstage the capital'.[18] And so, in the time-honoured tradition of opera house constructions, an international tender or competition was held to invite architects to present plans for the capital's new opera house.

But the stakes have changed somewhat since 1958 and the intelligentsia are more vocal.[19] Petitions have been raised and unusual controversy has centred around the support by the current Chinese power brokers for a Grand National Opera costing over half-a-billion dollars on 25 acres of land in one of the most historically significant places of the regime, 'the communist heart of Beijing', Tiananmen Square, close to the Great Hall of the People and Mao Zedong's mausoleum.[20] According to the French architect Paul Andreu, 'I met several officials during my recent trip to Beijing and none raised any problem'.[21] And so it is that the Chinese power brokers, the officials, have deemed that it is now time for China to have an emblematic European-designed opera house. It is claimed that 'More than 2,000 residents in traditional Chinese buildings were kicked out from the vast site next to the Great Hall of the People' to make way for this building, which will 'feature a titanium and glass-dome set in the center of a lake'.[22] The building is to house two large theatres, one for opera and one for concerts, and two smaller theatres and its spectacular entrance will be by way of a tunnel constructed under a lake. This is the inverse of the great monumental stairway. Instead of rising up to ascend the steps and enter the house, the select few will in ritualistic style enter its underground caverns (is this a pun on phantom of the opera?) only to appear in the sacred ground and join the 'happy few' to reach the other side.

Critics such as Alfred Peng suggest that the proposition 'isolates the theatre and the small elite of people who would be able to afford to go to the opera house from the mass of people',[23] and He Zuoxiu, fellow at the Chinese Academy of Sciences, considers that the building may not be economically viable which would 'mean that the tickets must be very expensive. If they are not, what is the point in building it?'[24] But they have fundamentally misunderstood the very nature of the theatre. What they claim is in fact true but it is the very intention of this house, like so many others, to separate out the 'small elite' from the greater group. That is why these houses exist, and no amount of lip service to inclusive behaviour by communist or modern democratic governments will change this. Opera's meaning is immutable. Power brokers understand this. In fact, most people understand this. Critics who choose to ignore this fact are simply avoiding the obvious. They know that in order to break even ticket prices would be valued at 'about half an average Beijing resident's monthly wage'.[25] The project's architect understands this intrinsically, making the statement 'ticket prices would depend on the cultural policy'.[26] That is entirely the basis upon which entrance to such an arena has always been founded.

Most recently, and in the light of the surprising opposition to the plan, the project has been kept from the newspapers, where reports about its construction differ. According to some, work has begun, and to others this is not so. The inauguration ceremonies did not take place but it is unlikely that this will affect the final result, the erection of a grand opera house in central Beijing in 2002. Ironically, the construction of this Grand National Opera will be 'the biggest construction job near Tiananmen Square since 1976, when Chinese workers built the mausoleum that houses the embalmed corpse of Mao Zedong'.[27]

This chapter has focused on what could appear to be an eclectic range of theatres from around the globe, from those of South America, to North Africa, Asia Minor and China. What they have in common is that they all in some way have taken opera from the European operatic tradition and translated it into their own environment. We have also observed the latest addition to the monumental operatic repertoire as we know it, which is a French-designed opera house to be placed next to the Great Hall of the People, off Tiananmen Square in central Beijing. What is the purpose of such a house and why would a titanium-plated building, complete with all the iconographic references of a European opera house, be supported by the officials of that uniquely communist state?

10

BACK TO THE FUTURE?

This study has endeavoured to answer the following questions: Why is it that, alone amongst the arts, opera seems to retain the same immutable form through wars, revolution and vast social changes? Why is it that governments of all kinds, while paying lip service to the need to develop new art forms and to support contemporary cultural forms, nevertheless continue to give priority to the funding of opera and to the maintenance of state opera houses, even if such action seems to involve the neglect of popular theatre, dance, poetry or music?

It has been argued that opera is properly viewed not just as an art, but also as an important part of the ceremonial trappings of the state.[1] The argument has laid particular emphasis on two aspects. First, that the ceremonies and rituals associated with the opera change little over time. Second, that those same ceremonies and rituals are remarkably similar, even between countries of quite different constitution.

This unchangeability is the most important part of opera's political significance. The argument has been made throughout that opera-going remains an immutable ritual in a way that visiting the theatre, for example, does not.[2] It could be said that their immutability is the real 'meaning' of the rituals and ceremonies associated with the opera.

National operatic institutions have been ever present in modern Western history.[3] Indeed, not only has opera been labelled the 'Ultimate Art',[4] but it might also be considered to be the 'ultimate institution', as the history of opera and the grand opera houses is undeniably bound up with that of governments. This is demonstrated by the fact that throughout the changing fortunes of the state, opera has remained constant and has at times not merely served as a ceremonial backdrop but also taken on an acute political dimension. Such elements are illustrated by the numerous political incidents which have taken place within its walls and the debates of a social and political nature which have occurred in its name, as well as the treatises written by incumbent powers as justifications for its continued political support.

Clearly, just as the notion of opera has changed during the period under examination, so too has the notion of the state. In France, for example, in 1669 under Louis XIV opera was a very small enterprise serving the direct interests of the monarch; in this century it now reflects the larger functions of a bureaucratic and democratic state. State power, control and authority have grown enormously in the countries in question. This changing state function is reflected in the changing nature of the operatic institution over this time.

An assessment of opera's subvention over the past three centuries demonstrates its relationship to the state. Opera has often been associated with the political forces in power and yet its actual funding has been held at arm's-length from power, except when the institution has been deemed to be in immediate jeopardy and the king, government or chancellor of the exchequer has directly intervened to save it.[5] The state has invariably determined that there will be opera and nominated its immediate supporters to organise the provision of adequate resources for it. In the eighteenth century this role fell upon the shoulders of the nobility;[6] in the nineteenth century the bourgeoisie and the new aristocracy in France, and the traditional aristocracy and new industrialists in Britain, were the mainstay of the operatic audience and supporters; in the twentieth century the arts councils and great corporations and patrons have been looked upon to secure its continued existence; and it would seem in the 21st century the private patron once more has a significant role to play, as long as his name is associated with the house. Whichever century is scrutinised it is beyond doubt that heads of state, be they monarch, emperor, president or prime minister, have supported this institution by attending its inner sanctum and bestowing on it pomp and ceremony and the endorsement of privilege invested with complex ceremonial traditions and manifested in elaborate social structures such as state galas.

Opera is so closely aligned with the state that on some occasions state ceremonial behavior could be mistaken for being operatic. Donald Horne suggests that certain non-operatic events, such as the opening of parliament in Denmark, so resemble opera that they should be interpreted as part of the opera experience. For the monarch's role is to sit in his box and preside over the occasion, much as he and his predecessors would have done at the opera house.[7]

A charge brought against opera throughout its history has been that it is very much an art designed to satisfy the 'happy few'. This is largely true but opera gains importance precisely because it is the entertainment of the élite. It has grown as an institution distinct from popular culture, a symbol of establishment culture,[8] a national showcase in which state ceremonies are performed with political consequences. Furthermore, it symbolises the continuity of governments both as an institution constantly supported by them but also within the content of the works themselves and the iconography contained within the state opera houses.

The claim that it is foreign has also been a charge against opera in all countries other than Italy. The aristocracy, the bourgeoisie, or even corporations in England, for example, often have foreign origins or are amalgamated with foreign interests, and opera has reflected such foreign interests in the same way as these influential groups have done. Their foreign sources are very often the strengths of these socio-political groups, which are to all intents and purposes national symbols. Joseph I of Austria and Catherine of Russia held that Italian opera was to be played in their kingdoms; opera in the vernacular was not deemed to be part of court ritual. The élite has usually been more 'international' throughout modern history than those serving it and thus nationalism in terms of opera has to be understood in this broader context.

More specifically, in England, when what was known as 'Italian opera' was first performed,[9] it was considered to be allied with nobility and grandness. From the eighteenth century to the early twentieth century 'Italian opera' was commonly understood to be opera. Unlike other musical forms, which have roots in English theatre, the notion of 'Italian opera' represented a specific musical and theatrical form and was considered to be exclusive. All this is clearly demonstrated by the fact that it was not until 1892 that 'Italian' was deleted from the official title of the Royal Opera in England.[10]

This book has highlighted opera's remarkable permanence and legitimacy and presented evidence that throughout its history it has represented something larger than a performed work or experience. The investigation has necessarily been limited to selective highlights of operatic history with the intention of illustrating opera's relationship with government from its origins to the present day in order to prove that its connection with the state is not accidental but by design.

Tradition and ceremony determine its presentation. The chronicler of royal performance, Bevan, remarks that the iconography of the opera house reminds public and monarchy of their respective roles. The traditional relationship between the monarch and the opera will continue to be played out as a reminder of the elaborate ceremonial significance of both opera and the state.

> The Queen must often be reminded of the long tradition which links royalty with the theatre, just as the public is reminded when, for instance, they go to the Royal Opera House at Covent Garden and see the royal cipher embroidered on the stage curtains. The crowd scenes at Covent Garden's elaborate opera productions offer another reminder – for this theatre has the privilege of calling on the Brigade of Guards to supply soldiers as stage extras.[11]

It is, however, even more critical in the context of the questions raised in this book to interpret why governments today persevere in the maintenance of expensive non-utilitarian monuments, as society has plainly moved in modern times towards a spirit of economic rationality. Palaces are no longer constructed and are essentially maintained as museums, their function having evolved in accordance with the ethos of the twentieth century.

Opera houses, however, continue to be preserved, ostensibly to perform their original function. Even more surprisingly, they are still being constructed to enable new European and Western-influenced states to provide monumental venues. The state opera house of Finland, opened in 1993, the opera in Seville, inaugurated for the World Expo in 1992, and the Beijing Opera are recent examples of this phenomenon.[12] Moreover, opera houses continue to be financed by states, even though they require the constant provision of significant revenue from the nations' coffers merely for their maintenance or, it would seem, the performance of an art for a select few.

An investigation focusing on the question of why these monuments appear rarely to resemble each other externally and yet conform to an understood convention (spatially they invariably contain the configurations necessary to receive dignitaries, display audiences, etc.) is required in order to answer this evident paradox. Certainly there is no single comprehensive explanation. In some respects it is the desire to amaze which has created such extravagant monumental fantasies. Thus opera houses were built in a sense to upstage each other, to establish themselves not only as the foremost theatre within a nation but as the most remarkable theatre in the Western world. This is reinforced by the position they hold within urban configurations or morphology. The eighteenth-century San Carlo Theatre in Naples was placed next to Charles III's palace and connected to it by private corridors.[13] The Palais Garnier was placed in the centre of the nineteenth-century commercial district in Paris, and the twentieth-century Sydney Opera House crowns that city's harbour. Monuments have also been created traditionally as tools of political design to fulfil spatial and ceremonial requirements of ascendant regimes. The grand staircases, foyers and boxes all attest to their function.

The form of great monuments is commonly acknowledged to be a physical manifestation of a building's meaning, especially if the building is designed to house a state institution, so that it is possible for contemporary historians to espouse as acceptable truths ideas such as: 'Institutions, like individuals, must parade and display their glamour if they are to keep their glory alive.'[14]

Andrew Riemer reminds us that it is not only in England that opera symbolises the image a state wishes to project of itself. Writing on post-war Hungary, he affirms that:

> Opera is one of the means – perhaps the crucial one – of such a society's celebrating itself as a superior civilisation.[15]

Such a statement could equally well describe the reasons for the restoration of Covent Garden after the war, the creation of the Opéra Bastille after the election of France's first socialist government in half a century and the desire behind the NSW state government's support for the radical design of the Sydney Opera House.

This book has attempted to prove by cumulative example that opera has many facets. It is a performed work combining voice, dance, allegory, great archetypical mythology and machinery, but the art of opera does not exist without an opera audience attending an opera house, until, that is, we have the total activity we have termed 'the opera'. The opera house is a modern-day state palace. The experience of going there is a participation in state ceremonial. The clothing, the adornments, the refreshments, the transport are designed to evoke, as the present Prince of Wales wrote, 'the feeling of being somewhere rather special'.[16] This mystique which surrounds both the opera house and the operatic institution has aroused passion, fascination, resentment, but it has not left indifference.

For centuries society has debated the value of opera, and the nature of the operatic experience. We have seen great literary figures in England and France spurn opera, only then to discover that they themselves were frustrated librettists. We have also seen, over and over again, the opera house and the opera experience used as targets of popular invective. The notions of opera and house have been challenged by many regimes, but they have remained. The poignant example of the idea, design and construction of the Sydney Opera House well illustrates this point. Furthermore, it is often at the opera that governments are challenged or leaders go to present themselves to prove their successful escape from assassination attempts or to celebrate military or political triumph.

Most significantly, the language used to describe opera has remained consistent. It remains within the register of the superlative. 'Magnificence', 'glory', 'prestige', 'extravagance', 'gold', 'diamonds', 'grand' and 'noble' are some of the most common terms used to describe it, whether the writer be defending opera or deriding it.

Throughout this investigation many theories have been explored which contribute to understanding opera. From an historical perspective the evidence is overwhelming that it has been a consistent symbol recognised by all Western societies since the seventeenth century. In terms of social critics and theorists, it is a highly charged art which frequently divides the worlds of debate. From a semiotic viewpoint, it is a complex carrier of signs and symbols. The work, the house, the social codes, all contribute to investing opera with a highly charged meaning. Furthermore, even when there are subtle differences in concepts such as the nature of a state institution, opera transcends such barriers, making it a representation of some of the more complex elements of the state.

This book argues that opera owes something to all of the above and even more. It is because of its chameleon-like nature that it is so powerful. Through the ages opera has represented the pinnacle of culture even when culture shifted its power base. Thus in France, for example, an opera house (the Palais Garnier) designed for the needs of an empire could so easily be adapted to serve as a grand symbol epitomising a new republic.

In official declarations and language on opera we see time and time again the same arguments used by the state in order to justify its existence. Monarchs and governments from Louis XIV to François Mitterrand like to say that opera should exist in their country because it exists in other countries which rival theirs culturally. They also promote the notion that it attracts foreigners to their capital cities and is a significant employer which creates spin-offs for many industries. These arguments have been used by monarchies, democracies and revolutionary governments alike. It is important that, although many powers have queried the need for opera, they have all concluded that it is a vital part of the nation's assets.

These arguments continue to hold true today but are clouded by the ambiguous terminology of public relations language. Today's 'arts world', as we have seen, is focused on demonstrating to the enfranchised public that it has the 'right' to partake in the nation's cultural fruits. This is problematic, as demonstrated by Clive Priestley in his report to government on the Royal Opera House in 1983. He clearly could not give a satisfactory response to the following question put to him by a disgruntled tax payer:

> In recommending a higher level of funding for the ROH [Royal Opera House] I am conscious that the ROH is an institution which attracts controversy. This is captured in a nutshell in a letter whose author said that she and her husband and their three children would dearly like to see the Royal Ballet at Covent Garden but that it was beyond their means. She wondered how it could be right for a company supported by public funds to be so far out of reach of ordinary families.[17]

The composite examples which make up the thrust of this book clearly explain Priestley's dilemma. The writer has pointed to the dichotomy now evident between the language of 'accessibility' and the reality of the public funding of culture. The nation needs its national institution, if only to demonstrate to others, including 'ordinary families', that there is a national standard. There is, however, no room to invite all of the nation to participate in the experience. The nation can share in its reflected glory, take tours of the theatres, on occasion enter the house through schools' programmes or the sale on the day of performance of cheaper seats in the gods. This allows just enough 'accessibility' for government to maintain its agenda and yet argue that opera is open to all. One recalls the Canning/Isaacs debate in Chapter 4, in which Isaacs defends the institution's existence by arguing that today opera is not only accessible but also relevant to all aspects of contemporary culture, whereas Canning spurns opera as representing only the interests of the élite.

A further example of this dichotomy occurred in 1964, when a replacement for Sir David Webster was being sought by the Board of Covent Garden. Lord Harewood describes this contentious scene vividly:

> ...the matter of David Webster's successor was considered. Arnold Goodman was indignant since he felt the Arts Council should know what was being discussed and insisted that the post must be advertised. He was told this was not to be. '*Those Bourbons!*' he exclaimed. 'They are besotted with their own power and don't see that people from outside may come to question it.'[18]

Power on this occasion can be seen as resting in hands outside those of the democratically elected government of the day. The question of who should head this major national institution was therefore seen to be more critical than other government nominations for public posts.

As the power brokers change, so too do attempts to support the opera. In September 2000 it was reported that:

> A Danish billionaire is footing the £118 million bill to build Copenhagen's first opera house, which will be named after Queen Margrethe.
>
> Maersk McKinney Moeller is paying for the concert house to be built on a defunct navy base near the royal palace. The 87-year-old shipping magnate had earlier bought the grounds where the opera house will be built. *The government has now approved the plans.*
>
> Forbes magazine estimates that he is worth £2.3 billion. (my italics)[19]

Clearly Mr Moeller and his approving government, tacitly uniting with monarchy both in title and location, understand the need for the new and old power brokers to join forces in such an important venture.

Opera houses, it has been maintained, are the state palaces of old, reflecting the intrigues of shifting power bases and demonstrating permanence and grandeur. They will be maintained in capital cities or major cities which rival capitals, and they will continue to be designed and constructed. Essentially, opera houses distinguish themselves from the other arts by occupying a very different role relative to the state. In fact they invariably receive preferred treatment from it. This is because they are maintained by the state for many reasons, the least of which are artistic. It can be said, therefore, that in the United Kingdom today the Royal Opera House is not really competing with the other 'arts' for lottery money or subvention from arts councils or public donations. Furthermore, for the reasons which have been given, it will certainly continue to be funded rather more extensively than the other arts. Richard Morrison, the arts editor in *The Times*, forcefully espoused such a view.

> What most depressed me about the lottery-funded schemes so far proposed, however, is their utter predictability. Cities vie with each other for prestige: hence all these opera house and museum proposals. Existing cultural giants – Covent Garden, the South Bank – rush to bolster their own status quo with vast redevelopments.
>
> Nobody, it seems, is willing to step outside the constraints of self-interest and take a hard look at what the British arts scene actually *needs*. Where is the nationwide initiative to put arts education and performing opportunities back into classrooms? Or the imaginative voucher scheme that would provide, say, four free tickets a year for top-class performances to all those under 25? Either initiative could transform the cultural face

of Britain and build audiences far into the 21st century. Both could easily be funded by lottery money.

Yet neither will happen: nor anything remotely like them. Why? Because old pals would not benefit. Old school ties would not be acknowledged. Vision might be required, and a concept of public service rather than self-service. Does such public service exist in modern Britain? One lives in faint hope – just like the people in the queue for the scratch cards.[20]

Opera represents something much more deeply ingrained and grand than merely an 'old-school-tie' network, or inadequate structure of subvention or patronage. It is an institution with roots that are inextricably linked with the very concept of the state, which provides its ceremonial core.

Opera reverberates with significance. It is an accretion of high symbolism, not just in music but in the opera house itself. This is strengthened by time. Its permanence through the vicissitudes of social and political change demonstrates its importance, for physical constructs accrue their symbolism by weight of association over the years.

Throughout this book reference has been made to instances where opera has functioned as a venue for state ceremonial. The many factors which make up opera's broadest meaning do not possess the same functions individually, as no one aspect replaces the whole construct. This reinforces the central hypothesis that opera is extremely important to the state and is not a substitute for something else. It is not only a venue where those in power parade themselves, nor is it only an art, nor just a building, nor simply an elaborate social concept. It is itself of distinct and separate importance and is greater than the sum of its parts.

NOTES

1 INTRODUCING THE POWER BROKERS

1 In Finland in 1991 the state subsidy for opera was 111,420 FIM for 243 performances compared with the state subsidy for the national theatre of 35,450,000 FIM for 850 performances. By 1993 the sum for opera had increased to 122,500,000 for 222 performances compared with a small drop in subsidy to the national theatre of 35,336,600 for 830 performances. Source: Council of Europe, Arts Council of Finland, Research and Information Unit, page 158, Table 13B.

2 'Securing the Future: Major Performing Arts Inquiry Discussion Paper', July 1999. Published by Dept of Communications, Information Technology and the Arts, Canberra, Australia. Figures are based on those published under Exhibit 3.4 'Distribution of total government funding by artform and company: 1997', page 59.

3 Figures are based on those published on the NEA website: http://www.arts.gov/artforms/Opera.

4 *Washington Post Foreign Service*, 'On the Bubble: Opera Building Divides Beijing', by John Pomfret, 8 July 2000. N.B. Official figures for the cost of the house vary. This article appeared a few months after the others and therefore probably indicates the rising costs for the project, as opera house costs rise exponentially.

5 The Royal Opera House received the largest grant (£55 million) awarded by the Arts Council. Furthermore, this sum will increase; the Royal Opera House is expected to receive £71 million (*Evening Standard*, 6 August 1996).

6 Gourret, *Histoire des salles de l'opéra de Paris*, pp. 105–6. See also Bartlett, p. 108.

7 Bradshaw, pp. x–xiii.

8 The President of the Republic announced, on 9 March 1982, the decision to construct a new opera at the Place de la Bastille in Paris. This was cited by the Minister of Culture, Jack Lang, in his press release of 17 January 1983 announcing an international architectural competition for the opera house.

9 The competition to design the opera house was announced on 13 September 1955 by the NSW Labor Premier, John Cahill.

10 During the Great Depression in the United States, the Metropolitan Opera House maintained its reserves.

11 Quoted by Weaver, p. 29.

12 Horne, *The Public Culture*, p. 156.

13 The original brief is set out in *Opéra de la Bastille. Concours international d'architecture. Dossier élaboré par la Mission de la Bastille*, 1983.

14 Quoted by Dizikes, p. 531; from *New York Times*, 17 Sept. 1966.

15 Lumley, pp. 48–9.

16 Clément, p. 3.

17 Sir Christopher Wren, *Parentalia* (1750); from Humphreys, p. 3.

18 Edelman; quoted by Horne, p. 18.
19 Barthes, p. 247.
20 Schwarz, p. 13.
21 Urfalino, p. 258 (my translation). This is also cited by Saint Pulgent, p. 256.
22 Bevan, p. 88.
23 Bevan, p. 29.
24 Bevan, pp. 219–20.
25 Alda, p. 110.
26 Eyre, *Report on the Future of Lyric Opera in London*, 1998.
27 Department of National Heritage, *Annual Report 1994: The Government's Expenditure Plans 1994–5 to 1996–7*. Presented to Parliament by the Secretary of State for National Heritage and the Chief Secretary to the Treasury by Command of Her Majesty the Queen, February 1994. Chapter 1: The Role of the Department, *Rationale* 1.7, p. 2.
28 Department of National Heritage, *Annual Report 1994*, Chapter 1: The Role of the Department, *Rationale* 1.4, p. 2.
29 Dickens, *Hard Times*, pp. 59–61.
30 Véron, *L'Opéra de Paris 1820–1835*, p. 64.
31 Klein, Hermann, *Thirty Years of Musical Life in London 1870–1900*, p. 231.
32 Beecham, p. 88.
33 Pascal, Marie, 'The Present Crisis in Argentine Opera', translated by Ossia Trilling, in Rosenthal, *Opera Annual No. 4*, pp. 106–8.
34 *Renaissance City Report. Culture and the Arts in Renaissance Singapore*, March 2000, Ministry of Information and the Arts, Singapore.
35 Cahill, J.J. Premier of New South Wales, *Ceremony to Commemorate the Commencement of the Building of the Sydney Opera House*, 2 March 1959.
36 Sachs, p. 76.
37 H. Dalton, letter to Sir John Anderson, 1 August 1946; quoted in Pick, *The West End*, p. 158.

2 PRINCELY PLEASURES

 1 See Burney, *Music, Man and Manners in France and Italy 1770*; Stendhal, *Rome, Naples et Florence en 1817* and *L'Opéra Italien*.
 2 Rosselli, *Music and Musicians in Nineteenth century Italy*, p. 16.
 3 Rosselli, *Music and Musicians in Nineteenth century Italy*, p. 17.
 4 Napoleonic domination (1796–1814).
 5 Hughes, p. 117.
 6 Hughes, p. 117; Weaver, p. 10; Hardin, p. 15.
 7 See Rosselli, *The Italian Opera Industry in Italy from Cimarosa to Verdi*, p. 136.
 8 Sadie, *The New Grove Dictionary of Opera*, Vol. II, p. 838.
 9 Leacroft, pp. 47, 60, 45.
10 See Lindenberger, p. 238.
11 Rosselli, *Music and Musicians in Nineteenth-century Italy*, p. 59.
12 Jellinek, pp. 256–7.
13 Burney, Ed. Percy A. Scholes, Vol. I, p. 66.
14 Hughes, p. 185.
15 * Note from Burney: The fourth of November is likewise celebrated as the name-day of the Queen of Naples and the Prince of Asturias.
16 Burney, *The Present State of Music in France and Italy*; quoted in Strunk, p. 695.
17 Burney, *The Present State of Music in France and Italy*; quoted in Strunk, p. 695.
18 Weaver, p. 31.
19 Hughes, p. 191.

20 Weaver, p. 28.
21 Weaver, p. 29.
22 Weaver, p. 29.
23 Hughes, p. 183.
24 Stendhal, *Rome, Naples et Florence en 1817*; quoted and translated by Dizikes, p. 30.
25 Stendhal, *Rome, Naples et Florence en 1817*, p. 319.
26 Stendhal, *Rome, Naples et Florence en 1817*, p. 333 (19 mars 1817).
27 Stendhal, *Rome, Naples et Florence en 1817*, p. 334 (20 mars).
28 Hughes, p. 201.
29 Hughes, p. 211.
30 Arici and Saspores, p. 214.
31 Gishford, p. 38.
32 Hughes, p. 218.
33 Hughes, p. 220.
34 Gishford, p. 29.
35 Arici and Saspores, p. 165.
36 Arici and Saspores, p. 163.
37 Following the fire of January 1996, which completely razed the theatre, the city of Venice has chosen to rebuild the Fenice as it was, thus demonstrating that its tradition and monumental stature will be recreated in an entirely new edifice. This signifies the importance which this monumental opera house holds for the city of Venice.
38 Stendhal, *La Vie de Rossini*, pp. 461–2.
39 Hughes, p. 90.
40 Hughes, p. 90.
41 Gishford, p. 20.
42 Rosselli, *Music and Musicians in Nineteenth-century Italy*, p. 21.
43 Gishford, p. 21.
44 Stendhal, *Rome, Naples et Florence en 1817*, p. 26 (10 novembre 1816).
45 Hughes, p. 96.
46 Hughes, p. 97.
47 Segalini, p. 31.
48 Weaver, p. 10.
49 Stendhal, *La Vie de Rossini*, pp. 458–9.
50 Segalini, p. 32.
51 Hughes, p. 102.
52 See Segalini, p. 55.
53 Hughes, p. 107.
54 Weaver, p. 156.
55 Hughes, p. 112.
56 Alda, p. 71.
57 Weaver, p. 235.
58 Hughes, p. 117.
59 Braddon, pp. 175–6.
60 Gishford, p. 23.
61 *The European*, 20 November 1992.
62 *The European*, 'Imperial baths overflow with opera lovers' by Chris Endean, July 1993.
63 *Daily Telegraph*, 11 December 2000.
64 Sachs, p. 71.

3 OF KINGS AND BARRICADES

1 Dent, *The Foundations of English Opera*, p. 44.
2 Isherwood, p. 150.

3 Isherwood, and Catherine Kintzler in Cicero.

4 'Privilège de Perrin' 28 June 1669, quoted by Gourret, *Ces hommes*, p. 251.

5 'Privilège de Perrin', quoted by Gourret, *Ces hommes*, p. 251.

6 'Privilège de Lully' March 1672, quoted by Gourret, *Ces hommes*, p. 253.

7 'Privilège de Lully', quoted by Véron, *L'Opéra de Paris 1820–1835*, p. 160; Gourret, *Ces hommes*, p. 26.

8 'Privilège de Lully', quoted by Véron, *L'Opéra de Paris 1820–1835*, p. 161; Gourret, *Ces hommes*, p. 253.

9 See Strunk.

10 *Querelle des Anciens et des Modernes* 1702–10; *Querelle des Bouffons* 1754–60; *Gluckist/Piccinist* 1770s.

11 Quoted in Strunk, p. 480.

12 Quoted in Strunk, p. 487.

13 Cerf de la Vieville; English translation in Strunk, p. 489.

14 Isherwood, pp. 53–4.

15 Quoted in Saint Pulgent, p. 151.

16 Saint Pulgent, p. 151.

17 Quoted in Strunk, p. 632.

18 Rousseau, 1993, p. 141.

19 Quoted in Strunk, p. 627.

20 Quoted in Strunk, p. 671.

21 Burney, Ed. Percy A. Scholes, Vol. I, p. 16.

22 Burney, Ed. Percy A. Scholes, Vol. II, p. 81.

23 Mueller von Asow, p. 31. From *Mercure de France*, February 1773, 'Lettre de M. le Chevalier Gluck sur la musique'; see also Strunk, p. 682.

24 Jellinek, p. 296.

25 Le Roux, J.J., Officier municipal, administrateur aux établissements publics, 17 August 1791, Report to 'faire connaître si ce théâtre était absolument nécessaire au commerce de la capitale'; quoted by Gourret, *Ces hommes*, p. 92.

26 Le Roux, J.J., Officier municipal, administrateur aux établissements publics, 17 August 1791, Report to 'faire connaître si ce théâtre était absolument nécessaire au commerce de la capitale'; quoted by Gourret, *Ces hommes*, p. 93.

27 Le Roux, J.J., Officier municipal, administrateur aux établissements publics, 17 August 1791, Report to 'faire connaître si ce théâtre était absolument nécessaire au commerce de la capitale'; quoted by Gourret, *Ces hommes*, p. 93.

28 Gourret, *Ces hommes*, p. 93.

29 It is interesting to note that one of the qualities sought from state leaders is to remain calm in the face of personal attacks. In 1993 in Sydney, Australia, when the Prince of Wales was lunged at by a crowd member toting a gun in his hand, the press praised the Prince for his lack of concern. The image that is projected is of a leader who is less concerned about their person than their duty and thus can and would willingly serve the nation before all else.

30 Barbier, p. 6.

31 See, for example, Johnson, p. 168; Duault, p. 21.

32 Crosten, p. 14.

33 Crosten, p. 14.

34 References to this document are from Gourret, *Ces hommes*, p. 104.

35 Gourret, *Ces hommes*, p. 104.

36 Gourret, *Ces hommes*, pp. 104–5.

37 Gourret, *Ces hommes*, p. 104.

38 Quoted in Gourret, *Ces hommes*, p. 105.

39 Quoted in Gourret, *Ces hommes*, p. 104.
40 'Cahier des charges de la direction de l'opéra en régie intéressée (arrêté en commission et approuvé par M. Le ministre de l'intérieur, du 28 février 1831): Article premier – L'administration de l'Académie royale de musique, dite *Opéra*, sera confiée à un directeur-entrepreneur qui l'exploitera pendant six ans à ses risques, périles et fortune.' Quoted by Véron, *Mémoires d'un bourgeois à Paris*, p. 54 (full text reproduced pp. 269–77).
41 Véron, *Mémoires d'un bourgeois à Paris*, p. 54.
42 Véron, *Mémoires d'un bourgeois à Paris*, pp. 58.
43 Véron, *Mémoires d'un bourgeois à Paris*, p. 59.
44 Gourret, *Ces hommes*, p. 108.
45 Gourret, *Histoire des salles de l'Opéra de Paris*, p. 113.
46 This house was meant to be temporary but remained in use for the next fifty years until the Palais Garnier was completed in 1875.
47 Véron, *Mémoires d'un bourgeois à Paris*, pp. 65–6.
48 'Cahier des charges de la direction de l'opéra en régie intéressée (arrêté en commission et approuvé par M. Le ministre de l'intérieur, du 28 février 1831): Article 4. L'entrepreneur sera tenu de maintenir l'Opéra dans l'état de pompe et de luxe convenable à ce théâtre national.'
49 Véron, *L'Opéra de Paris 1820–1835*, p. 70.
50 Véron, *L'Opéra de Paris 1820–1835*, pp. 64–5.
51 Véron, *L'Opéra de Paris 1820–1835*, p. 196.
52 Véron, *L'Opéra de Paris 1820–1835*, p. 197.
53 Patrick Barbier advances the theory that opera was so allied in the minds of the public with those holding the reins of power that it was closed down by the rioters because of this: Barbier, p. 133.
54 Walsh, p. 48.
55 The policy initiated by the Ministère de la Culture in 1993 is now that opera is to be performed again at the Palais Garnier.
56 Gourret, *Histoire des salles de l'Opéra de Paris*, p. 185.
57 Patureau, *Le Palais Garnier*, p. 10.
58 Patureau, *Le Palais Garnier*, p. 10.
59 Mission de la Bastille, *Opéra de la Bastille. Concours international d'architecture. Dossier élaboré par la Mission de la Bastille*, 1983: Press Release, Ministère de la Culture, Jack Lang, Paris, 17 Jan. 1983.
60 Patureau, *Le Palais Garnier*, p. 431.
61 Patureau, *Le Palais Garnier*, p. 19. Patureau describes the way in which this 'palace', designed and constructed for one regime, was to so well serve and endorse the legitimacy of another, which in many senses represented antithetical political and social mores.
62 Saint Pulgent, pp. 153–4.
63 Boysse, pp. iii-iv.
64 Fumaroli, p. 24.
65 Fumaroli, p. 60.
66 Adorno, p. 80.
67 Boll, p. 47.
68 'Décret de nomination' of André Malraux as Ministre d'Etat chargé des affaires culturelles, 3 February 1959.
69 Lebovics, pp. 54–5.
70 Soubie, *Rapport 1987*, p. 67.
71 Soubie, *Rapport 1987*, p. 67.

72 Boll, p. 47.

73 *Le Monde*, 17 October 1967. 'Les subventions aux scènes lyriques sont d'une évident nécessité.'

74 'Opera Houses? – Blow them up! Pierre Boulez versus Rolf Liebermann', in *Opera*, June 1968, p. 445. Boll supports this view and with less emotive language explains the connection between opera and the state, describing opera as having the possibility of being a political instrument which could be used in the service of the state. See also Littlejohn, p. 28.

75 Jouffray, Alain. 'Avons-nous encore une académie nationale de musique? II. Le temps des désillusions', *Opéra, la revue française de l'art lyrique*, Mensuel numéro 115, 1 June 1976, p. 17.

76 Patureau, *Les Pratiquants de l'art lyrique aujourd'hui*, p. 1.

77 Mission de la Bastille; Fumaroli, p. 300. Fumaroli explains that even the term 'modern' is in the French sense a euphemism for traditional notions and habits, of which opera is one, its antecedents dating from notions established under the highly stylised reign of Louis XIV.

78 Soubie, *Rapport 1986*, p. 63.

79 Soubie, *Rapport 1986*, p. 63.

80 Soubie, *Rapport 1986*, p. 64.

81 Urfalino, p. 44. (M. Audon).

82 Urfalino, p. 217.

83 Saint Pulgent, p. 124.

84 Mission de la Bastille. Press Release, Jack Lang, Ministère de la Culture, Paris, 17 Jan. 1983.

85 Rémy, *Bastille*, p. 43.

86 Urfalino, pp. 149–50.

87 Soubie, *Rapport 1987*, p. 26.

88 Urfalino, p. 67 (Charlet).

89 Urfalino, p. 149.

90 *Time Magazine*, 18 September 1989, 'Paris à la Mitterrand' by Robert Hughes.

91 *Time Magazine*, 17 January 1994, 'Storming the Bastille'.

92 *Sunday Times Magazine*, 26 November 1994, 'Phantoms of the Opera' by Charles Bremner.

93 Saint Pulgent, pp. 244–5.

94 *Sunday Times Magazine*, 26 November 1994, 'Phantoms of the Opera' by Charles Bremner.

95 Urfalino, p. 218.

96 Urfalino, p. 223 (Audon).

97 Urfalino, p. 292 (Audon).

98 Urfalino, p. 271 (Dittman).

99 Saint Pulgent, pp. 304–5.

100 *Sunday Times Magazine*, 26 November 1994, 'Phantoms of the Opera' by Charles Bremner.

4 THE DISUNITED KINGDOM

1 Rodney Milne in *The Times*, 21 June 2000.

2 Philip Hensher in *The Independent*, 12 January 2001.

3 Report by the Culture, Media and Sport Committee, House of Commons Session 1997–98, First Report *The Royal Opera House, Vol. I, Report and Proceedings of the Committee*, 25 November 1997, p. xxviii.

4 BBC four-part documentary, *The House: Inside the Royal Opera House, Covent Garden.* Double Exposure, BBC, 1995.

5 Examples of such intervention are: Louis XIV's establishment of opera; the letter from the chancellor of the exchequer to the Arts Council of Great Britain (i.e. 'see that opera is not let down'); the maintenance of opera by the Paris Commune; the Bolshoi after the Russian Revolution.

6 The so-called democratisation of opera, which focuses on accessibility of opera, will be discussed later. Although 'an opera' is performed in this context, 'opera' is not fully represented in the grand public democratic arena.

7 Steele and Addison, pp. 74–5.

8 Similarly, it is valid to ask the question whether Rousseau, prompted by the success of his libretto *Le Devin du Village*, was not emboldened to lay scorn upon the French opera of his day, based as it was on different precepts from his own.

9 Joseph Addison, *The Spectator* (1710); quoted by Arundell, pp. 202–4.

10 Nalbach, p. 17.

11 Nalbach, p. 35.

12 This did not mean that the Italian opera performed was necessarily brought from Italy. It was the understanding that it had been written in Italian, or in an 'Italian spirit', and was performed often by English singers, or singers of many nationalities singing in a number of tongues.

13 Saint, p. 97.

14 Dent, *The Foundations of English Opera*, p. 104.

15 Nalbach, p. 36.

16 Nalbach, p. 36.

17 Hogarth, *Memoirs of the Opera*, Vol. 1, pp. 362–3.

18 Nalbach, p. 39.

19 Nalbach, p. 39.

20 Burney, Ed. Percy A. Scholes, Vol. II, pp. 91–2.

21 Nalbach, p. 42.

22 Burney, Ed. Percy A. Scholes, Vol. II, p. 92.

23 Nalbach, p. 46.

24 See, for example, White, *The Rise of English Opera*, p. 49.

25 White, *The Rise of English Opera*, p. 49.

26 Raynor, *Music in England*, p. 126.

27 Castil-Blaze, vol. 2, pp. 414–15.

28 Hobsbawm, p. 271.

29 *Morning Chronicle*, 26 March 1802.

30 Howe, Ed. p. 92.

31 Howe, Ed. p. 94.

32 Dent, *A Theatre for Everybody*, p. 59.

33 Ebers, pp. xviii–xxi.

34 White, *A History of English Opera*, pp. 295–6.

35 White, *A History of English Opera*, pp. 295–6.

36 Mackerness, p. 189.

37 Raynor, *Music in England*, p. 137.

38 Mapleson, pp. 42–3.

39 Hobsbawm, p. 271.

40 Mackerness, p. 187.

41 Mapleson, p. 142.

42 *London Illustrated News*, 11 June 1844.

43 The text of this prospectus is taken from *An Opera Souvenir* by Richard Northcott, specially written and published (by the Opera Publishing Co. London) for the 1919 Beecham Opera Season Covent Garden.' White, *A History of English Opera*, p. 399.

44 *Illustrated London News*, 1862 season; quoted by Rosenthal, *The Opera at Covent Garden*, pp. 53–4.

45 Ebers, pp. xix–xx.
46 Ebers, pp. xxi–xxii.
47 Macready, p. 104.
48 Mapleson, pp. 180–81.
49 Mapleson, pp. 180–81.
50 White, *A History of English Opera*, p. 298.
51 Haltrecht, pp. 51–2.
52 Dent, *Opera in English*, p. 9.
53 Dent, *Opera in English*, p. 10.
54 Drogheda, *The Covent Garden Album*, p. 22.
55 *The Times*, March 1946.
56 *The Times*, 21 February 1946.
57 *The Times*, 21 February 1946.
58 *The Times*, 8 February 1940 (review of *Don Giovanni* at Sadler's Wells).
59 Leventhal, F.M., ' "The Best for the Most" CEMA and State Sponsorship of the Arts in Wartime, 1939–1945', in *Twentieth Century British History*, Vol. 1, No. 3, 1990, pp. 316–17.
60 Leventhal, F.M. ' "The Best for the Most" CEMA and State Sponsorship of the Arts in Wartime, 1939–1945', in *Twentieth Century British History*, Vol. 1, No. 3, 1990, p. 316.
61 H. Dalton, letter to Sir John Anderson, 1 August 1946, quoted in Pick, *The West End*, p. 158.
62 'Crisis at Covent Garden', in *Opera Now*, March 1991, p. 14.
63 'English Composers at Covent Garden' by Eric Walter White, in Osborne, p. 43.
64 'The Resident Opera Company – Karl Rankl' by Frank Howes, in Osborne, p. 25.
65 'The Resident Opera Company – Karl Rankl' by Frank Howes, in Osborne, p. 25.
66 Littlejohn, pp. 27–8.
67 *The Times*, 12 April 1991, Lord Harewood reflecting on *Gloriana*.
68 Bevan, p. 22.
69 Braddon, p. 154.
70 Drogheda, *The Covent Garden Album*, 'Royal Galas' by Michael Wood, p. 50.
71 Drogheda, *The Covent Garden Album*, 'Royal Galas' by Michael Wood, p. 50.
72 Drogheda, *The Covent Garden Album*, 'Royal Galas' by Michael Wood, p. 50.
73 Lumley, p. 75.
74 Drogheda, *The Covent Garden Album*, 'Royal Galas' by Michael Wood, p. 50.
75 Drogheda, *The Covent Garden Album*, 'Introduction' by Harold Rosenthal, p. 19.
76 *The Times*, 17 June 1946.
77 *The Times*, 17 June 1946.
78 Drogheda, *The Covent Garden Album*, 'Royal Galas' by Michael Wood, p. 50.
79 Accessibility is not of course an easy term, as Mary Warnock seems to imply (Wallinger and Warnock). She makes the claim that the opposite of 'accessibility' is, of course, élitism. This is no foregone conclusion and a rather ambitious suggestion.
80 Adorno, p. 81.
81 Crispian Palmer in *The Guardian*, 27 October 1992.
82 Letter to the Editor, *Sunday Times*, 30 October 1994.
83 Letter to the Editor, *Sunday Times*, 30 October 1994.
84 Royal Opera House, Covent Garden Ltd, Annual Report, Press Notice 1985/1986, p. 2.
85 Robert Maycock, 'Crisis at Covent Garden – The Poverty Trap', in *Opera Now*, March 1991, p. 14.
86 Rémy, p. 14.
87 Advertisement 'The ladies who have become men's trophies', publicity for the book *The First Wives Club* by Olivia Goldsmith, *Daily Express*, 14 April 1992.
88 *Observer Magazine*, 5 May 1991.

89 David Mellor, former Secretary of State for National Heritage, writing in *High Life* (British Airways Inflight Magazine), September 1994 – the myth of the ordinary music lover as traditional opera-goer.
90 *The Guardian*, 20 April 1991.
91 Lebrecht, p. 495.

5 ALONG THE DANUBE AND THE RHINE

1 Prawy, plate xvii/1.
2 Hughes, p. 54; Osborne, *1966 Opera*, p. 154.
3 Prawy, p. 154.
4 Hughes, p. 30.
5 Hughes, p. 31.
6 Leopold's marriage was celebrated in 1669 by a performance of Cesti's *Il pomo d'oro*. At Louis XIV's marriage in 1662 Cavalli and Lully's *Ercole amante* was performed. At Charles VI's coronation in 1723 in Prague Fux's *Costanza e fortessa* was performed. Leopold 'contributed music to the gigantic operatic spectacle provided to celebrate his own marriage in 1666 to the Infanta Margareta of Spain' (Hughes, p. 32).
7 Hughes, p. 33.
8 Hughes, p. 33.
9 Sadie, *The New Grove Dictionary of Opera*, Vol. I, Vienna.
10 Bruce Alan Brown, 'Maria Theresa's Vienna', in Zaslaw, p. 101.
11 Hughes, p. 34.
12 Bruce Alan.
13 Hughes, p. 38.
14 Riemer, *The Hapsburg Café*, p. 72.
15 Hughes, p. 47.
16 Prawy, p. 28; Hughes, p. 47.
17 Prawy, p. 24.
18 See the film *The Edge of the Possible: The Story of Jørn Utzon and the Design and Construction of the Sydney Opera House*. Co-written and directed by Daryl Dellora. Produced by Sue Maslin. Film Art Doco Pty Ltd and The Australian Film Finance Corporation, Videocover Ronin Films, 1998.
19 Prawy, p. 24.
20 Prawy, p. 214.
21 Klein, Rudolf, *The Vienna State Opera*, p. 53.
22 Gishford, p. 150.
23 Prawy, p. 24.
24 Gishford, p. 153.
25 Gishford, p. 153.
26 Prawy, p. 100.
27 Prawy, p. 100.
28 Hughes, p. 53.
29 Prawy, p. 155. See also Saunders, Frances Stonor, pp. 14–16 for an account of Furtwängler's post-war status and Lebrecht *The Maestro Myth*, chapter 4.
30 Prawy, p. 155.
31 See Lebovics, chapter 1.
32 See Spotts, pp. 189–93.
33 Hughes, p. 54.
34 Prawy, p. 214.
35 Prawy, p. 153.
36 Hughes, p. 55.

37 Riemer, *The Hapsburg Café*, pp. 62–3. Riemer further develops this analogy by linking the Staatsoper to an historical and pan-European interpretation of the meaning of the house:

> The present theatre, though somewhat different from the original structure, preserves the social, cultural and spiritual assumptions on which the regal or ducal opera houses of Europe – from London to Moscow, from Stockholm to Lisbon – were based.

38 Littlejohn, p. 28.
39 Klein, Rudolf, *The Vienna State Opera*, p. 30.
40 Klein, Rudolf, *The Vienna State Opera*, p. i.
41 Klein, Rudolf, *The Vienna State Opera*, p. 6.
42 Osborne, p. 148.
43 Karl Ruppel, in Rosenthal, *Opera Annual No. 4*, p. 84.
44 Zaslaw, p. 242.
45 Koegler, in Gishford, p. 85.
46 Sadie, *The History of Opera*, p. 29.
47 Zaslaw, p. 242.
48 Zaslaw, p. 245.
49 Koegler, in Gishford, p. 83.
50 Sadie, *The New Grove Dictionary of Opera*, Vol. I, Berlin, p. 424. This account differs from Jellinek in terms of titles and years: 'The new, spacious Königliches Opernhaus (Royal Opera House) (was built) on the site of the old Festungswerken ... it included a canal system for cascades and waterfalls and also provided fire protection. It stood until 1843, when it burnt down. .... Inaugurated on 7 December 1742 ... Two years later ... the new Schlosstheater at Potsdam was completed and in service until Friedrich Wilhelm III had it dismantled in 1800.'
51 Jellinek, p. 257.
52 Koegler, in Gishford, p. 83.
53 Koegler, in Gishford, p. 83.
54 Burney, Ed. Percy A. Scholes, Vol. II, pp. 161–2.
55 Burney, Ed. Percy A. Scholes, Vol. II, p. 163.
56 Reichardt, in Strunk, p. 700.
57 Opera houses have often been enlisted by the state in times of national crisis because of their size and central locations. Dresden's opera house was used as a storage depot by the Prussians during the Seven Years War and England's Covent Garden served as a furniture repository during the Second World War.
58 Sadie, *The New Grove Dictionary of Opera*, Vol. I, Berlin, p. 427.
59 Hardin, p. 17: 'In 1919 it became the Staatsoper, or State Opera. Its most notorious remodelling to date occurred in 1935, when Paul Baumgarten (1900–1984) was commissioned by the Nazi Party to redecorate the vestibule and foyer in a manner becoming to the Third Reich. These have since been removed.'
60 Osborne, *Opera 66*, pp. 187–90, 191–3, 194–5.
61 MacDonogh, pp. 72–3. Quotation from Klaus Mann, *Mephisto*, Reinbek, 1981, p. 11.
62 Carey, p. 199.
63 Sadie, *The New Grove Dictionary of Opera*, Vol. I, Berlin, p. 430.
64 Koegler, in Gishford, p. 84.
65 Hans Busch, 'Trends in Post-war Germany', in Rosenthal, *Opera Annual 1954–1955*, p. 74.
66 Hans Busch, 'Trends in Post-war Germany', in Rosenthal, *Opera Annual 1954–1955*, p. 75.
67 Karl Ruppel, in Rosenthal, *Opera Annual No. 4*.
68 Carey, p. 208.

69 Leiris, *Opératiques*, p. 185.
70 Sadie, *The New Grove Dictionary of Opera*, Vol. I, Berlin, p. 431.

6 THE JEWEL IN THE CROWN

1 Schwarz, p. 15.
2 Schwarz, p. 11.
3 Schwarz, p. 14.
4 Schwarz, p. 12.
5 See Fitzpatrick, *The Commissariat of the Enlightenment*, p. 139.
6 Chaliapin, p. 30.
7 Buckler, p. 3. Julie Buckler comments that: 'It has been noted that the Russian Monarchy itself resembled a theatrical institution during the eighteenth century, staging elaborate coronations and pageants that extended across the entire city of St Petersburg.'
8 See Gishford, p. 214.
9 Jellinek, p. 275.
10 Jellinek, p. 277.
11 Buckler, p. 16.
12 Buckler, p. 4.
13 Buckler, p. 16.
14 Hardin, p. 29.
15 www.bolshoi.ru/eng/
16 www.bolshoi.ru/eng/
17 www.bolshoi.ru/eng/
18 Buckler, p. 8.
19 Buckler cites David J. Levin's view p. 8.
20 See Buckler, p. 8.
21 See Gishford, p. 214.
22 See Buckler, p. 27.
23 www.bolshoi.ru/eng/
24 Buckler, p. 4.
25 Benois, p. 40.
26 Buckler, pp. 8–9.
27 Benois, p. 131.
28 Volkov, p. 96.
29 Gishford, p. 215.
30 Volkov, p. 96.
31 Jellinek, p. 31.
32 Buckler, p. 9.
33 Volkov, p. 192.
34 Gishford, p. 220.
35 Volkov, p. 248.
36 Hardin, p. 30.
37 See Magarshack.
38 Benois, p. 40.
39 www.bolshoi.ru/eng/
40 www.bolshoi.ru/eng/
41 Schwarz, p. 465.
42 Bovier-LaPierre, p. 78.
43 Pick, *Off Gorky Street*, p. 30.
44 The Ministry Council of USSR Decree of 9 March 1987, 'About the measures of reinforcing material and technical base of the Bolshoi Theatre'.

45 This contemporary account in *The Times* has been verified by discussion with Graham Walne, one of the designers.
46 www.bolshoi.ru/eng/
47 www.bolshoi.ru/eng/
48 Maryinsky Theatre. St Petersburg 214th Season, Annual Publication No. 1.
49 *The Times*, 11 March 2000.

7 MAGNIFICENCE OF THE MET

1 See Da Ponte.
2 See Barnum.
3 See Mapleson.
4 There were other opera houses; see Ahlquist for a thorough account of the history of opera performance in New York.
5 See Ahlquist, p. 148.
6 Dizikes, p. 217.
7 Kolodin, p. 2.
8 Kolodin, p. 3.
9 Preston, p. 12.
10 Kolodin, p. 11.
11 Kolodin, p. 11.
12 Wharton, p. 13.
13 See Merkling *et al.* and Preston.
14 Merkling *et al.*, p. 23.
15 Merkling *et al.*, p. 23.
16 Wharton, pp. 147–8.
17 James, Henry, *The American Scene*, p. 124.
18 James, Henry, *The American Scene*, p. 124.
19 Briggs, John, p. 72.
20 Alda, p. 109.
21 Bonner, p. 26.
22 Bonner, p. 12.
23 Bonner, p. 14.
24 Bonner, p. 14.
25 Bonner, p. 17.
26 Kolodin, p. 53.
27 Bonner, p. 34.
28 See Preston, pp. 16–17; Briggs, John, p. 67.
29 Alda, p. 110.
30 Alda, pp. 109–10.
31 Kolodin quotes Gatti's memoirs, p. 140.
32 Kolodin, p. 239.
33 Kolodin, p. 260 and Alda, pp. 236–7.
34 Bonner, p. 67.
35 Alda, p. 288.
36 Alda, pp. 288–9.
37 Bonner, p. 73.
38 Merkling *et al.*, p. 97.
39 Merkling *et al.*, p. 198.
40 See Bonner, pp. 68–9.
41 Rubin, p. 39.
42 Rubin, p. 39.
43 Briggs, John, p. 261.

44 James Hinton Jnr, in Rosenthal, *Opera Annual 1954–1955*, p. 101.
45 Briggs, John, p. 295.
46 Braddon, p. 229.
47 Kolodin, pp. 365–6.
48 Bing, *Five Thousand Nights at the Opera*, p. 284.
49 Briggs, John, p. 326.
50 Briggs, John, p. 331.
51 Briggs, John, p. 332.
52 Merkling *et al.*, p. 281 (Epilogue by Anthony A. Bliss).
53 Dizikes, p. 531.
54 Dizikes, p. 531.
55 Martorella, p. 114.
56 Rubin, p. 38.
57 Saint Pulgent, p. 35.
58 Rémy, *Bastille*, p. 81.
59 Rémy, *Bastille*, p. 81.
60 Bing, *Five Thousand Nights at the Opera*, p. 338.
61 Bing, *A Knight at the Opera*, pp. 48–9.
62 Bing, *A Knight at the Opera*, Introduction by Garson Kanin, p. 17.

8 THE CHIP IN THE HARBOUR

1 It could be perceived as even more strange when Aboriginal civilisation has lasted, it is claimed, 40,000 years, and Aboriginals were the original settlers of the site on which the opera house now stands.
2 *The Sun*, front page, 17 October 1973.
3 By John Yeomans, author of the most definitive study of the house, who puts a most pertinent question (p. 3): 'How, then, did such a city become the possessor of an unforgettable palace built not for sports but for the arts, a palace which, whether you like or dislike this or that detail, gives off such an indestructible aura of magnificence that it is hard not to think of it as another Taj Mahal?'
4 Waites.
5 Cargher, *Opera and Ballet in Australia*, p. 117.
6 Cargher, *Opera and Ballet in Australia*, p. 117.
7 Cargher, *Opera and Ballet in Australia*, p. 117.
8 *Sydney Morning Herald*, 7 October 1948; quoted by Yeomans, p. 8.
9 Yeomans, p. 3.
10 Smith, *The Sydney Opera House*, p. 50.
11 Yeomans, pp. 1–2.
12 Yeomans, p. 160.
13 Smith, *The Sydney Opera House*, p. 65.
14 Smith, *The Sydney Opera House*, p. 65 (on the judges' criteria).
15 Arup and Zunz, p. 4.
16 Waites.
17 Smith, *The Sydney Opera House*, p. 77.
18 See Pick and Anderton for a more complete study of the relationship between lotteries and arts funding in the United Kingdom.
19 Examples of similar projects are the various attempts in England at funding opera by groups of gentlemen, e.g. Handel and Opera of the Nobility.
20 Cahill, Programme, 2 March 1959. *Ceremony to Commemorate the Commencement of the Building of the Sydney Opera House.*
21 Programme, 2 March 1959. *Ceremony to Commemorate the Commencement of the Building of the Sydney Opera House.*

22 Pick, *Managing the Arts*. Pick follows Titmuss in suggesting 'models' of behaviour by which governments achieve their aims in cultural planning. Governments create great emblematic cultural institutions because they wish to be remembered, and this is described by him as the 'Glory Model'. Professor Hampshire has said that it is ultimately a government's only valid motive for supporting the arts.

23 Cahill, August 1957, and Programme, 2 March 1959. *Ceremony to Commemorate the Commencement of the Building of the Sydney Opera House.*

24 Cahill, Programme, 2 March 1959. *Ceremony to Commemorate the Commencement of the Building of the Sydney Opera House.*

25 Jensen, H.F., Lord Mayor of Sydney. Programme, 2 March 1959. *Ceremony to Commemorate the Commencement of the Building of the Sydney Opera House.*

26 Hughes, Davis, leader of the NSW Country Party. Programme, 2 March 1959. *Ceremony to Commemorate the Commencement of the Building of the Sydney Opera House.*

27 Morton, P.H., leader of the State opposition, the Liberal Party. Programme, 2 March 1959. *Ceremony to Commemorate the Commencement of the Building of the Sydney Opera House.*

28 Moses, Charles, General Manager, Australian Broadcasting Commission. Programme, 2 March 1959. *Ceremony to Commemorate the Commencement of the Building of the Sydney Opera House.*

29 Walford, Leslie, in *Sun Herald*, 14 October 1973.

30 Cargher, *Opera and Ballet in Australia*, p. 119.

31 Transcript from videotape of the speech delivered by HM Queen Elizabeth II on the occasion of the opening of the Sydney Opera House, 20 October 1973.

32 *Sydney Morning Herald*, Editorial, 20 October 1973.

33 *Sun Herald*, 21 October 1973.

34 'Bennelong's Speech' by Victor Carell, Sydney Opera House Opening, 20 October 1973.

35 *Glasgow Evening Times*, 17 October 1973.

36 Smith, *The Sydney Opera House*, p. 141.

37 Hoffman, W.L., in *Canberra Times*, 23 January 1974.

38 Hoffman, W.L., in *Canberra Times*, 23 January 1974.

39 *The Bulletin*, 27 October 1973.

40 *The Bulletin*, 27 October 1973.

41 Yeomans, pp. 12–13.

42 Hughes, Gary, in *Melbourne Herald*, 20 September 1973.

43 Hughes, Gary, in *Melbourne Herald*, 20 September 1973.

44 *The Sun*, 23 October 1973.

45 *Sun Herald*, 21 October 1973.

46 *Daily Telegraph*, 25 September 1973.

47 *The Sun*, 5 November 1973.

48 Yeomans, p. 216.

49 Walford, Leslie, in *Sun Herald*, 21 October 1973.

50 Arup and Zunz, p. 4.

51 Kerr, p. 37.

52 Kerr, p. 28.

53 Smith, *The Sydney Opera House*, p. 36.

54 Pererauer, Maria, in *The Bulletin*, Arts, 7 November 1995.

55 Yeomans, p. 2.

9 OTHER OPERAS – OTHER WORLDS

1 Sadie, *The New Grove Dictionary of Opera*, Vol. I, Buenos Aires, p. 633.

2 Sadie, *The New Grove Dictionary of Opera*, Vol. I, Argentina, p. 166.

3 'A Short Historical Note on the Teatro Colon, Buenos Aires', in Rosenthal, *Opera Annual No. 4*, p. 109.

4 Hardin, p. 55.

5 'The Present Crisis in Argentine Opera', by Marie Pascal (translated by Ossia Trilling), in Rosenthal, *Opera Annual No. 4*, p. 106.

6 'The Present Crisis in Argentine Opera', by Marie Pascal (translated by Ossia Trilling), in Rosenthal, *Opera Annual No. 4*, p. 107.

7 Sadie, *The New Grove Dictionary of Opera*, Vol. I, Brazil, p. 590.

8 Sadie, *The New Grove Dictionary of Opera*, Vol. I, Brazil, p. 590.

9 Hardin, p. 55.

10 Hardin, p. 55.

11 Said, p. 155.

12 Sadie, *The New Grove Dictionary of Opera*, Vol. II, Istanbul, p. 833.

13 Sadie, *The New Grove Dictionary of Opera*, Vol. II, Istanbul, p. 833.

14 Sadie, *The New Grove Dictionary of Opera*, Vol. II, Istanbul, p. 833.

15 Sadie, *The New Grove Dictionary of Opera*, Vol. IV, Teheran, p. 674.

16 Sadie, *The New Grove Dictionary of Opera*, Vol. IV, Teheran, p. 675.

17 *South China Morning Post*, 'Pitch for Kowloon Opera House' by Alex Lo, 8 March 2000.

18 *Washington Post Foreign Service*, 'On the Bubble: Opera Building Divides Beijing' by John Pomfret, 8 July 2000, p. A11.

19 *Financial Times*, 'Beijing Opera House Plans Attacked' by James Kynge, 28 March 2000.

20 *Washington Post Foreign Service*, 'On the Bubble: Opera Building Divides Beijing' by John Pomfret, 8 July 2000.

21 *China Times*, 'Beijing Opera House: French Architect Expects Approval in a Month', 18 April 2000.

22 *China Times*, 'Beijing Opera House: French Architect Expects Approval in a Month', 18 April 2000.

23 *China Times*, 'Beijing Opera House: French Architect Expects Approval in a Month', 18 April 2000.

24 *Financial Times*, 'Beijing Opera House Plans Attacked' by James Kynge, 28 March 2000.

25 *Financial Times*, 'Beijing Opera House Plans Attacked' by James Kynge, 28 March 2000.

26 *China Times*, 'Beijing Opera House: French Architect Expects Approval in a Month', 18 April 2000.

27 *Washington Post Foreign Service*, 'On the Bubble: Opera Building Divides Beijing' by John Pomfret, 8 July 2000, p. A11.

10 BACK TO THE FUTURE?

1 The symbols and rituals associated with the opera are akin to high state ceremonies in another sense. Their derivation is often lost in the mists of time; it is their longevity, and the fact that they are always enacted at particular points in the ceremonies, which give them their significance and meaning. Few people, for instance, would recall the historical incident which gives rise to Black Rod beating on the doors of the House of Lords at the annual opening of the British Parliament, but the ceremony is invested with high significance nevertheless.

2 Until the Second World War everyone attending a theatrical first night in London or Paris wore formal evening dress (and many did so at other performances in the fashionable theatres). This is no longer the case, although significantly people still dress distinctly for opera-going. A random survey in London, Paris and Sydney showed that, out of 112 people questioned, *none* was prepared to say that they would go to the

opera wearing the same casual clothes they would wear to the theatre, or for visiting a major exhibition (1993/94).

3 Vincent, p. 6

4 See Littlejohn.

5 Examples of such intervention are: Louis XIV's establishment of opera; the letter of 1946 from the chancellor of the exchequer to the Arts Council of Great Britain, i.e. 'see that opera is not let down'; the maintenance of opera by the Paris Commune; the survival of the Bolshoi after the Russian Revolution.

6 In eighteenth-century France the opera of the court and the city were separated. In England the opera was financed by rival groups of nobility. In nineteenth-century France Véron stated that the opera of the 1830s was the triumph of the bourgeoisie. Later in the century the opera was to be very much an image of Napoleon III's prestige and, although the Palais Garnier was designed under his reign, it was to house the leading names of the Third Republic. In England opera was financed in the public domain by entrepreneurs but supported as an aristocratic pastime. Harris comments upon its need for support by the aristocracy as well as the effect that visits from the Prince of Wales had on the tone of the house. In the twentieth century opera has become the responsibility of the state in both England and France. In France it is financed through the Ministère de la Culture, the state department which is responsible for cultural expenditure. Opera, not surprisingly, is one of its greatest sources of expenditure. In England the Arts Council of England is the major supporter of opera, although there are quite substantial contributions from donors and sponsors. The notion of patronage, however, over the three centuries of opera's existence has been constant: one class supporting opera, which, in turn, supports the state.

7 Horne, *The Public Culture*, p. 157: 'In Denmark, although the Foketing meets in a royal palace, the monarch's only role in the opening of parliament is to sit in a royal box, as if parliament were an opera.'

8 The so-called democratisation of opera, which focuses on the accessibility of opera, has already been discussed. Although 'an opera' is performed in this context, 'opera' is not fully represented in the grand public democratic arena.

9 This did not mean that the Italian opera performed was necessarily brought from Italy. It was the understanding that it had been written in Italian or in an 'Italian' spirit and was performed often by English singers, or singers of many nationalities singing in a number of tongues.

10 Saint, p. 97.

11 Bevan, p. 261.

12 The state opera house in Finland, a glorious building in glass and white marble, is constructed in the most prestigious part of Helsinki, on the city's edge.

13 Lindenberger, p. 238.

14 Edelman, Murray. *Politics as Symbolic Action*; quoted in Horne, *The Public Culture*, p. 18.

15 Riemer, *Inside Outside*, p. 76.

16 Boursnell, p. 7.

17 Priestley, p. 51.

18 Harewood, p. 174.

19 Ananova virtual broadcaster: www.ananova.com, 7 September 2000.

20 Richard Morrison, in *The Times*, 29 April 1995.

BIBLIOGRAPHY

Adorno, Theodor W. *Introduction to the Sociology of Music*. The Seabury Press, New York, 1976.

Ahlquist, Karen. *Democracy at the Opera. Music, Theater and Culture in New York City, 1815–60*. University of Illinois Press, 1997.

Alda, Frances. *Men, Women and Tenors*. Houghton Mifflin Company, Boston, 1937, reprinted New York, 1971.

Allen, John and Watkins, Dennis. *The Eighth Wonder*. An Opera Australasia Libretto, No. 27, Pelliner Pty. Ltd, Sydney, 1995.

Allen, Mary. *A House Divided: The Diary of a Chief Executive of the Royal Opera House*. Simon and Schuster, 1998.

Amis, John and Rose, Michael, Eds. *Words About Music: An Anthology*. Faber and Faber, London, 1989.

Arici, Romanelli Pugliese and Saspores, Veroli, Ed. *Gran Teatro La Fenice*. Benedikt Taschen Verlag GmbH, 1999.

Arts Council of Great Britain. *Glory of the Garden: The Development of the Arts in England. A Strategy for the Decade*. Arts Council of Great Britain, London, 1990.

Arts Council of Great Britain. *Housing the Arts in Great Britain: Annual Report 1959*. Arts Council of Great Britain, London, 1959.

Arts Council of Great Britain. *Opera and Dance: Report of the Study Group*. Arts Council of Great Britain, London, 1983.

Arundell, Dennis. *The Critic at the Opera*. Ernest Benn, London, 1957.

Arup, Sir Ove and Zunz, Jack. *Sydney Opera House: A Paper on Its Design and Construction*. Sydney Opera House Reprint Series, No. 1, Sydney Opera House Trust, 1988.

Australia Council for the Arts. *Artburst! Growth in Arts Demand and Supply over Two Decades*. Hans Hoeh Gulberg Economic Strategies Pty. Ltd., 1992.

Australian Liberal/National Parties policy document (March 1996). 'For Arts Sake – A Fair Go for All of Us: The Importance of the Arts. Policies for a Coalition Government'. Australia.

Avery, Emmet L. and Scouten, Arthur H. *The London Stage 1660–1700: A Critical Introduction*. Southern Illinois University Press, 1968.

Barbier, Patrick. *La Vie Quotidienne à l'Opéra au temps de Rossini et de Balzac: Paris 1800–1950*. Hachette, Paris, 1987. Trans. by Robert Luoma as *Opera in Paris 1800–1950*, Amadeus Press, Oregon, 1995.

Barnum, P. T. *Barnum's Own Story: The Autobiography of P.T. Barnum*, combined and condensed from the various editions published during his lifetime by Waldo R. Browne. Gloucester, Mass., Peter Smith, 1972.

Barthes, Roland. 'The Eiffel Tower', in Susan Sontag, Ed. *Selected Writings*. Fontana, 1982.

Bartlett, M. Elizabeth. 'The New Repertory of the Opera during the Reign of Terror: Revolutionary Rhetoric and Operatic Consequences', in M. Boyd, Ed. *Music and the French Revolution*, Cambridge University Press, 1992.

Baumol, W.J. and Bowen, W.G. *The Performing Arts: The Economic Dilemma*. Twentieth Century Fund, New York, 1966.

Beaudouard, Jack. *Mourir à l'Opéra. Essai*. Société de Musicologie de Languedoc, Béziers, 1990.

Beavert, T. and Parmty, M. *Les Temples de l'Opéra*. Découvertes Gallimard, Paris, 1990.

Beecham, Sir Thomas. *A Mingled Chime: Leaves from an Autobiography*. Hutchinson & Co. Ltd., Essex, 1944.

Benois, Alexandre. *Memoirs*. The Lively Arts. Columbus Books, London, 1988.

Bergé, Pierre. *Liberté, j'écris ton nom*. Bernard Grasset, Paris, 1991.

Berlioz, Hector. *The Memoirs of Hector Berlioz including His Travels in Italy, Germany, Russia and England*. Trans. and Ed. by David Cairns. Panther Arts, London, 1970.

Bevan, Ian. *Royal Performance: The Story of Royal Theatregoing*. Hutchinson, London, 1954.

Bing, W.J., Sir. *Five Thousand Nights at the Opera*. Doubleday and Co., New York, 1972.

Bing, W.J., Sir. *A Knight at the Opera*. G.P. Putnam and Sons, New York, 1981.

Blaug, Mark. *Why are Covent Garden Seat Prices So High?* Royal Opera House, London, 1976.

Blom, E. *Music in England*. Pelican Books, Wyman and Sons, London, 1942.

Boll, André. *L'Opéra de l'avenir. Etude polémique*. Olivier Perrin, 1968.

Bonner, Eugene. *The Club in the Opera House: The Story of the Metropolitan Opera Club*. Princeton University Press, Princeton, New Jersey, 1949.

Boursnell, Clive. *The Royal Opera House Covent Garden*. Hamish Hamilton, London, 1982.

Bovier-Lapierre, Bernard. *Opéras: Faut-il fermer les maisons de plaisir?* Presses Universitaires de Nancy, 1988.

Boysse, Ernest. *Les Abonnés de l'opéra. 1783–1786*. A Quantin, Paris, 1881.

Braddon, Russell. *Joan Sutherland*. Collins, London, 1962.

Bradshaw, Martha, Ed. *Soviet Theaters 1917–1941: A Collection of Articles*. Research Program on the USSR, Brooklyn College, New York, 1954.

Briggs, Asa. *BBC: The First Fifty Years*. Oxford University Press, Oxford, 1985.

Briggs, John. *Requiem for a Yellow Brick Brewery: A History of the Metropolitan Opera*. Little, Brown and Company, Boston, 1969.

Brody, E. *Paris: The Musical Kaleidoscope 1870–1925*. George Bazilles Inc., Paris, 1987.

Brown, E., Ed. *The London Theatre 1881–1886: Selections from the Diary of Henry Crabb Robinson*. The Society for Theatre Research, London, 1966.

Buckler, Julie A. *The Literary Lorgnette: Attending Opera in Imperial Russia*, Stanford University Press, 2000.

Burford, E.J. *Wits, Wenchers and Wantons: London's Low Life. Covent Garden in the 18th Century*. R. Hale, London, 1986.

Burney, Charles. *Dr Burney's Musical Tours in Europe*. Ed. Percy A. Scholes. Oxford University Press, Oxford, 1959. First published as Vol. I *The Present State of Music in France and Italy* (1770), and Vol. II *An Eighteenth-Century Musical Tour in Central Europe and the Netherlands being Dr. Charles Burney's Account of his Musical Experiences* (1772).

Burney, Charles. *Music, Man and Manners in France and Italy 1770*. Ed. H. Edmund Poole. Folio Society, 1969.

Cahill, J.J., Premier of New South Wales. *Ceremony to Commemorate the Commencement of the Building of the Sydney Opera House*. Programme. Government Printer, Sydney, 2 March 1959.

Carey, John. *The Intellectuals and the Masses: Pride and Prejudice among the Literary Intelligentsia 1880–1939*. Faber and Faber, London, 1992.

Cargher, John. *Opera and Ballet in Australia*. Cassell, Sydney, 1977.

Cargher, John. *There's Music in My Madness and Opera as Well*. Thomas Nelson, Australia, 1984.

Carlson, Marvin. *Places of Performance: The Semiotics of Theatre Architecture*. Cornell University Press, Ithaca, 1989.

Castil-Blaze, François Henri J. *L'Académie Impériale de Musique de 1645 à 1855: Histoire littéraire, musicale, chorégraphique, pittoresque, morale, critique, facétieux, politique et galante de ce théâtre*. Vols I and II. Castil-Blaze, Paris, 1855.

Catchcart-Borer, Mary. *Covent Garden*. Abelard Schuman, London, 1967.

Central Opera Service Conference/Bulletin, Vol. 27, No. 1. (Spring/Summer 1986). Central Opera Service National Conference: An International Symposium. New York – November 1 and 2, 1985. Sponsored by the Metropolitan Opera National Council. In Collaboration with *Opera News*, celebrating the Metropolitan Opera Guild's Fiftieth Anniversary.

Chaliapin, Fedor. *An Autobiography as Told to Maxim Gorky*. Trans. and Ed. by N. Froud and J. Hanley. Macdonald, London, 1967.

Charlet, Gérard. *L'opéra de la Bastille: genèse et réalisation*. Editions du Moniteur, Paris, 1989.

Chesterfield, Philip Dormer Stanhope, Earl of. *Lord Chesterfield's Letters*. Oxford University Press, Oxford, 1992.

Chorley, Henry F. *Music and Manners in France and Germany: A Series of Travelling Sketches of Art and Society*. 3 Vols. Brown, Green and Longman, London, 1844.

Chorley, Henry F. *Thirty Years' Musical Recollections*. Ed. Ernest Newman. Alfred A. Knopf, London, 1926.

Christianson, Rupert. *The Grand Obsession: A Collins Anthology of Opera*. Collins, London, 1988.

Cibber, Colley. *An Apology for the Life of Mr. Colley Cibber, Comedian*. Ed. John Maurice Evans. London, 1987.

Cicero, Ed. *La Tragédie Lyrique: Les carnets du Théâtre des Champs-Élysées*. Paris, 1991.

Clément, Catherine. *Opera, or the Undoing of Women*. Virago Press, London, 1989; translation by Betsy Wing of *L'Opéra ou la défaite des femmes*, 1988.

Conrad, Peter. *A Song of Love and Death: The Meaning of Opera*. The Hogarth Press, London, 1987.

Council of Europe. *Cultural Policy in Europe, National Report*. European Programme of National Cultural Policy Reviews, Arts Council of Finland, Research and Information Unit, 1995.

Crabb-Robinson, H. *The London Theatre 1811–1866*. Ed. E. Brown. The Society for Theatre Research, London, 1966.

Crofton, Ian and Fraser, Donald. *A Dictionary of Musical Quotations*. Routledge, London, 1985.

Crosten, William L. *French Grand Opera: An Art and a Business*. King's Crown Press, New York, 1948.

Culture, Media and Sport Committee. House of Commons Session 1997–98, First Report, *The Royal Opera House, Vol. I, Report and Proceedings of the Committee*, 25 November 1997, The Stationery Office, London.

Culture, Media and Sport Committee. House of Commons Session 1997–98, Second Report, *The Royal Opera House: Responses by the Government and the Arts Council of England to the First Report from the Culture, Media and Sport Committee Session 1997–1998*, 5 February 1998, The Stationery Office, London.

Da Ponte, Lorenzo. *Memoirs of Lorenzo Da Ponte*. Introduction by Charles Rosen. New York Review of Books, 2000.

Dahlhaus, Carl. *Nineteenth-century Music*. University of California Press, Los Angeles, 1989.

Davidson, Jim. *Lyrebird Rising*. Melbourne University Press, Melbourne, 1994.

Davidson, Jim. 'Opera and Power', in *Meanjin*, Vol. 52, No. 2 (Winter 1993), pp. 313–24.

Demuth, Norman, Ed. *An Anthology of Musical Criticism*. Eyre and Spottiswood, London, 1947.

Dent, E.J. *The Foundations of English Opera*. Cambridge University Press, Cambridge, 1928.

Dent, E.J. 'The Nomenclature of Opera', in *Music and Letters*, No. 25 (1944), pp. 132–46.

Dent, E.J. *Opera*. Penguin, London, 1949.

Dent, E.J. *Opera in English*. Penguin, London, 1946.

Dent, E.J. *The Rise of Romantic Opera*. Ed. W. Dean. Cambridge University Press, Cambridge, 1976.

Dent, E.J. *A Theatre for Everybody: The Story of the Old Vic and Sadler's Wells*. T.V. Boardman and Co. Ltd, London, 1945.

Department of Communications, Information Technology and the Arts, Canberra, Australia. 'Securing the Future: Major Performing Arts Inquiry Discussion Paper'. July 1999.

Department of National Heritage. *Annual Report 1994*. HMSO, London, 1994.

Dickens, Charles. *Hard Times*. Oxford Paperbacks, Oxford, originally published 1854.

Diderot, Denis. *Le Neveu de Rameau*. Gallimard, Paris, 1972.

Dizikes, John. *Opera in America: A Cultural History*. Yale University Press, New Haven and London, 1993.

Donaldson, Frances. *The Royal Opera House in the Twentieth Century*. Weidenfeld and Nicolson, London, 1988.

Donington, Robert. *The Opera*. The Harbrace History of Musical Forms. Harcourt Brace Jovanovich, New York, 1978.

Donington, Robert. *Opera and Its Symbols: The Unity of Words, Music and the Myth*. New Haven, Connecticut, 1991.

Donington, Robert. *The Rise of Opera*. Faber and Faber, London, 1981.

Drew, Philip. *The Masterpiece: Jørn Utzon, A Secret Life*. Hardie Grant Books, Victoria, Australia, 1999.

Drogheda, Garrett Moore, Earl of, Ed. *The Covent Garden Album: 250 Years of Theatre, Opera and Ballet*. Routledge and Kegan Paul, London, 1981.

Drogheda, C.G., Lord. *Double Harness*. Weidenfeld and Nicolson, London, 1978.

Drummond, John D. *Opera in Perspective*. University of Minnesota Press, Minneapolis, 1984.

Duault, Alain. *L'Opéra de Paris: Histoire, mythologie, divas*. Editions Sand, Paris, 1989.

Duek-Cohen, E. *Utzon and the Sydney Opera House: Statement in the Public Interest*. Morgan Publications, Sydney, 1967.

Dupechez, C. *Histoire de l'Opéra de Paris*. Librairie Académique de Perrin, Paris, 1984.

Ebers, John. *Seven Years of the King's Theatre 1821–1827.* W.H. Ainsworth, London, 1828.

Edelman, Murray. *The Symbolic Uses of Politics.* University of Illinois Press, Chicago, 1964.

Edmond, Mary. *The Rare Sir William Davenant.* Manchester University Press, Manchester, 1987.

Ehrlich, Cyril. *The Music Profession in Britain since the Eighteenth Century: A Social History.* Clarendon Press, Oxford, 1985.

Evans, Ifor and Glascow, Mary. *The Arts in England.* Falcon Press, London, 1949.

Eyre, Sir Richard, CBE. *Report on the Future of Lyric Opera in London,* 30 June 1998, HMSO, London.

Federal Ministry for the Arts, Australia, *Creative Nation,* Commonwealth of Australia, October 1994.

Fenner, Theodore. *Opera in London: Views of the Press 1785–1830.* Southern Illinois University Press, Carbondale, 1994.

Fiske, Roger. *English Theatre Music in the Eighteenth Century.* Oxford University Press, Oxford, 1973.

Fitzpatrick, Sheila. *The Commissariat of the Enlightenment: Soviet Organization of Education and the Arts under Lunacharsky October 1917–1921.* Cambridge University Press, Cambridge, 1970.

Fitzpatrick, Sheila. *The Cultural Front: Power and Culture in Revolutionary Russia.* Cornell University Press, Ithaca, 1992.

Forsyth, Cecil. *Music and Nationalism: A Study of English Opera.* Macmillan, London, 1911.

Forsyth, Michael. *Buildings for Music: The Architect, the Musician and the Listener from the Seventeenth Century to the Present Day.* Cambridge University Press, Cambridge, 1985.

Foucher, Michel, Ed. *Les Ouvertures de l'Opéra: Une nouvelle géographie culturelle?* Collection Transversales, Presses Universitaires de Lyon, 1996.

Fulcher, Jane. *French Grand Opera as Politics and Politicised Art.* Cambridge University Press, Cambridge, 1987.

Fumaroli, Marc. *L'État Culturel: Essai sur une réligion moderne.* Editions de Fallois, Paris, 1992.

Gammond, Peter. *How to Bluff Your Way in Opera.* Ravette Publishing, West Sussex, 1989.

Geissmar, Berta. *The Baton and the Jackboot.* Hamish Hamilton, London, 1944.

Gishford, Anthony, Ed. *Grand Opera: The Story of the World's Leading Opera Houses and Personalities.* Weidenfeld and Nicolson, 1972.

Gorce, Jérome de la. *L'Opéra à Paris au temps de Louis XIV: Histoire d'un théâtre.* Editions Desjonquères, Paris, 1992.

Gourret, Jean. *Ces hommes qui ont fait l'Opéra 1669–1984.* Editions Albatros, Paris, 1984.

Gourret, Jean. *Histoire des salles de l'Opéra de Paris.* Guy Trédaniel, Editions de la Maisnie, Paris, 1985.

Grout, Donald Jay. *A Short History of Opera.* Revised edition by H.W. Williams. Columbia University Press, New York and London, 1988.

Gruneisen, C.L. *The Opera and the Press.* Robert Hardwicke, London, 1869.

Guthrie, Tyrone. *The Opera in English.* Bodley Head, London, 1946.

Gyger, Alison. *Opera for the Antipodes.* Currency Press, Sydney, 1990.

Haltrecht, M. *The Quiet Showman: Sir David Webster and the Royal Opera House.* Collins, London, 1975.

Hardin, Terri. *Theatres and Opera Houses: Masterpieces of Architecture.* Totdri Productions Limited, New York, 1999.

Harewood, George Lascelles, Earl of. *The Tongs and the Bones: The Memoirs of Lord Harewood.* Weidenfeld and Nicolson, London, 1981.

Hayworth, Peter. 'The End of Opera?', in *Opera*, September 1968, pp. 696–702.

Hazlitt, William. *Hazlitt on Theatre: Selections from the View of the English Stage, and Criticisms and Dramatic Essays*. Hill and Wang, New York, 1957.

Henze, H.W. *Music and Politics*. Faber and Faber, London, 1982.

Hobsbawm, E.J. *The Age of Revolution: Europe from 1789–1848*. Weidenfeld and Nicolson, London, 1962.

Hobsbawm, E.J. and Ranger, Terence, Eds. *The Invention of Tradition*. Cambridge University Press, Cambridge, 1983.

Hogarth, George. *Memoirs of the Opera in Italy, France, Germany and England*. Volumes I and II. Da Capo Press, Music Reprint Series, 1969.

Hogarth, George. *Musical History, Biography and Criticism*. Da Capo Press, Music Reprint Series, 1969.

Horne, Donald. *The Great Museum: The Re-presentation of History*. Pluto Press, London, 1984.

Horne, Donald. *The Public Culture: The Triumph of Industrialism*. Pluto Press, London, 1986.

Howe, P.P. Ed. *Complete Works of William Hazlitt. Centenary Edition*. After the edition of A.R. Waller and Arnold Glover. Volume Twenty. Miscellaneous Writings, *On The Opera*. J.M. Dent and Sons Ltd, London and Toronto.

Hubble, Ava. *More than an Opera House*. Landsdowne Press, Sydney, 1983.

Hubble, Ava. *The Strange Case of Eugene Goosens*. Collins Australia, 1988.

Hughes, P.C. (Spike). *Great Opera Houses: A Traveller's Guide to Their History and Traditions*. Weidenfeld and Nicolson, London, 1956.

Humphreys, Arthur. 'The Arts in Eighteenth-century Britain', in Boris Ford, Ed. *Cambridge Cultural History of Britain*, Vol. 5. Cambridge, Cambridge University Press, 1992.

Isaacs, Jeremy. *Never Mind the Moon: My Time at the Royal Opera House*, Bantam Press, 1999.

Isherwood, Robert M. *Music in the Service of the King: France in the Seventeenth Century*. Cornell University Press, Ithaca, New York, 1973.

James, Henry. *The American Scene*. Penguin Classics, 1994.

Jellinek, George. *History through the Opera Glass*. Kahn and Averill, 1994.

Johnson, James H. *Listening in Paris: A Cultural History*. University of California Press, Los Angeles, 1995.

Kahane, Martine. *Le Foyer de la Danse*. Les Dossiers du Musée d'Orsay, 22. Ministère de la culture et de la communication, Editions de la réunion des musées nationaux, Paris, 1988.

Kerman, Joseph. *Opera as Drama*. Random House, New York, 1952.

Kerr, James Semple. *Sydney Opera House: An Interim Plan for the Conservation of the Sydney Opera House and its Site*. Sydney Opera House Trust, Sydney, 1993.

Keynes, John Maynard. 'The Arts Council: Its Policy and Hopes.' Text of BBC broadcast, reprinted from *The Listener*, 12 July 1945.

Kleberg, Lars. *Theatre as Action: Soviet Russian Avant-garde Aesthetics*. Trans. from Swedish by Charles Rougle. Macmillan, London, 1993.

Klein, Hermann. *The Golden Age of Opera*. G. Routledge and Sons, London, 1933.

Klein, Hermann. *Thirty Years of Musical Life in London 1870–1900*. Da Capo Press, Music Reprint Series, Century and Co., New York, 1978.

Klein, Rudolf. *The Vienna State Opera: An Account of the Opera House and Its Hundred Years' History*. Verlag Elisabeth Lafite, Vienna, 1969 (second edition) [1967].

Koestenbaum, Wayne. *The Queen's Throat: Opera, Homosexuality and the Mystery of Desire*. Poseidon Press, New York, 1993.

Kolodin, Irving. *The Metropolitan Opera 1883–1966: A Candid History*. Alfred A. Knopf, New York, 1966.

Lane, J., Ed. *Opera in English: Sadler's Wells Contributions by T. Guthrie, E. Evans, J. Cross, E.J. Dent, N. de Valois*. Opera Books, The Bodley Head, London, 1945.

Le Huray, Peter and Day, James. *Music and Aesthetics in the 18th and early 19th Centuries*. Cambridge Readings in the Literature of Music, Cambridge University Press, Cambridge, 1981.

Leacroft, R. and H. *Theatre and Playhouse: An Illustrated Survey of Theatre Building from Ancient Greece to the Present Day*. Methuen, London, 1984.

Lebovics, Herman. *Mona Lisa's Escort: André Malraux and the Reinvention of French Culture*. Cornell University Press, Ithaca, 1999.

Lebrecht, Norman. *Covent Garden, the Untold Story: Dispatches from the English Culture War 1945–2000*. Simon and Schuster, 2000.

Lebrecht, Norman. *The Maestro Myth: Great Conductors in Pursuit of Power*. Simon and Schuster, 1991.

Leiris, Michel. *L'Age d'homme*. Editions Gallimard, Paris, 1946. Trans. as *Manhood* by Richard Howard. Jonathan Cape, London, 1963.

Leiris, Michel. *Opératiques*. P.O.L. Editeur, Paris, 1992.

Leventhal, F.M. ' "The Best for the Most" CEMA and State Sponsorship of the Arts in Wartime, 1939–1945', in *Twentieth Century British History*, Vol. 1, No. 3, 1990, pp. 289–317.

Levin, David J., Ed. *Opera Through Other Eyes*. Stanford University Press, 1993.

Lidderlow, Eden. 'Mozart, Europe and Economic Rationalism: A Digression', in *Meanjin*, Vol. 52, No. 2 (Winter 1993), pp. 325–33.

Liebermann, Rolf. *En passant par Paris*. Gallimard, Paris, 1980.

Lindenberger, Herbert. *Opera: The Extravagant Art*. Cornell University Press, Ithaca, 1984.

Littlejohn, David. *The Ultimate Art: Essays Around and About Opera*. University of California Press, Berkeley and Los Angeles, California, 1992.

Lumley, Benjamin. *Reminiscences of the Opera*. Da Capo Press, Music Reprint Series, New York, 1976.

MacDonnell, Justin. *Arts, Minister? Government Policy and the Arts*. Currency Press, Sydney, 1992.

MacDonogh, Giles. *Berlin: A Portrait of Its History, Politics, Architecture and Society*. St Martin's Press, New York, 1998.

Mackerness, E.D. *A Social History of English Music*. Routledge and Kegan Paul, London, 1964.

Macqueen Pope, W.J. *Theatre Royal Drury Lane*. W.W. Allen, London, 1945.

Macready, William Charles. *The Journal of William Charles Macready, 1832–1851*. Ed. J.C. Trewin. London, Longmans, 1967.

Magarshack, David. *Stanislavski: A Life*. Faber and Faber, London, 1950.

Mander, Raymond and Mitchenson, Joe. *Theatres of London*. Hart-Davis, London, 1961.

Mapleson, James Henry. *The Mapleson Memoirs 1848–1888*. 2 vols. Remington & Co., Covent Garden, London, 1888.

Martinoty, Jean-Louis. *L'Opéra Imaginaire*. Editions Messidor, Paris, 1991.

Martorella, Roseanne. *The Sociology of Opera*. Praeger Special Studies, New York, 1982.

Matthews, Thomas. *The Splendid Art: A History of Opera*. Crowell Collier Press, Macmillan, New York, 1970.

Mellers, Wilfrid Howard. *The Masks of Orpheus: Seven Stages in the Story of European Music*. Manchester University Press, Manchester, 1987.

Mellers, Wilfrid Howard. *Music and Society: England and the European Tradition.* Whitehall Printers Limited, London, 1946.

Merkling, Frank, Freeman, John W., and Fitzgerald, Gerald, with Stolin, Arthur. *The Golden Horseshoe: The Life and Times of the Metropolitan Opera House.* The Viking Press, New York, 1965.

Merlin, G., Fribourg, S.A. and Lessing, E. *L'Opéra de Paris.* Hatiers Editions, 1975.

Messent, David. *Opera House Act One.* David Messent Photography, Sydney, 1997.

Minihan, Janet. *The Nationalisation of Culture.* Routledge, London, 1977.

Ministry of Information and the Arts, Singapore. *Renaissance City Report: Culture and the Arts in Renaissance Singapore*, March 2000.

Mission de la Bastille. *Opéra de la Bastille. Concours international d'architecture. Dossier élaboré par la Mission de la Bastille.* Press Release, Jack Lang, Ministère de la Culture, Paris, 17 Jan. 1983.

Montagu-Nathan, M. *A History of Russian Music.* The New Temple Press, Norbury, 1914.

Mount Edgcumbe, Richard, 2nd Earl of. *Musical Reminiscences: Containing an Account of the Italian Opera in England from 1773.* F.W. Wall, Richmond, Surrey, 4th edition, 1834.

Mueller von Asow, H. and E.H. Eds. *The Collected Correspondence and Papers of Christoph Willibald Gluck.* Barrie and Rockliff, London, 1962.

Nalbach, D. *The King's Theatre 1704–1867.* The Society for Theatre Research, London, 1972.

Nicoll, Allardyce. *World Drama from Aeschylus to Anouilh.* Harrap, London, 1947.

Nietzsche, F. *Le Cas Wagner*, suivi de *Nietzsche contre Wagner.* Gallimard, Collection Folios Essaies, 1974. Original title: *Der Fall Wagner, Nietzsche Contra Wagner 1888–1889* (1888).

Novelli, Luigi. *Shanghai Architecture & the City between China and the West.* Edizioni Libreri Dedalo, Rome, 1999.

Nuitter, Charles. *Le Nouvel Opéra (Garnier).* Claude Tchou pour la Bibliotheque des Introuvables, 1875.

Opera, June 1968, 'Opera Houses? – Blow them up! Pierre Boulez versus Rolf Liebermann', pp. 440–50; articles reprinted from *Der Spiegel* and *Die Welt.*

Orrey, L. *Opera.* Updated by R. Milnes. Thames and Hudson, London, 1987.

Osborne, Charles, Ed. *Opera 66.* Alan Ross, London, 1966.

Osborne, Charles, Ed. *The Opera House Album: A Collection of Turn-of-the-century Post Cards 1897–1914.* Robson Books, London, 1979.

Palisca, Claude V. *The Florentine Camerata: Documentary Studies and Translations.* Yale University Press, 1989.

Patureau, Fréderique. *Le Palais Garnier dans la Société Parisienne 1875–1914.* Mardaga, Liège, 1991.

Patureau, Fréderique. *Les pratiquants de l'art lyrique aujourd'hui: Une étude du public actuel de l'opéra de Paris.* Editions de la Maison des Sciences de l'Homme, Paris, 1991.

Pick, John. *Off Gorky Street.* City Arts, London, 1984.

Pick, John, Ed. *The State and The Arts.* City Arts, London, 1980.

Pick, John. *Vile Jelly: The Birth, Life, and Lingering Death of the Arts Council of Great Britain.* Brynmill Press, Norfolk, 1991.

Pick, John. *The West End: Mismanagement and Snobbery.* City Arts, London, 1983.

Pick, John and Anderton, Malcolm. *Building Jerusalem: Art, Industry and the British Millennium.* Harwood Academic Press, London, 1999.

Pistone, Danièle. *Nineteenth-century Italian Opera from Rossini to Puccini.* Trans. by E. Thomas Glasow. Amadeus Press, Portland, Oregon, 1991. (Orig. *L'Opéra italien au XIXe siècle de Rossini à Puccini,* Editions Champion, Paris, 1986.)

Pitou, Spire. *The Paris Opéra: An Encyclopedia of Operas, Ballets, Composers and Performers, Rococo and Romantic 1715–1815.* Greenwood Press, 1983.

Pleasants, Henry. *Opera in Crisis: Tradition, Present, Future.* Thames and Hudson, London, 1989.

Poizat, M. *L'Opéra ou le cri de l'ange: Essai sur la jouissance de l'amateur d'opéra.* Editions Métailié, Paris, 1986.

Prawy, Marcel. *The Vienna Opera.* Weidenfeld and Nicolson, London, 1970.

Preston, Stuart, Ed. *Farewell to Old House: The Metropolitan Opera House 1883–1968.* Doubleday and Company Inc., New York, 1966.

Price, Curtis A. *Henry Purcell and the London Stage.* Cambridge University Press, Cambridge, 1984.

Priestley, Clive. *Financial Scrutiny of the Royal Opera House, Covent Garden Ltd.* Vols I & II, Report to the Earl of Gowrie, Minister for the Arts. HMSO, London, 1984.

Prod'homme, J.-G. *L'Opéra 1669–1925.* Librairie Delagrave, Paris, 1925.

Prunières, Henry. *L'Opéra italien en France avant Lulli.* Librairie Ancienne Honoré Champion, Edouard Champion, Paris, 1913.

Raynor, Henry. *Music and Society since 1815.* Anchor Press, London, 1976.

Raynor, Henry. *Music in England.* Robert Hale, London, 1980.

Raynor, Henry. *A Social History of Music from the Middle Ages to Beethoven.* Barrie and Jenkins, London, 1992.

Reid, C. *The Music Monster: A Biography of James William Davison, Music Critic of The Times of London 1846–1878.* Quartet Books, London, 1984.

Rémy, Pierre-Jean. *Bastille: Rêver un opéra. Carnets.* Plon, Paris, 1989.

Rémy, Pierre-Jean. *Covent Garden: Histoire, mythologie, divas, renseignements pratiques.* Editions Sand, Paris, 1989.

Riemer, Andrew. *The Hapsburg Cafe.* Angus and Robertson, Sydney, 1993.

Riemer, Andrew. *Inside Outside.* Angus and Robertson, Sydney, 1994.

Rio, M.-N. and Rostain, M. *L'Opéra mort ou vif?* Editions Recherches/Encres, Paris, 1982.

Rosenthal, Harold. *Covent Garden: Memories and Traditions.* Joseph, London, 1976.

Rosenthal, Harold. *My Mad World of Opera.* London, Weidenfeld and Nicolson, 1982.

Rosenthal, Harold, Ed. *Opera Annual 1954–1955.* John Calder, London, 1954.

Rosenthal, Harold, Ed. *Opera Annual No. 4.* John Calder, London, 1957.

Rosenthal, Harold. *Opera at Covent Garden: A Short History.* Victor Gollancz Ltd, London, 1967.

Rosenthal, Harold, Ed. *Royal Opera House, Covent Garden, 1858–1958.* London, 1958.

Rosenthal, Harold. *Two Centuries of Opera at Covent Garden.* Putnam and Co. Ltd., London, 1958.

Ross, A., Ed. *Richard Steele and Joseph Addison: Selections from* The Tatler *and* The Spectator. Penguin Classics, 1988.

Rosselli, John. *The Italian Opera Industry in Italy from Cimarosa to Verdi: The Role of the Impresario.* Cambridge University Press, Cambridge, 1984.

Rosselli, John. *Music and Musicians in Nineteenth-century Italy.* Amadeus Press, Portland, Oregon, 1991.

Rousseau, Jean-Jacques. *Essai sur l'origine des langues ou il est parlé de la mélodie et de l'imitation musicalle suivi de Lettre sur la musique français et examen de deux principes avancés par M. Rameau.*

(1753) Reprinted Flammarion, Paris, 1993. Abridged Eng. translation in Strunk, *Source Readings in Music History*.

Rubin, Stephen E. *The New Met in Profile*. Macmillan Publishing Co. Inc., New York, 1974.

Sachs, Harvey. *Music in Fascist Italy*. W.W. Norton & Co., New York, 1987.

Sadie, Stanley, Ed. *The History of Opera*. The New Grove Handbooks in Music. Macmillan, London, 1989.

Sadie, Stanley, Ed. *The New Grove Dictionary of Opera*. 4 vols. Macmillan, London, 1992.

Said, Edward. *Culture and Imperialism*. Chatto and Windus Ltd, London, 1993.

Saint, Andrew, Ed. *A History of the Royal Opera House, Covent Garden 1732–1982*. The Royal Opera House, London, 1982.

Saint-Geours, Jean-Philippe. *Le Théâtre national de l'Opéra de Paris*. Que sais-je? Presses Universitaires de France, 1992.

Saint Pulgent, Maryvonne de. *Le Syndrome de l'Opéra*. Editions Robert Lafont, Paris, 1991.

Salazar, P.J. *Idéologies de l'Opéra*. Presses Universitaires de France, 1980.

Saunders, Frances Stonor. *Who Paid the Piper? The CIA and the Cultural Cold War*. Granta Books, London, 1999.

Saxe Wyndham, Henry. *Annals of Covent Garden Theatre from 1732–1897*. 2 Volumes, Chatto and Windus, London, 1906.

Scannell, Paddy. 'A conspiracy of Silence: The State, the BBC and Public Opinion in the Formative Years of British Broadcasting', in G. McLennan, D. Held and S. Hall, Eds. *State and Society in Contemporary Britain: A Critical Introduction, 1922–39*. Polity Press, 1994.

Scholes, Percy A. *The Mirror of Music 1844–1944: A Century of Musical Life in Britain as Reflected in the Pages of the Musical Times*, Vols I & II. Novello & Co., London, 1947.

Schwarz, Boris. *Music and Musical Life in Soviet Russia 1917–1970*. W.W. Norton & Co., New York, 1972.

Seebohm, Andrea, Ed. *The Vienna Opera*. Rizzoli International Publications, New York, 1987.

Segalini, Sergio. *La Scala: Histoire, mythologie, divas, renseignements pratiques*. Editions Sand, Paris, 1989.

Shaw, George Bernard. *London Music in 1888–1889 and Music in London, 1890–1894*. (1932) 3 Vols. Constable, London, 1937.

Shaw, Sir Roy. *Élitism versus Populism in the Arts*. City Arts Series, General Ed. John Pick. John Offord Publications, no year of publication.

Shawe-Taylor, Desmond. *Covent Garden*. Max Parish & Co., London, 1948.

Simpson, Adrienne E. *Opera in New Zealand: Aspects of History and Performance Arts*. The Witham Press, 1990.

Smith, Vincent. *The Sydney Opera House*. Paul Hamlyn, Sydney, 1974.

Smith, William C., Ed. *The Italian Opera and Contemporary Ballet in London 1789–1820: A Record of Performances and Players with Reports from the Journals of the Times*. The Society for Theatre Research, London, 1955.

Soubie, Raymond. *Rapport au Ministre de la Culture et de la Communication sur la situation et les perspectives de l'Opéra*. 1987. Préstenté par Raymond Soubie. Président du Conseil d'Administration du Théâte National de L'Opéra de Paris.

Spotts, Frederic. *Bayreuth: A History of the Wagner Festival*. Yale University Press, New Haven and London, 1994.

Stanford, Charles V. *Interludes: Records and Reflections*. John Murray, London, 1922.

Stendhal. *L'Opéra Italien: Notes d'un dilettante par Henri Beyle, dit Stendhal*. Editions Michèle de Maule, Paris, 1824.

Stendhal. *Rome, Naples et Florence en 1817*. Julliard Littérature, Paris, 1817.

Stendhal. *La Vie de Rossini*. Editions Gallimard, 1992 [1824].

Stone, Marla Susan. *The Patron State: Culture and Politics in Fascist Italy*. Princeton University Press, New Jersey, 1998.

Strunk, Oliver. *Source Readings in Music History from Classical Antiquity through the Romantic Era*. W.W. Norton & Company, New York, 1959.

Swanston, Hamish E.G. *In Defence of Opera*. Penguin, Harmondsworth, 1968.

Sydney Opera House. *Draft Strategic Plan 1995–2000*. March 1995.

Sydney Opera House. *Draft Business Objectives and Priorities 1995–96*. March 1995.

Sydney Opera House officially opened by Her Majesty, Queen Elizabeth II, accompanied by His Royal Highness, the Duke of Edinburgh, on Saturday, October 20, 1973. *Official Souvenir*.

Sydney Opera House Trust. *Corporate Plan 1993–1997*. 30 June 1993.

Thorncroft, Anthony. 'Opera Elite', 'Opera Costs and Ticket Prices', 'Opera for the Masses of Europe', in *The Economist*. World Press Review, 1994.

Throsby, D. and Withers, G. *The Economics of the Performing Arts*. Edward Arnold, 1979.

Tolstoy, Leo. *Anna Karenina*. (1877) Trans. by Rosemary Edmonds. Penguin Classics, London, 1954.

Tooley, John. *In House: Covent Garden 50 Years of Opera and Ballet*. Faber and Faber, London, 1999.

Urfalino, Philippe. *Quatre voix pour un opéra: une histoire de l'Opéra Bastille racontée par M. Audon, F. Bloch-Lainé, G. Charlet, M. Dittman*. Editions Métailié, Paris, 1990.

Véron, Louis Désiré. *L'Opéra de Paris 1820–1835*. Les silences compacts, 1835, and Editions Michel de Maule, Paris, 1987.

Victoria and Albert Museum. *25th Anniversary of Opera and Ballet at Post-war Covent Garden*. Exhibition Catalogue, 1971.

Vincent, Andrew. *Theories of the State*. Basil Blackwell, Oxford, 1987.

Volkov, Solomon. *St Petersburg: A Cultural History*. Trans. by Antonina W. Bouis. Simon and Schuster, 1997.

Waites, James. 'The Sydney Opera House: A Cultural Complex or Sacred Site?', in the Programme by Alan John and Dennis Watkins for *The Eighth Wonder* World Première, 14 October 1995, The Australian Opera, 1995.

Wallinger, Mark and Warnock, Mary, Eds. *Art for All? Their Policies and Our Culture*, PEER, London, 2000.

Walsh, T.J. *Second Empire Opera*. John Calder, London, 1981.

Wangermee, Robert, Ed. *Les Malheurs d'Orphée: Culture et profit dans l'économie de la musique*. Pierre Mardaga, Brussels and Liège, 1990.

Weaver, William. *The Golden Century of Italian Opera from Rossini to Puccini*. Thames and Hudson, London, 1980.

Weber, William. *Music and the Middle Class: The Social Structure of Concert Life in London, Paris and Vienna between 1830 and 1848*. Croom Helm, London, 1975.

Wechsberg, Joseph. *The Opera*. Macmillan, New York, 1972.

Wells, H.G. *Russia in the Shadows*. George H. Doran Company, New York, 1921.

Wharton, Edith. *The Age of Innocence*. D. Appleton and Co., New York, 1920.

White, Eric Walter. *A History of English Opera*. Faber and Faber, London, 1983.

White, Eric Walter. *The Rise of English Opera*. John Lehmann, London, 1985.

Withington, R. *English Pageantry: An Historical Outline.* 2 vols. Oxford University Press, 1918.

Wolff, S. *L'Opéra au Palais Garnier 1875–1962.* L'Entracte, Paris, 1962.

Wood, Sir Henry. *My Life of Music.* Victor Gollancz Ltd, London, 1938.

Yeomans, John. *The Other Taj Mahal: What Happened to the Sydney Opera House.* Longman, Sydney, 1968.

Yorke-Long, Alan. *Music at Court. Four Eighteenth Century Studies.* Weidenfeld and Nicolson, London. 1954.

Zaslaw, Neal, Ed. *The Classical Era: From the 1740s to the End of the Eighteenth Century.* Man and Music Series, Macmillan, London, 1989.

Ziegler, Oswald L. *Sydney Builds an Opera House.* Oswald Ziegler Publications, Sydney, 1973.

INDEX